IMMERSIVE THEATRES

nacy and Immediacy in Contemporary Performance

uely comprehensive and valuable text that I would have no
on in recommending to my students. The critical commentary
s with the rich collection of interviews to make an excellent
for undergraduates, postgraduates, researchers and general
readers.' – **Sita Popat**, *Chair in Performance and Technology,*
of Leeds

prehensive survey, Josephine Machon explores the theory,
practice of immersive theatre. Part One introduces concepts
n, situating them within a historical context and estab-
ear critical vocabulary for discussion. Part Two presents
tterviews with artists from major companies, including:

Punchdrunk
eamthinkspeak
WildWorks
ngel

an Howells

The ies introduced in Part One are clearly demonstrated through the
exar es of practice in Part Two.

Assu no prior knowledge, *Immersive Theatres* invites readers to
create, alyse, debate and appreciate this extraordinary form of
thea tice. It is an ideal resource for students at all levels, as well
as pr ners and researchers alike.

Josephine Machon is Senior Research Fellow in Contemporary
Performance Practi Midd University London. She is the author
of *(Syn)aesthe* ditor of the
Palgrave Mac

Immersive Theatres

Intimacy and Immediacy in Contemporary Performance

Josephine Machon

palgrave
macmillan

First published 2013 by
PALGRAVE MACMILLAN

Palgrave Macmillan in the UK is an imprint of Macmillan Publishers Limited, registered in England, company number 785998, of Houndmills, Basingstoke, Hampshire RG21 6XS.

Palgrave Macmillan in the US is a division of St Martin's Press LLC, 175 Fifth Avenue, New York, NY 10010.

Palgrave Macmillan is the global academic imprint of the above companies and has companies and representatives throughout the world.

Palgrave® and Macmillan® are registered trademarks in the United States, the United Kingdom, Europe and other countries.

ISBN: 978–1–137–01984–4 hardback
ISBN: 978–1–137–01983–7 paperback

This book is printed on paper suitable for recycling and made from fully managed and sustained forest sources. Logging, pulping and manufacturing processes are expected to conform to the environmental regulations of the country of origin.

A catalogue record for this book is available from the British Library.

A catalog record for this book is available from the Library of Congress.

10 9 8 7 6 5 4 3 2 1
22 21 20 19 18 17 16 15 14 13

Printed in China

For my father
Roy William Machon
(1940–2011)
who instilled in me a passion for the arts

and for my son
Rufus John Machon Pendleton
for whom I hope to do the same

Contents

Contents

Part Two   Immersion, Intimacy and Immediacy in Practice

Contents

List of Illustrations and Tables

Illustrations

Tables

Acknowledgements

I wish to give heartfelt and special thanks to my friend and sounding board, Janet Free, who has been so generous with time, support and expert advice in the drafting of this book. Glenda Cooper has been a constant support in so many ways and provided last-minute professional advice when it was needed. Paul Woodward asked some pertinent questions and made useful suggestions in developing certain ideas. To my creative comrade, Amelia Cornish, who took me to *The Crash of the Elysium* and let me quiz her about it all the way home. I am grateful to Lyn Gardner, David Jubb, Maria Oshodi and Roberto Sanchez-Camus with Ffion Aynsley and Saul Eisenberg, for the interviews they gave as research for this book. My sincere thanks to Alice Nash and Ebony Bott at Back to Back Theatre, Thea Jones at Battersea Arts Centre, Alexandra Rowse at Coney Headquarters, Jennie Hoy and Steph Allen at Punchdrunk and Sunita Pandya at WildWorks, all of whom patiently assisted me in organising interviews and obtaining image permissions. Thanks to Jenna Steventon at Palgrave for initial interest in the project to Jenni Burnell, for support and advice and to Penny Simmons who was essential to the successful completion of the project. I am indebted to Felix Barrett, Owen Calvert-Lyons, Janet Evans, Bruce Gladwin, Pete Higgin, Sue Hill, Sam Holdsworth, Adrian Howells, Christer Lundahl, Silvia Mercuriali, Bill Mitchell, Michael Morris, Ralph Savoy, Martina Seitl, Tristan Sharps, Tassos Stevens, Jen Thomas and Louise Ann Wilson, who were so generous with their time, thought and practice and have granted me the privilege of sharing their work and reflections. Lastly my thanks and deepest love to Andrew and Rufus who have put up with me being 'a bit stressed' during the writing of this book. I'm just going to immerse myself in you two for a while.

Preface

Take a dip...

Remember what it is like to be immersed in water; to lie back slowly and put your head underwater in the bath. The muted sensation of being submerged in another medium, where the rules change because if you were to breathe as normal your lungs would fill with water; so you have to hold your breath, feeling the buoyancy of your body in this new realm, attending to every moment of what this new experience offers. At once being able to relax within that otherworldly feeling but always alert, ready to respond to your body's eventual need for oxygen.

Remember what it is like to jump in at the deep end, plummeting through air in a way that sends your stomach into your mouth, scary, exhilarating, reliance on the body to respond instinctively in order to do-as-needs-be-done.

Remember tumbling under a crashing wave as a child, gasping for air as you emerge; scared, dishevelled, overwhelmed by your unpreparedness for the event; keen to return to the thrill of it or unwilling to try again.

Immersion in water can be a pleasant, powerful experience. It places us in a strange environment that can be comforting or potentially dangerous. It makes us utterly aware – in that moment – of our body and its instinctive response to the medium. It is notable that immersion in water is used as a figurative and physical element in rites of passage; ablutions in Hindu, Islamic, Judaic ceremonies or Christian baptism, not only as an act of cleansing but a deeper, spiritual act of transformation.

We understand what it is to be immersed in water; the action of plunging your whole body into an alternative medium and its subsequent sensations. We all have some grasp of the – actual and metaphoric – transformational implications that immersion in water holds in religious and cultural situations. So might this help us to understand what it is to be immersed in a theatre experience; to determine what 'immersive theatre' actually is?

... Immerse yourself

This book is offered as an attempt to get to the heart of what it is that makes up those immersive theatres that are physical, sensual and participatory. It surveys a strand of immersive practice that arises from the fusion of installation art and physical and visual theatres of the 1980s and owes its sensual aesthetic primarily to a mix of ingredients involving landscape, architecture, scenography, sound and direct, human contact. I accept from the outset that this area of study is broad and contestable, yet my intention is that ideas and descriptions shared in this book will enable you to identify where immersive experiences exist in your own journey through the arts. The title refers to 'theatres' in recognition of the pluralities of practice that exist under this banner whilst also placing it firmly within the realm of performance and theatre studies.[1] I intend to show how current immersive theatre is distinguishable in a range of work, including those produced by Artangel in the early 1990s and through to the present day, and is exemplified in a great deal of the performance work of a wide range of internationally recognised practitioners. These include Blast Theory, Brith Gof, De La Guarda, Dogtroep, FuerzaBruta, Ontroerend Goed, Reial Companyia de Teatre de Catalunya, Royale de Luxe, Shunt and Sound & Fury. It aims to show how you might identify where companies such as Extant Theatre Company, Forster & Heighes, Lotos Collective, Oily Cart, Periplum, Redmoon Central, Secret Cinema, Skewed Visions or Walkabout Theatre are artfully exploiting immersive techniques to intimate and experiential ends. It was my previous research into the work of Marisa Carnesky, Curious, Punchdrunk and Shunt, examined in *(Syn)aesthetics*, that emphasised the power of immersive practice and served as a springboard for this project; a meditation on what 'defines' immersive theatre. This book has come about from a desire to honour the significance of the artists and work under scrutiny as much as from an ambition to understand and articulate the peculiar power of this practice.

Some of the above named are mentioned in Part One to elucidate certain ideas discussed. However, this book is only so long and cannot cover every company or artist exploring immersivity in practice. Instead, it points towards those that offer models of practice according to the parameters set by this book. The contributing artists to Part Two have been chosen as leading exponents of paradigmatic practice, namely; Artangel, Back To Back Theatre, Coney, dreamthinkspeak, Adrian Howells, Lundahl & Seitl, Silvia Mercuriali, Nimble Fish, Punchdrunk, WildWorks and Louise Ann Wilson. These are British-based companies with international appeal (save for Back to Back Theatre; an Australian company that has long-standing relationships with partners in Europe and Britain).

Although diverse in approach, the range of work under scrutiny all prioritises human contact. In this regard as much as I reference theories from Virtual Art and Games Studies in defining immersive practice, it is not my intention to explore these forms in depth, particularly the practice of Pervasive Gaming (device-led game-play in physical locations, exploiting digital gaming environments that fuse real-life and online worlds). Such transmedia play is an important influence on immersive theatres and for this reason I touch upon Blast Theory, a company that explores this practice in performance. I also cover the digital and online experimentations of Coney and Punchdrunk. In this regard, the Recommended Reading and Research Section at the end of the book offers guidance towards companies and areas that are connected with yet beyond the specific scope of this book.

I started this venture with a fairly clear idea, albeit fuzzy around the edges, of what I believed immersive performance to be, and what I knew it was not. I am now certain that 'immersive theatre' is impossible to define as a genre, with fixed and determinate codes and conventions, because *it is not one*. However, immersivity in performance does expose qualities, features and forms that enable us to know what 'it' is when we are experiencing it. I know when I have experienced a wholly immersive event I am totally submerged in it for the length of time that the work lasts, aware of nothing other than the event itself and only actions, feelings (both emotion and sensation) and thoughts related to that event are of consequence in that time. I can be surprised, delighted, inspired and, in the most powerful instances, genuinely transformed by the event; a rare and precious experience in theatre and one that, when it does happen, reminds me why I stick with it, why I believe in the power and potential of the discipline. I have had immersive experiences where I have zoned in and out of total immersion for various reasons, including a lack of authenticity in execution or frustration at not being able to get to 'where I want to be' (within large-scale events). I have also experienced work that holds brief moments of immersion within a wider artistic experience and performances that incorporate immersive techniques to 'un-immersive' ends. What is apparent is that certain productions display distinctive, defining features that are accepted as immersive, such as the now cult-status experience of *You Me Bum Bum Train* (2010–12) created by Kate Bond and Morgan Lloyd or all of Punchdrunk's work. Equally, there are companies and artists renowned for their immersive encounters such as dreamthinkspeak, Nimble Fish or WildWorks, yet this does not mean that all the work they produce is, or will continue to be, fully immersive.

This book embraces the fuzziness around the edges in engaging in the debate about what immersive theatre is. I would hope that as you read, you understand the term as it is intended; as shorthand, not jargon; as a way of sharing an appreciation for the work under consideration without pussyfooting around what we might or might not want to call it; to give it a name in order to interrogate and celebrate the range of work the term embraces. The analysis offered acknowledges the significance of this work to contemporary practice and recognises its potential to inspire the innovators of the future to new ends in the ongoing timeline that charts theatrical experimentation.

As these opening paragraphs indicate there is both expediency and contradiction involved in the act of defining. I have always been somewhat resistant to definitions and categorisation when it comes to appreciating theatre and am mindful to draw attention to this whenever I have a need to use them, whether in relation to my teaching or in general conversation regarding certain types of theatre. I am all too aware of the trickiness of contested terms, the difficulties of 'fixing' ideas and practices around the pliable forms involved where the 'shades of grey', the blurring of boundaries that exist across theatre, are what makes it such an exciting medium to experience. I recognise the frustrations that can be encountered in attempting to describe and examine interdisciplinary practice and am acutely aware that anyone involved in making or experiencing and appreciating performance work may be opposed to 'reducing' the interpretative possibilities and power of an event through definitions (as is illustrated in certain conversations in Part Two). Yet, despite my own resistance, I know that definitions, as simplified terms, can benefit the user in appropriate situations (i.e. when there is a need to talk or write about the work) in order that she or he might engage in a dialogue with others around the area; as shorthand to describe the work, and the experience of that work, after the event. In such instances, words – useful, explanatory words – are, mostly, all we have. It came as no surprise to me that in talking with Lyn Gardner, theatre critic for *The Guardian*, about this practice, she and I shared our mistrust of definitions yet proceeded to use them wilfully throughout the ensuing conversation in order to explore the ideas under consideration, clearly sharing a vocabulary in relation to the theatre pieces to which we referred. Look back (in languor) at many a critic's back catalogue of reviews and you will find them peppered with definitions, summarised descriptions and drawing categorised conclusions all over the place.

So why then write a book with a focus on defining when so resistant to that act? Well, very simply because, as a long-time appreciator of theatre, across my time as a student of theatre and in my role as an educator in theatre, I am aware that definitions can assist in the art of creating, analysing, arguing over and appreciating theatre practice. Because it is important to have a purchase on the words that are employed to describe the practice in which we are engaged, because the words are there to help us *understand the ideas behind the work*. Because it is fun to talk about it and in talking about it we need a shared vocabulary so we can be as clear with each other and can understand each other as much as we 'do or don't' understand the work. It is also useful to note that contemporary performance definitions themselves are often pleasurably shifting and open to a range of ideas and works therein. Overall, the main precept is to encourage debate between audience members and practitioners regarding the significance of immersive performance events and to establish a lexicon with which to do this.

Take the helm...

I would like to close this Preface by suggesting ways in which the reader may choose to navigate her or his way through the book. This is intended for those new to reading books such as this, which fuse theory and analysis within and across practice, so please ignore this next passage if that is not you.

If you are in this for the ride, then take your time and read each section in bite-size morsels taking in the full, overarching discussion; read in a linear fashion from start to finish to understand the developing ideas around, approaches to and experiences of immersive practice. Alternatively, follow a non-linear, taking-the-dog-for-a-walk route, that gets to the heart of the areas that most interest you; as you read sections that touch on a particular outlook related to this practice, it may be beneficial to you to cross-reference these sections with relevant interviews from Part Two. You will note that the analysis throughout Part One refers to various conversations of Part Two from a range of perspectives. With this in mind it would be useful to familiarise yourself with the following section on Contributing Artists and Referenced Work and then read and reread the interview material as you engage with the analysis of Part One.

If you prefer a quick fix, simply head straight to the 'scale of immersivity' that closes Part One, Chapter 2. This identifies and describes the central traits of immersive theatre practice. You can then back this up by reading those interviews that are highlighted as examples of such practice. Finally, if you prefer to let practice speak for itself, turn first to the Contributing Artists and Referenced Practice and then straight to Part Two where the conversations with each contributor contextualises a particular approach to immersive practice. Each dialogue provides illustration of the contributor's ideas around forms and a methodology for practice. These discussions encourage the practitioners to question the term 'immersive' and to describe their own particular intentions, approach and style in creating such work.

Note

1. I use 'theatres' as a generic term for the purposes of defining. 'Immersive performance' is used interchangeably with 'theatres' whereas 'immersive practice' widens the field to refer to immersive approaches including and beyond theatre.

Contributing artists and referenced work

This introduction to each of the contributing artists, and respective companies, alongside the conversations of Part Two, is not intended as an exhaustive overview of all the companies and artists working in this realm at present. Instead, the aim of each overview is to provide a context for the artists who offer reflection on the distinctive approaches each takes with the immersive form in Part Two of this book. Each profile follows the order of the interviews and provides a brief background and history to the artists. Each includes a précis of two works from those that are discussed across Part One and during the conversations of Part Two, in order to give a flavour of the range of work under consideration. For sources from which these overviews have been compiled and more detailed information on the history and practice beyond that proffered in these sketches, please refer to the Recommended Reading and Research section at the end of this book alongside the Bibliography. Any direct quotations used in these profiles are taken from the artist's authorised website or from personal correspondence following the interviews.

Michael Morris, Joint Artistic Director of Artangel

Morris and James Lingwood established Artangel in 1991 to commission and produce innovative projects by artists working across forms and disciplines in unique ways. Artangel is based in London and collaborates with artists and organisations nationally and internationally. Since its inception Artangel has consistently supported work that explores the boundaries of art and life. From early on Morris and Lingwood recognised the potency of the immersive form. All Artangel projects demonstrate an idiosyncratic exploration of site and subject matter where ideas, themes and narratives are uncovered through an array of interdisciplinary practice. Artangel's approach is unique in that the commissioning process arises from open-ended conversations with the artist that enables an initial idea to be imagined and then realised; an approach that immerses itself in the process as much as product. The following examples were commissioned and produced by Artangel.

H.G.

H.G. (1995) was ground-breaking in terms of Artangel's practice, the first commission in Britain by Robert Wilson and sound and light architect Hans Peter Kuhn. Collaborating with British film production designer Michael Howells, Wilson and Kuhn made palpable the idea of *encountering time* via an immersive installation that was housed in Clink Street Vaults; musty, interconnected, underground spaces that were the site of London's medieval dungeons. Audience-immersants entered alone or in pairs, the doorway providing a strange portal to an 'otherworld'. Inside they came across a series of tableaux from room to room, joined by darkened corridors that could be navigated in any order. Certain scenes suggested just-missed activity; an abandoned dinner party or a hospital desk with a Medical Officer's notes. In addition to rooms that could be fully entered, there were also glimpses of alternative lands through brickwork and doorways; lush gardens, ancient ruins. This immersion exploited chiaroscuro effects. Intricate scenography fused with sound to create otherworldly and uncanny scenarios. Evocative accounts and images of the experience exist in the *H.G.* archive on the Artangel website.

The Missing Voice (Case Study B)

The Missing Voice (Case Study B) (1999) by Janet Cardiff was a 50-minute immersive audio-walk experience for individual audience-participants. Starting at Whitechapel Library, where visitors were given a portable CD-player to listen to the adventure, the journey was routed through London's East End. It played on the idea of blurring the lines between reality and imaginative fantasy, ensuring that the 'everyday' became a heightened reality; 'part urban guide, part detective fiction, part *film noir*'. This aural experience can now be downloaded via the Artangel web archive.

Felix Barrett, Founder and Artistic Director of Punchdrunk

Barrett has conceived, designed and directed all of Punchdrunk's productions since founding the company in 2000, working closely with members of the company to realise his vision. Punchdrunk's work is exemplary of immersive practice in both epic and intimate forms. The company has pioneered a form of immersive theatre in which roaming audiences experience intimately epic storytelling inside sensory theatrical worlds. In the large-scale works all audience-participants are required to wear a carnivalesque mask that encourages liberation, can imply an invitation to role-play and ensures the audience adds an organic scenographic dimension within the work. The Punchdrunk aesthetic in masked productions plunders the themes forms and narratives in classic literary, cinematic and visual art forms with physical performance and intricate scenography within found sites to blur the boundaries between space, performer and audience. Punchdrunk works open up the narratives and themes that exist in classic texts; characters that only have brief moments in the original literary work extend these moments in a three-hour cyclical run, all are under scrutiny throughout, focus shifting away from one protagonist; narratives and experiences are to be found on different floors, behind every door; audience-participants shape and discover their own throughlines. This deconstructive play with the text causes time to kaleidoscope. Within these grand narratives it is also possible to encounter clandestine one-on-ones, where the audience-immersant is unmasked for a brief moment, an electric experience. Punchdrunk have recently begun to experiment with online technologies in collaboration with Massachusetts Institute of Technology (MIT). Wider plans in development are to explore how audio-technology might enable an uncanny fusion of the Punchdrunk aesthetic within everyday environments and to establish Punchdrunk Travel, a mind-altering blurring of art and life for the participant-adventurer.

Masque of the Red Death

Masque of the Red Death (2007–8), followed the masked format of Punchdrunk's epic work; an adaptation of Edgar Allen Poe's novella of the same title, interweaving other tales from Poe's short stories. Punchdrunk's reinvention of the space opened up areas of Battersea Arts Centre (BAC) that had rarely been seen by the public, completely reawakening the architectural and historical space. The design was woven into the fabric of the performance and the unique physicality of Maxine Doyle's choreography fused with site and scenography to carry the experiential power of the piece, suffusing the space with a palpable *sensation* of having taken laudanum with Poe and (meta)physically entered his *Tales of Mystery and Imagination*. The collaboration between BAC and Punchdrunk aimed to create an experience that inspired collaboration and participation; artist to artist as much as artist to audience. Within the epic narrative of *The Masque of The Red Death*, there ran specially commissioned work from companies such as Coney and WildWorks, individual artists and BAC's youth theatre who embedded work within the wider piece, embellishing the rich layers of detail across the space. Some of these developed over the course of the entire run (as with Coney's *The Gold-bug* described below) others changed on a weekly basis.

The Crash of the Elysium

The Crash of the Elysium (2011, 2012) is the first purpose-built portable experience created by Punchdrunk, designed within a massive marquee. It is an ongoing collaboration between Punchdrunk and Steven Moffat, chief scriptwriter for the BBC's *Doctor Who*. A Punchdrunk Enrichment project as well as a Punchdrunk production, this was created primarily for children aged 6–12 (adults are allowed to accompany the younger age group); an immersive event that exploits the action-led, mystery-solving narratives of *Doctor Who* via the Punchdrunk process to encourage high-paced interactivity. The format borrows from Punchdrunk's recent explorations in pervasive game-playing as much as its innovation in theatrical performance. The adventure begins with an educational talk at an exhibition that documents the mysterious disappearance of a Victorian steamship, *The Elysium*, in 1888, interrupted by the British army bursting in and forcing the audience to follow them, don white biohazard suits and masks, as an alien spaceship has crash-landed in the vicinity. Once inside we discover, revealed in a video message from the Doctor himself, the ship is an ancient alien gallery that holds a vast number of Weeping Angels, living statues that kill with a single glance and cannot be defeated without the help of children. Rather than via Punchdrunk's trademark complex layering in form and content, audience-participants are engaged by the dynamic clue-solving participation, involving interaction with the Doctor via a series of video messages, and sensory stimulation.

Bruce Gladwin, Artistic Director of Back to Back Theatre

Back to Back Theatre was founded in Geelong, Australia, in 1987 with a mission to create theatre events with people who are perceived to have a disability. With Gladwin as Artistic Director, Back to Back's work examines moral, philosophical and political questions about the value of individuals' lives. It explores immersive techniques within an all-encompassing design aesthetic, using audio-technologies to make the audience experience the event in an intimate and immediate manner. This evolves out of a belief that 'theatre should engage all senses, visual, tactile and olfactory' and through the 'endeavour to allow form to define itself, to deliver dynamic and enhanced performance that exists in endless suspension and oscillation'. With an ensemble of performers who are perceived to have intellectual disabilities, the company have sought to establish an aesthetic and outlook that explores experience from a position of marginality. The narratives the company explore start from this position of marginality yet open out to confront and explore what it is to be human, both incorporating, and irrespective of, perceived disability. The play with the physical proximity of live(d), performing bodies forces the audience-immersant to *attend* to the details of the event and the *experiences* that underpin the narratives and themes. Consequently, the work can be transformative for audience-immersants; the audio play allowing access to an alternative sensual perception as well as the ideas confronting changing attitudes to notions of difference.

Soft

Soft (2002) was a large-scale theatrical performance that explored the social implications of genetic technologies, specifically the ethical dilemmas of prenatal screening. Three performers are the physical representation of Down's Syndrome, a genetic condition that society seeks to screen and eradicate. Designed within a specially made giant inflatable bubble – suggestive of a sci-fi world, a potential utopia, a dystopian clinic, a womb – *Soft* merges architectural design, live performance, animation and 3D surround-sound delivered to the audience via individual headphones (see Illustration 7).

Small Metal Objects

Small Metal Objects (2005–8) establishes an immersive world via the intricacies of the performing style within an active and colourful existing cityscape, heightened as a consequence of being the backdrop to the world of the event. The London premiere was presented at Stratford Station, East London, within the bustle of commuter traffic. Sat on a raised seating bank with individual headphones, the audience listens in to a situation unfolding somewhere in the crowd. The action, played out ahead of you, often at a distance, demanded that the audience-observer pan across the activity, hone in on action, focus on the finer details and nuances of the work against this busy and unyielding backdrop. The intimacy is accentuated by the dialogue occurring through the headphones; at once an individual and a shared experience with the rest of the audience (delightfully strange to laugh together at both the humour in the speech and the serendipitous 'real' action of the commuters which happens to coincide with the performance). This piece explores how respect is withheld from those on the margins, the disabled and unemployed, deemed 'unproductive'. Set against a backdrop of finance and the city commute, the notion that everything has a price, little has a value, becomes immediately visceral (see Illustration 14).

Christer Lundahl and Martina Seitl, Founders and Artistic Directors of Lundahl & Seitl

Lundahl & Seitl was formed in 2003, based in London and working across Europe, to create immersive events with a strong foundation in research and process. Using audio-instruction, choreography by Seitl and technology, Lundahl & Seitl investigates space, time and perception, collaborating within the areas of architecture, fashion, cognitive neurology and classical music. They cite the Artangel-produced *Stifter's Dinge* by Heiner Goebbels (2008) amongst wider influences on their own practice.

Symphony of a Missing Room

Symphony of a Missing Room (2011b; ongoing), is a 30-minute piece for six audience members at a time, sited in a museum (the Birmingham Museum and Art Gallery for the UK premiere). You are blindfolded by whiteout goggles, led by a voice in wireless headphones and delicately dancing hands, physically and imaginatively to believe that you are moving across space and time; through tunnels, forests; a series of subtle effects and scenarios created by the sensations of movement, sound and torches shone onto these goggles. The work involves you in a constant dialogue between the real, the sensual and the imagined, reminding you that there is a way to appreciate art that comes from within and is based on instinctual responses rather than on guidance dictated by site or curation (see Illustrations 9 and 15).

Rotating in a Room of Moving Images

Rotating in a Room of Moving Images (2011a; ongoing) is a 15-minute performance for one audience-participant. An audio-instructed experience located in a room where scale is played with and perspective manipulated. Ivory drapes are suspended from the ceiling to the floor, creating corridors which change each time the experience shifts to total blackout, to film projections of a child or ethereal costumed characters, reminiscent of Caravaggio or Velázquez portraits, then suddenly, you are guided (in blackout) to turn around, by the playful voice in your ear, to discover live performers behind you; a disquietingly lit tableau vivant, ghostly, smiling, kind. The length of the floor is extended through this play between the live and mediated image, all of which are accentuated by a repeated shifting from gentle light to total darkness and the inter-action from the invisible dancing hand, twirling you around, guiding you, always in artful conjunction with the childlike voice in your ear through headphones. The assorted tableaux, art-world fragments, remain seared on your retina as afterimages, the visual remains of a dream, just as the fleeting touch (an interaction which involves a tangible sensation of *waiting for physical connection* in the absence of movement) remains as an embodied memory in your hand and limbs.

Silvia Mercuriali

Italian-born Mercuriali trained at the Arsenale, Milan, as a physical performer, studying with Marina Spreafico, a teacher of Jacques Lecoq methods. Mercuriali also cites Commedia dell'arte, Dario Fo and Franca Rama as influences. She moved to the United Kingdom to work with Ant Hampton as Rotozaza (1999–2010), creators of 'Autoteatro', which they describe as 'interactive installations'. This is theatre that occurs outside of the theatre space, is self-generated by the audience-participant so unique to that individual. In 2009 she set up Inconvenient Spoof with Matt Rudkin. With Gemma Brockis she founded Berlin Navada and created *Pinocchio* (2007) and *Still Night* (2012). Mercurilali also collaborates with Simon Wilkinson as Il Pixel Rosso, founded in 2010, exploring the potential of audio and video technologies within intimate and outlandish immersive experiences. All of her collaborations demonstrate her wider influences, owing much to cinema alongside her theatrical training; the expressionist aesthetic of Federico Fellini and the absurd-political resonance of Pier Paolo Pasolini (especially his attention to landscape and the beauty of real people). John Smith's *Girl With Chewing Gum* has heavily shaped her work, particularly with Berlin Nevada. The cinematic influences are clear in Il Pixel Rosso's video work, a strong visual aesthetic, offering a beautiful-grotesque. The framing of Smith's work through audio-description overlaid on an image is clear in *Wondermart* and the Jean Luc Godard reference is delightful in Rotozaza's *Etiquette*. In each case, the intimacy of the audio causes the immersant to re-perceive the mundane as otherworldly and special.

Etiquette

Etiquette (Rotozaza, 2004; ongoing) a half-hour experience for two people, who might or might not know each other, that occurs in the public space of a bar, restaurant or cafe. A young girl and an old man lead you as guest-performers/audience-participants to your table. You are assured no-one will be, knowingly, watching you; other diners in the space will not be aware of your performance as it is intimately shaped to be clandestine, quiet. You wear headphones that tell you what to say, to use objects on the table, making 'easy' your interactions but also allowing space for improvised flourishes during this interplay; for the piece to work, and the liberation to occur, you need to listen and respond accordingly – carefully boundaried 'play' (see Illustration 16).

And the Birds Fell From the Sky...

And the Birds Fell From the Sky... (Il Pixel Rosso, 2011) is a 15-minute immersion for two people, that combines the theatrical strategy of Autoteatro with film. You are shown to a small 'waiting room', where your partner already sits. Around you are strange objects, like a rag-and-bone storeroom; a Parish Newsletter details information about a strange Faruk Clown Tribe who are terrorising local towns; mobile numbers to call, with strange voices speaking an impenetrable language on the other end. You are then given headphones and video-goggles and have been kidnapped by the Faruk; sat in a wheel chair, then on a car seat, where you are sprayed with whiskey from the mouth of your Faruk driver, the ensuing anarchic behaviour is both unsettling and exhilarating until you are let out onto a vast, beautiful landscape, a green hill in the distance against a blue sky, a non-Faruk figure ahead of you holding a bird extends his hand, you return the gesture and a rolled, carrier-pigeon message lands in your palm. As the goggles are removed you find yourself at a shrine to the Faruk, sent on your way to call the number on the message if you dare.

Tassos Stevens, Co-Founder and Co-Director of Coney

Stevens is a founding member and Co-Director of Coney, and rumoured to have been involved in most of their work. Coney is an 'Agency of Adventure', making live interactive, interdisciplinary work across a community of artists and practitioners. The Agency of Coney may or may not have connections with Rabbit; a mysterious agent. Nobody knows who or what Rabbit is. (It is known that Stevens is also a game-designer – he designed *Papa Sangre*, an audio-only game for the iPhone – and that he has a doctorate in Psychology.)

The Gold-bug

The Gold-bug (2007–8) was both treasure-hunt and performance-adventure inspired by Poe's short story, devised and produced by Coney within Punchdrunk's *The Masque of the Red Death*. *The Gold-bug* was a six-month adventure where an online community of 80 players, aged between 18 and 57, played out the final three months in detail, with 300 totally immersed in the 'Gold-bug' world plus over 3000 'casual players' (passing visitors within the larger Punchdrunk world) discovering the hunt through a mysterious hooded and masked figure playing tarot in the bar. Players shared findings and stories online; solved puzzles and codes set by characters; uncovered narratives, broke into the theatre one Sunday night to disturb a spirit, and eventually dug up the box that revealed the final location of the treasure and the source of the haunting. Rabbit sent a postcard to alert players to the hunt, and forwarded a telephone message at its conclusion thanking them for helping to lay his tormented friend, William Moray, to rest. If you engage with all the material in the Recommended Reading and Research on *The Gold-bug* a potent sense of this immersive experience comes through; piecing together the archive narratives feels like immersive game-play in itself.

A Small Town Anywhere

A Small Town Anywhere (2009; ongoing) is inspired by Henri-Georges Clouzot's film *Le Corbeau*. The story of the town is both revealed and pieced together through the interactions of the playing-audience and is responsive to the decisions they take; individually and collectively. As with all of Coney's work, the life of this immersive experience begins days or weeks prior to the entering of the space, via an advance inter-action with the Small Town Historian (either online or in person) which gives you the opportunity to cast yourself into the town, to set your personal history, and to confide a dark secret which ultimately ends up in the story of the event, as part of the destructive gossip (see Illustration 2).

Samantha Holdsworth, Co-Founder and Co-Artistic Director of Nimble Fish

Holdsworth formed Nimble Fish in 2006 with Greg Klerkx. Defining themselves as 'cultural producers', they establish and manage creative projects using immersive techniques to 'animate or re-interpret public spaces in the context of the communities they serve'. A feature that comes across clearly within Holdsworth's conversation is Nimble Fish's concern with process as much as product. Within its original immersive performance and installation work, Nimble Fish have a wide array of influences from artistic and philosophical realms. Holdsworth's own physical performance style developed through studying Directing at the Central School of Speech and Drama, and Clowning at L'Ecole Philippe Gaulier, alongside her experiences working with other performance companies including Geraldine Pilgrim's Corridor.

The Container

The Container (2007), a play by Clare Bayley, directed by Tom Wright, produced and designed by Nimble Fish, examined human trafficking for an audience of twenty. You meet on the street and then are shouted at to get into a parked, articulated lorry, where you are plunged into darkness, sitting knee-to-knee on containers. Torchlight reveals that you are amongst five migrants who share their stories; who they are, from where they have come geographically, physically and emotionally, what they will encounter on arrival. The confines of the lorry became increasingly suffocating, making live(d) the conditions of those trafficked to work in Britain.

re:bourne

re:bourne (2010) was a site-responsive, interactive performance and art event created with the community of Sittingbourne, Kent (UK), co-produced with Workers of Art. It involved a number of 'mini-commissions' and intimate immersions that encouraged the local residents to reperceive the immediate environment in which they lived. This was initiated by 'Sparky' (see Illustration 11) who 'appeared' from another time and place (a side alley, filled with smoke) and was travelling back from the future to discover what the town of Sittingbourne was like in the present day. Sparky's purpose was to interact and gently connect with the shyest or most cynical of community members; a visual, interactive yet gentle invitation to 'come and play'. Participants loved Sparky because of his otherworldly quality; Holdsworth retains a memory of Sparky waving through the window to shoppers and a woman remarking, 'bloody hell, I never thought an alien would be watching me buy my frozen peas'. With *re:bourne* Nimble Fish took the community on a journey through the past, present and future of the city via otherworldly happenings in the high street, under carriageways, inside historic buildings and revitalised disused commercial spaces.

Punchdrunk Enrichment led by Pete Higgin, Enrichment Director

Punchdrunk Enrichment was set up in 2008 by Higgin, a founding member of Punchdrunk. Having witnessed how his A Level student's work developed in response to Punchdrunk's *Sleep No More* (2003), he realised the huge potential for transformative engagement within the confines of immersive practice. Punchdrunk Enrichment aims to build on the captivated nature of Punchdrunk audiences and channel this into creative learning, producing extraordinary experiences for children, schools and community groups. The signature Punchdrunk aesthetic is key to the working processes of the Enrichment Team. Higgin also cites as personal influences his own work with Eudemonic (a London-based arts agency exploring collaborative innovation and development), the practice of Oily Cart and PS1 (the more experimental arm of the Museum of Modern Art, New York), all of which demonstrated how sensory performance, installation, architecture and 'real life' can fuse together. Punchdrunk Enrichment, as with all Punchdrunk's work, is inspired by childhood curiosity, fuelled by Higgin's own formative years; 'an early installation of a space ship is still one of my overriding memories of Primary School. It is the creation of this lifelong memory that inspires me the most'.

Under The Eiderdown

Under The Eiderdown (2011; ongoing) was devised to address speaking and listening and creative writing, inspired by the book *Who are You Stripy Horse?* by Jim Helmore, set in a bric-a-brac shop. The project begins with a Punchdrunk Enrichment workshop based on the book, which elicits from pupils what the shop looks, smells, feels and sounds like. Designers observe the workshop, recording all of the pupils suggestions and, unbeknownst to them, install this bric-a-brac shop in their school over the weekend, complete with all of their suggestions and the characters from the story. On the Monday pupils receive a letter inviting them to come and visit the shop and to meet with the shopkeepers, The Weevils, who believe that every object in the world has a history and the potential to tell many stories; that it is stories that keep the world and the shop alive. Pupils are entrusted with the job of looking after the shop for the next two weeks by writing stories about its objects. Punchdrunk Enrichment leaves the shop in the school to facilitate imaginative learning and to inspire creative writing.

The Uncommerical Traveller

The Uncommerical Traveller (2011c; ongoing) was a professionally executed immersive event created in collaboration between Punchdrunk Enrichment and Arcola 50+, part of community Creative Learning at the Arcola Theatre, London. The idea originated in Dalston, London, where Arcola and Punchdrunk worked with local performers over the age of 50, capturing stories from their experiences of living in the area to create an audio journey and an immersive performance in a disused shop. Audience-immersants could begin the experience with an audio journey that took you through East London streets, narrated by Dickens, which encouraged you to attend to the details of the environment, imagine the narratives that might exist behind closed doors, the final destination being the door to this 'Self-Supporting Cooking Depot' in Hackney. As the audience of 15 or so arrive, they enter the depot in groups of three, to a small front room of impoverished Victoriana, seated alongside a Dickensian character and handed a cup of broth, the aroma of which suffuses the environment. The woman with whom I and partner-immersants was sat refrained from chatting too much, continued gazing into the middle-distance, would gently nod or tell you to sup up, ask you if you have children, whilst all around the laughter and talk from other tables filled the space and merged into the soundscape which suddenly swells, chiming clocks, horse-drawn carriages, a curtain is pulled around us, and she subtly pulls us into her world, slowly revealing her chilling story, fragments of a narrative about her daughter, Alice, with the beautiful hair as she repeatedly strokes the silk of the ribbon in her hand, then breathtakingly penetrates time and space by looking me straight in the eye, placing the ribbon in my hair and for that split-second I am her long-lost Alice, and I have shocked her to her core which brings her back to our surroundings and she sends us on our way. We exit to discover others around us had been taken below stairs to witness violent secrets in dingy rooms, hidden under floorboards. Then and now I am acutely aware of her delicately aging skin, her distinct physiognomy, her eyes looking at me, the sensation of the wood of the table beneath my fingers, resting on my knees, the silvery white colour and texture of her hair and the mesmerised expressions of my witnessing partners. The discussion of *The Uncommercial Traveller* in Part Two takes place between myself, Higgin, Jen Thomas, Punchdrunk's Enrichment Officer and Owen Calvert-Lyons, the Creative Learning Manager at The Arcola Theatre, London, both co-directors of the project with Higgin, alongside Ralph Savoy and Janet Evans, performers with Arcola 50+ (see Illustrations 18 and 19).

Louise Ann Wilson

Wilson is a performance-maker, scenographer and artist. Her work offers a unique approach to immersive events within, and arising out of, landscape, made through an extended period of immersion in a chosen place. Since 2008 her practice has focused on rural landscape as a place for performance in which the relationship between the personal and the environment can be re-imagined. Each piece is evolved in close collaboration with artists from a broad range of creative disciplines and experts from fields not usually associated with performance, including scientists and people with local knowledges. Prior to 2008 Wilson was Co-Artistic Director, with Wils Wilson, of wilson+wilson (1997–2008) who created unique sensory, immersive events, collaborating with artists and the people of the places that inspired each production. Like Wilson's current practice, wilson+wilson's work transcended conventional boundaries (between artistic disciplines, between performers and audience, between individual artists and members of the public, between memory and imagination) and generated an intense connection between audiences, artists, participants, site and performance.

House

House (1998) by wilson+wilson, transformed two nineteenth-century terraced houses in the centre of Huddersfield into an extraordinary performance event. These houses were discovered to hold relics of former inhabitants, many of which became important inspiration for the piece, alongside meticulous research that uncovered the site's fascinating past. Links with nineteenth-century naturalist Seth Mosley, Charles Darwin and the former Methodist mission next door became central to the development of the piece. *House* combined installation with live spoken and physical performance, incorporating poetic speech written by Simon Armitage and an evocative soundscore composed by Scanner. An audience of fifteen journeyed from room to room, 'from stone cellar to airy attic', discovering characters, piecing together fragments of stories, examining objects, immersed in a world of unusual images and sound. *House* evoked powerful memories and emotions associated with notions of home and workplace, as well as exploring ideas of evolution, expedition, scientific investigation and religious belief (see Illustration 20).

Fissure

Fissure (2011), devised by Wilson in memory of her late sister, was a unique walking performance that unfolded over three days in the Yorkshire Dales. It was an extraordinary encounter between artists, scientists, audiences and landscape that explored life, death, grief and renewal. With undertones of myths inscribed in the collective psyche, in particular Eurydice's and Ariadne's stories, alongside religious narratives that mark death and rebirth, in *Fissure* haunting figures (pairs of sisters), emerged, danced and vanished into caves to lyrical poetry by Elizabeth Burns set to mournful music by composer Jocelyn Pook. Wilson provides evocative detail of this work in her discussion in Part Two, illustrating how *Fissure* became performance-pilgrimage for artist and audience-participants alike (see Illustration 21).

Bill Mitchell, Artistic Director, and Sue Hill, Associate Director of WildWorks

WildWorks is an internationally renowned theatre company, pushing boundaries of participatory performance through large-scale immersive projects. WildWorks' practice is always sited in found landscapes rather than theatre spaces; places that reflect and embrace the host communities from which the work draws its themes. Mitchell established the company in 2005, following a career as a designer, then Artistic Director of KneeHigh Theatre (1995–2005). Hill is a founding member of WildWorks. Prior to this she worked with Welfare State International, joining Kneehigh Theatre from 1988–2001. From 2000 until 2006 she was Artistic Director for the Eden Project, Cornwall, United Kingdom. The wider company of WildWorks is made up of artists from different cultures and performance traditions. Mitchell notes a shared influence amongst the company of magic realism. Equally, the idiosyncratic practice of KneeHigh Theatre, with its roots in Lecoq's approach to creating work, and inspiration taken from John Fox and Welfare State, is fundamental to WildWorks' productions. Hill and Mitchell also cite as personal influences; the visual theatre of Dogtroep, especially *Noordwester Wals*, as well as the artwork of Louise Bourgeois, and (like Mercuriali) Fellini films, in particular *Amarcord*.

Souterrain

Souterrain (2006–7), a work that was conceived as a journey within different communities in England (Brighton, Hastings, Colchester, Cornwall) and France (Gosnay, Amiens, Sotteville-les-Rouen), re-imagined through the different (hi)stories of each new place. Each community brought new skills, narratives and meaning to the existing work, which was based on the myth of Orpheus and Eurydice and explored themes of love, loss and regeneration. These themes resonated with the host communities, each of which had 'lost traditional industries, countries of birth and a collective memory'. An important moment in each performance was the invitation to the audience-participants to leave their most precious memories at the mouth of Hades, 'in the care of the angels of death' during their journey through the underworld (see Illustration 22). This 'archive of the human heart' amounted to over 10,000 memories and was exhibited at London's Victoria & Albert Museum in 2008.

The Passion

The Passion (2011), based on the Easter story, was a three-day, uninterrupted event (waking to sleeping the action continued); beginning on the afternoon of Good Friday and concluding powerfully on Sunday evening, performed by Michael Sheen (a native of Port Talbot), members of the community and WildWorks. For six months prior to production, WildWorks collaborated in the streets, malls and social clubs of Port Talbot, finding stories, memories and images of the place. The final event was staged across the town, from the beach to under the motorway, in locations where The Passion story resonated with the past and present narratives of the place and its inhabitants; the passions of Port Talbot people. Over 1200 community members took part as writers, musicians, singers, performers, makers, stewards, messengers, angels and demons.

Adrian Howells

Howells is a leading artist in the realm of intimate performance and one-to-one encounters. He creates theatrical experiences in non-traditional performance spaces, often in a one-to-one, autobiographical or confessional context. Howells has a unique capacity to engage on a deeply personal level with each individual audience-participant with whom he works, establishing highly ritualised, unquestionably safe spaces for authentic and profound encounters to occur. He is currently Artist-in-Residence at the Arches, Glasgow and is also collaborating with TouchBase, Sense Scotland, an organisation that provides specialised services and support for disabled children, young people and adults, to create work around ideas of tactile communication.

Foot Washing for the Sole

Foot Washing for the Sole (2010; ongoing) is a one-to-one performance that lasts for 30 minutes, always sited in peaceful settings. Whilst washing and massaging the feet with choreographic care, Howells quietly shares thoughts on the symbolic relevance of feet washing, and its spiritual and cultural associations. This allows Howells to reflect on the situation in the Middle East, and on notions of 'peace' and 'service'. All the while he shares these thoughts, Howells completes a careful choreography of washing, drying, anointing and massaging the participant's feet in frankincense oil. As a consequence of the intimacies and philosophies shared, it concludes with Howells requesting permission to kiss the feet (see Illustration 6).

The Pleasure of Being: Washing, Feeding, Holding

The Pleasure of Being: Washing, Feeding, Holding (2011; ongoing) is a unique one-to-one piece. The audience-participant begins by privately reading guidelines before being led to disrobe in an antechamber. Once undressed (down to a bathing costume if preferred) you knock on a door which is answered by Howells, dressed in white, who welcomes you to the inner sanctum of the bathroom, with an ivory, roll-top bath raised on a platform centre-stage surrounded by lit candles. The experience is charged with a heightened sense of ritual. Howells makes you feel instantly safe, calm, protected and the busy-ness and business of everyday life is immediately forgotten. Howells suggests closing the eyes, which immediately allows a giving-in-to sensation and a release of the imagination. He begins with a gentle dripping of water over the face and body, accentuating the simultaneously sacred and practical attitude in each action. He then washes you, face, neck, limbs, back; very clearly choreographed. This piece takes the act of bathing out-of-the-ordinary to become a journey that allows thoughts to transcend the everyday, into the precious, the pampered, the profound. When the bath is over he directs you to a screen, behind which you dry yourself. He then invites you to be cradled by him, where at some point, you are offered chocolate or fruit (see Illustration 12). Although it feels like a long time, you are only in there for twenty minutes. This intensely intimate work is epic in so many ways; epic in the power of the imaginative plane traversed, the thematic voyages taken and profound in the level of commitment between Howells and his participants alike.

Tristan Sharps, Founder and Artistic Director of dreamthinkspeak

dreamthinkspeak was formed in 1999 by Tristan Sharps. The company creates immersive work, inspired by classical texts, that is always site-responsive and interweaves live performance with film, installation and sound, to create artful worlds through which an audience-immersant journeys. As the descriptions below detail, dreamthinkspeak have a unique approach to the immersive form which exploits the sensual details of architecture, scenography, film and live performance as immersive installation.

Before I Sleep

Before I Sleep (2010) was a multi-sensual journey through the hidden interiors of The Co-operative Building, a long-forgotten department store, in the centre of Brighton, United Kingdom. It was based on Chekhov's *The Cherry Orchard*, a story about a debt-ridden aristocratic family who sell their estate to a serf-turned-entrepreneur. The narrative of *Before I Sleep* belongs to Firs, the old footman who the family have left behind, boarded up inside the house. Groups of five or so enter at a time, meet Firs at the entrance, a stooped man who stares from a doorway and jabbers at you in Russian before beckoning you into the dark. From there you are directed by the space itself through a series of rooms containing images of arresting power; a journey through a liminal space that shifts between Firs' memories of rose-coloured scenarios from Ranyevskaya's lost world – afternoon tea on the veranda, clandestine conversations in the orchard; a waltz in evening dress – to a stark vision of his future/our present, sparse department stores indicating both the splendours of the Chekhovian ballroom and the materialism of the modern world. The thematic twists of this world are interwoven by mirroring, repetition; as if you have become caught in Firs' limbo state, between the past and the future, in an uncanny present that exposes the repetitions and repercussions of history within socio-economic structures (see Illustrations 10 and 25).

The Rest Is Silence

The Rest Is Silence (2012) fuses space, live performance and film in a cinematic deconstruction, a clinical installation, of *Hamlet*. The audience is placed in a black box, which becomes lit by chiaroscuro effects, from the subtle to the stripped. We are both separated from and at the heart of the action in this construction; four vast screens in which we are enclosed. The audience can pivot, creep around, spy on the action as it is intercut across all four walls; characters and audience alike are observing, witnessing, plotting outcomes, submerged in psychologies, complicit in action. Scenes and visual sequences are interwoven or interrupt each other to expose the unfolding psychologies, interrogating the play's themes and characters from a variety of angles. In the midst of this play between space, speech, image and live and (beautifully) mediated action, we are immersed in Hamlet's mind.

Introduction

**Illustration 1 Punchdrunk's *Sleep No More*, NY (2010–).
Performer, Matthew Oaks**
[Photo credit: Yaniv Schulman. Image courtesy of Punchdrunk]

Immersive Theatre

'Immersive' is a term once solely used as an adjective, and now increasingly applied to suggest a 'genre' of theatre. There are several aspects to the word and its related forms: to 'immerse' is 'to dip or submerge in a liquid', whereas to 'immerse oneself' or 'be immersed', means to involve oneself deeply in a particular activity or interest. 'Immersion' thus defines the action of immersing or the state of being immersed; whereas 'immersive', developed from computing terminology, describes that which 'provides information or stimulation for a number of senses, not only sight and sound'. These definitions help to highlight how immersive experiences in theatre combine the act of immersion – being submerged in an alternative medium where all the senses are engaged and manipulated – with a deep involvement in the activity within that medium.

In theatre discourse 'immersive' is now attached to diverse events that assimilate a variety of art forms and seek to exploit all that is experiential in performance, placing the audience at the heart of the work. Here experience should be understood in its fullest sense, to feel *feelingly* – to undergo. From the word (under)go, I wish to be clear that a lot of theatre is experiential and works on its audience in a visceral manner, immersive practice is simply one strand of that. I will elaborate on this point in greater detail below.

This book surveys both large-scale and minimalist immersive works in order to explore the diversity of practice that exists under this banner. Within immersive theatre there has been a recent upsurge in intimate encounters in the performance experience; 'one-on-one' or 'one-to-one' performance, which explores the direct connection between performer and audience member, space and individual interaction. 'One-on-one' and 'one-to-one' defines work where the piece is designed for one audience member. This may involve one artist performing for/with you within the piece or could involve any number of performers in the work to facilitate the individual experience as with *You Me Bum Bum Train* (2010–12), performed by a vast company of volunteers for one audience-participant at a time.[1] One-on-one experiences can also be designed as clandestine moments for a lone member of the crowd within the structure of large-scale works such as with Punchdrunk's epic works. In some instances the intimacy of a one-on-one experience can open out to being partnered audience-participant interaction, rather than artist/audience interaction, as is the case with Mercuriali's work. With Il Pixel Rosso productions you are assigned a partner whose presence cannot always be seen due to video goggles yet it is felt physically via her/his responses as the piece progresses, whereas Rotozaza's *Etiquette* casts two strangers in the one-to-one experience, who follow audio-described instructions to enable the interaction and entertainment to proceed.

As I discuss in more depth in Chapter 1, the rise in such intimate work is arguably because a new, non-traditional theatre audience is attracted to the work on offer and the forms explored. One need only look at the range of work that was presented as part of the London 2012 festival and the Cultural Olympiad to realise that this type of practice, because it blurs artistic boundaries and is widely accessible in its participatory nature, has been embraced as ground-breaking and important in a national celebration of community and culture. David Jubb, the Joint Artistic Director of BAC notes that, due to its mission to 'reinvent the future of the theatre', BAC was the first venue to host an international one-on-one festival. He asserts that this proved a desire amongst non-mainstream audiences for 'conviviality and congregation'.[2] For Jubb, theatrical situations where genuine human connection occurs holds the greatest potential for transformation; 'which is why it's good theatre, because theatre ought to be transformative':

> In a relatively secular society perhaps theatre can provide that place where people come together, explore their differences and by putting differences and creativity together, invent something new, invent a future... [BACs] interest in [immersive practices] comes out of that; its about people and it's about putting the audience at the heart of the experience.
>
> (Jubb and Machon, 2012: n. pag.)

The mention of non-mainstream audiences is of interest here in that it indicates that immersive theatres attract an alternative audience; those who would not necessarily consider themselves theatregoers.[3] Similarly, a number of the artists highlighted in Part Two identify how their work is attended by a diverse demographic. The tastes and types of audience members responding to these works may have something to do with the ways in which these events are marketed; people feel involved, invited or even do not perceive the work to be 'theatre'. Immersive events are often advertised via unusual methods, relying on word-of-mouth and social media for advertising, using e-flyers that are akin to personal invitations, treasure hunt clues or secret society missions (see Illustrations 2 and 17). What is evident with such strategies is that the immersive experience begins the moment you first hear about it. This idea is fundamental to the ethos of Coney, an organisation that believes the experience starts when you first hear about it and only ends when you stop thinking and talking about it. At every stage of this process the work is responsive to the actions of its audience, moulding them as co-authors of their experience.

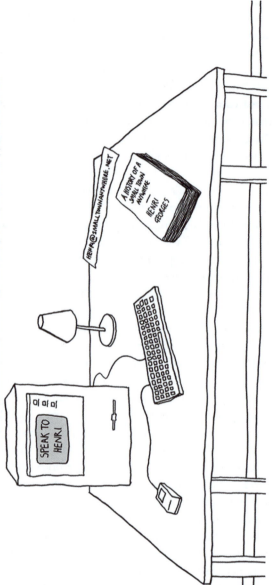

Illustration 2 Coney's *A Small Town Anywhere* (2009)
[Image by Joe Davis and Tassos Stevens. Image courtesy of Coney]

All of the discussions in Part Two refer to a range of ways in which the work evolves, exists and lasts beyond the immersive moment. Holdsworth shares how, with Nimble Fish events, the work begins from the moment she and Klerx have the initial idea where proposals are written as if the person reading it is in the experience, 'they're already playing the game, already part of that process'. She also highlights how worlds created between Nimble Fish and participating communities continue to exist after the event; lasting artworks that physically remain inscribed upon the place as well as affectively within an individual's memory. Barrett, in his conversation, draws attention to his fascination with the point at which 'the show' starts and finishes, 'that murky hinterland that is the space between the show and real life' and how that can be 'theatricalised'. Similarly, Stevens refers to 'the principle of minimum fiction' required to play with the real world and, in so doing, recast it as otherworldly in the imagination and experience of the beholder.

Each conversation in Part Two draws similar observations regarding audience diversity and points out that this can have as much to do with the nature of the work, the involvement of communities in evolving the form and content, as with the playful practices explored. Coming out of this is the observation that the increasing desire for this kind of practice and growing fan-bases have come about due to a desire for genuine physical connection. A need to feel sensually and imaginatively alive in the way that one does after a revitalising walk, experiencing a fairground ride, engaging in extreme sports, pushing oneself to the front at a gig. Technologically driven forms of communication, so predominant in work and socialising today, mean that the opportunities for sentient human interaction have been greatly reduced. This idea is analysed across Chapters 1 to 3 and all of the practitioners interviewed in Part Two highlight how the responses they receive from their audiences suggest there is a genuine wish to make *human* contact, often with another human as much as with the work itself; an enthusiasm for undergoing experiences that both replace and accentuate the live(d) existence of the everyday world. In Part Two, Stevens notes how this form can be addictive and thus evolves a particular fan-base, intoxicated by 'that first thrill of immersion', who can easily become dulled to its pleasures and challenges. This places an onus on practitioners to be inventive, to surprise; not to be complacent nor rely on formulaic approaches.

Matt Trueman, theatre critic and blogger, suggests:

> [The] desire to experience more fully is at the heart of immersive theatre, which can place us in situations that we are unlikely to encounter in our everyday lives, rather than merely placing them before us…. It stands to reason, then, that immersive theatre might be well-suited to tackle the extremities of human existence.
>
> (2010: n. pag.)

The possibility of experiencing more fully can be achieved during the most intimate of one-to-one performance as much as within the large-scale works of Punchdrunk or WildWorks. The alienation from real intimacy in our workaday lives, via such forums as Facebook, can be addressed by immersive practice, which demands bodily engagement, sensually stimulates the imagination, requires tactility. There is a special quality to this work that allows the intimate to be uncovered in the epic and points out where the epic lies within the intimate in human endeavour. By 'epic' in this practice I intend that which is both grand in execution and profound in appreciation; as Hill puts it in Part Two, epic is 'spectacular but it also has powerful meaning'. This underlines the unique potential this form of practice holds for *felt*, transformative behaviour within, and as a consequence of, the work.

The overriding focus of this book is to foreground current immersive practice that ensures the audience, their presence and sentient involvement within the work is the central concern. With immersive theatre the audience is removed from the 'usual' set of rules and conventions expected from 'traditional' theatrical performances. To be clear, 'traditional' or 'conventional' in this particular context (and accepting that these are contestable terms themselves) is a theatre experience, whether in a large Victorian theatre with a proscenium arch, the open-plan theatres of The National or in smaller studio spaces, where audiences enter an auditorium, sit in their assigned seat in a given row, obediently hush as soon as the house-lights dim and stage lights come up, perhaps, even still, a red, velvet curtain is raised.[4] Audience members applaud at the end of each act, take a drink in an interval, after which they return to their seats and, as the performance ends, there is final applause for the 'curtain call' and they leave. These rules and conventions can be understood to be in place in any spectatorial, theatre production where the audience/ actor (us/them) relationship is defined by the delineation of space (auditorium/stage) and role (static-passive observer/active-moving performer) where the audience is viewing the action ahead of them. This is a theatre experience which, on analysis, suggests it does not matter if you are there or not; the audience could get up and walk out and it would carry on. Such habits and preconceptions are actively investigated and overturned by Mercuriali in her Autoteatro investigations with Hampton or Brockis, as her conversation in Part Two makes clear. Wilson highlights how, with the traditional theatre set up, 'there's something about the lights going down that means you can be present and not present at the same time'. Janet Evans of Arcola 50+, discussing her experience of *The Uncommerical Traveller* in Part Two, muses on these customs and behaviours from the perspectives of both actor and audience member:

> I went to see *Betrayal* by [Harold] Pinter, expensive seats at the front and I just thought, they're over there and I'm over here; after doing [*The Uncommercial Traveller*] it made that division seem much greater.

In contrast, with immersive practice the audience is thrown (sometimes even literally) into a totally new environment and context from the everyday world from which it has come. These environments are seemingly outside of 'everyday' rules and regulations and always have expectations of physical interaction. All elements of theatre are in the mix, establishing a multidimensional medium in which the participant is submerged, blurring spaces and roles. Here there are unusual and intriguing rules of engagement; the wearing of masks, as with Punchdrunk's large-scale work, is a prerequisite for the audience's experience (see Illustration 1); rowdy interactivity akin to a gig or festival is encouraged, as with the audience for *Fuerza Bruta* (created by Diqui James, De La Guarda's founding director); ethical guidelines are shared and private agreements are made, as with Howells and his audience/ subject/collaborator in *The Pleasure of Being: Washing, Feeding, Holding*. What these experiences ensure is that each particular environment has its own order and logic; a logic that encourages a spontaneous response from its audience, and requires a personal abandonment of everyday boundaries. Such performances can offer lawbreaking conditions to roam free, take risks, be adventurous. They are specifically designed to immerse the individual in the unusual, the out-of-the-ordinary, to allow her or him, in many ways, to *become* the event. With immersive theatre, a childlike excitement for curiosity and adventure, perhaps equally a wariness of compliance, is activated in each participant. Whatever the scenario, the rules of play may be offered secretly before entering the world of the event or inferred by the audience as they experience the work moment-by-moment. More often than not it is a combination of the two. Rediscovery is central to the experience; of space, narrative, character, theme and sometimes even of unknown depths, or hidden emotions and memories specific to that individual participant. This rediscovery through active decision making is transformative; in terms of the way the individual audience member influences the shape of the 'show'; and transformative, like a rite of passage, where one can be personally and positively changed through the thematic concerns of the event, communicated via its experiential form.

An immersive inheritance

Immersive theatre is inherently interdisciplinary. An immersive form has evolved from the innovators of performance practice across generations. A range of practice has actively sought to create total, communal experiences for an audience. Participatory practice has existed in religious festivals and ceremonial pageants for centuries. Within the broad church of physical and visual theatres, in which immersive practice resides, techniques employed owe much to ancient and international rituals and theatre practices including: the embodied intoxication of African Dance Dramas, the shadow puppetry of Indonesia and Thailand, the democratic and ludic subversions of Commedia dell'arte alongside other worldwide traditions of street theatre; the breathtaking power and environmental practice of Butoh; and the conceptual and site-specific art of Europe and the Americas. Certain historic forms can be seen to remain vital to a communal, experiential methodology of practice, as evidenced in WildWorks' or Wilson's practice. They perhaps offer something inchoate in relation to spatial design and audience participation that is instinctively sensitive to the collective experience, both on a human and environmental level.[5] Bearing this in mind, and drawing on Nicolas Bourriaud's argument, it is important to remember that immersive practice as a 'relational art'

> is not the revival of any movement, nor is it the comeback of any style. It arises from an observation of the present and from a line of thinking about the fate of artistic activity … interactivity is anything but a new idea.

> (2002: 44)

Rather than give an exhaustive account of relevant practices and practitioners, the following inheritance shows an artistic trajectory and identifies possible origins of current immersive practice, highlighting inspirational forms and underpinning philosophies of practice.

Modernism, Antonin Artaud and 'total theatres'

Certain techniques and sensibilities attached to immersive theatre can be seen to have directly emerged from the Modernist period (roughly 1905–59) onwards, owing much to the interdisciplinary fusions across theatre, dance, film, visual/conceptual and installation art, and into current explorations in interactive gaming. Modernist practice arguably evolved from Richard Wagner's *Gesamtkunstwerk* (meaning 'total artwork') and early Romantic arguments for the inherent unity of all the arts. As Rose-Lee Goldberg points out, such cross-fertilizing of various aesthetic disciplines, developed from the Romantic forebears and explored by Modernist artistic practitioners (Dadaists, Expressionists, Surrealists and so on), established the effectiveness of 'an exchange between the arts' in the pursuit of the 'development of a sensibility' (1996: 46, 9). Equally, the element of fun, flux and furore that exists in immersive practice begins with Commedia dell'arte and European street theatre traditions which arose out of, and influenced, contemporary, carnival and festival. It traverses Dadaism and its radical experimentation with mixed-media hybridity and installation, which influenced the Assemblages, Environments and Happenings of the mid-twentieth century.

In highlighting the influence of Modernism and its various aesthetics, it is important to flag up the significance of Artaud's 'total theatre' where:

> theatre will recapture from cinema, music-hall, the circus and life itself, those things that always belonged to it...the magnitude and scale of a show aimed at the whole anatomy...an intensive mustering of objects, gestures and signs used in a new spirit.
>
> (Artaud, 1993: 66)

Immersive theatre can be seen as a paradigm of this as it puts much of his manifesto for theatre into glorious, sensual practice (see Artaud, 1993). Artaud is predominant in this lineage because his theories inspired the theatrical experimenters of the 1960s and beyond. Artaud's theory and practice directly influenced the inspirational practice of Jerzy Grotowski in Poland, Julian Beck and Judith Malina the instigators of the Living Theatre in North America, Richard Schechner and The Performance Group, Tatsumi Hijikata with Kazuo Ono in the creation of Butoh Theatre in Japan and Peter Brook in Britain. All were working at around the same time, sometimes collaborating or influenced by each other, all with Artaud's principles at the heart of the work. This was due to the fact that there was something in his manifesto that concurred with their beliefs about what theatre could and should be. Artaud's writings in particular, alongside a wider list of innovators of the Modernist period, hugely influenced the performance theory and practice that was to follow in terms of scenographic design, actor–audience relationships and highly physical performance styles.

Since the 1960s there has been a wealth of interactive and experiential practice that took forward Modernist principles of practice which are vital to current immersive theatre forms. These include 'Happenings' as documented by Allan Kaprow, Schechner's manifesto for 'Environmental Theatre' and the mid- to late twentieth-century movements in installation art. More recent experimentation with immersive technologies in performance have developed Artaudian ideals and influenced artistic concerns with interactivity to heighten sensual and imaginative engagement.

Happenings and Environmental Theatre

Kaprow states, *'the line between art and life should be kept as fluid, and perhaps indistinct, as possible'* (1995: 235; emphasis original). In this way the Happenings and environmental practice of the twentieth century find close affinity with the thinking and practice of current immersive theatre. As Claire Bishop summarises, with the Happenings, Kaprow sought 'a heightened experience of the everyday, in which viewers were formally fused with the space-time of the performance and thereby lost their identity as "audience"' (Bishop, 2006: 102). A key feature of Happenings was that they should occur 'over several widely spaced, sometimes moving and changing, locales. A single performance space tends toward the static and...resembles conventional theatre practice' (Kaprow, 1995: 236). Here the relationships formed between 'audience' and event involved 'new kinds' of interaction. Duration was a central feature of Happenings; time was perceived as '"real" and "experienced" time as distinct from conceptual time' (Kaprow, 1995: 237). Time was key to the sensual impact of the work and the differing qualities of time according to actions and spaces inhabited.[6] Happenings were ephemeral artworks, only to be performed once. In terms of 'composition' (and Kaprow uses this term in place of 'form', see 1995: 241–5) Happenings could not, indeed *should not*, be repeated, which connects closely with principles of immersive theatre.[7]

At the purest point of this sits Wilson's *Fissure*, which was created and performed for one weekend only in May 2011. Alternatively, Punchdrunk's work ensures that, as much as the 'form' of the event is repeated within the duration of any given performance night and across the performance run, the nature of each moment of this performance for each individual audience member is different and diverse and would be unrepeatable were they to attend every performance across the entirety of said run. Similarly, the intimate and exact composition of Howells's one-to-one performance, although precise and specific in certain actions, can never be the same by the very nature of the uniqueness of the encounter between Howells and his audience. Such practice connects with Kaprow's guidelines which propose the criteria or 'regulations' for the event 'provide for a variety of moves that make the outcome always uncertain' (1995: 239). Impulse and immediacy is a natural condition of the Happenings, 'the form emerge[s] from what the material can do' which ensures that openness to experience and interpretation becomes key (Kaprow, 1995: 243).

Happenings were Dionysian in form and attitude; instinctive, impromptu and random in nature rather than following more Apollinian forms of measure and restraint as with 'formal art' (Kaprow, 1995: 243).[8] Formal concerns with the 'finding of themes, subthemes, and counter themes' comes about directly via the lack of clear resolution and open quality of the composition, which leads to both general and specific meanings in experience and interpretation for the audience member (see Kaprow, 1995: 243). The concurrent and consequent affects of form and event are instinctive *and* intellectual, the intellectual often arising from the instinctive experience of the work. Ultimately, the composition and mission of the Happenings encouraged non-intellectualised, non-culturalised experience to be opened to the artist 'to use his mind anew in connecting things he did not consider before' (Kaprow, 1995: 243).

In considering Happenings it is important to highlight Schechner's work with The Performance Group. Schechner outlines a manifesto for environmental practice that describes the work of such companies as Living Theatre and The Performance Group and also provides a manifesto for any ensemble wanting to work in this way (see Schechner, 1994). His 'Six Axioms' within his wider treatise on 'Environmental Theatre' elucidate much about the intention, form and impact of immersive theatre, connecting notions of encounter between audience, performance and space:

> The kind of work I'm talking about can't happen if one territory belongs to the audience and another to the performers. The bifur-cation of space must be ended. The final exchange between performers and audience is the exchange of space, spectators as scene-makers as well as scene watchers.
>
> (Schechner, 1994: xxvi)

Maya E. Roth highlights how the 1960s practice from which Schechner's theorising developed, including that of the Living Theatre, The Performance Group, the Open Theatre and Anna Halprin's San Francisco Dancers' Workshops, looked to a 'revisioning of spatial and tactile physical relations' and was part of a movement in North American and British practice towards models of performance that were 'based less on presentation' and 'more explicitly on experiential encounter', acknowledging that such an approach can be seen to have existed across African, Asian and certain European traditions of performance prior to this time. Roth highlights how Schechner's analysis of Environmental Theatre practice implies an ecological sensibility that exists within the very form of this work (see Roth, 2007: 160–2). Arguably, then, an exploration of ecological and environmental issues automatically arises when *place* is a key feature of the immersive experience.

Installation and intimacy

Alongside the Happenings there was a correlational movement in conceptual art, which can be seen to foreshadow the more intimate aesthetic and participatory relationships of the immersive theatre experience, especially one-to-one performance practice. Practitioners from the 1960s onwards, in particular the ritualised performance/body art of the likes of Carolee Schneeman, Yoko Ono, Marina Abramović, Chris Burden and Franko B, can be seen directly to herald the one-to-one performance of today.[9] The rise of installation and site-specific art in Europe and the Americas since the 1960s has also influenced the aesthetic of immersive practice in the world of performance:

> 'Installation art' is a term that loosely refers to the type of art in to which the viewer physically enters, and which is often described as 'theatrical', 'immersive' or 'experiential'.
>
> (Bishop, 2010: 6)

Bishop provides a useful analysis of this practice and surveys a breadth of installation art processes and pieces (see 2010). Most significant to understanding the form and experience of immersive theatre is her reference to the Russian artist Ilya Kabakov, who has been working with what he refers to as 'total installation' since the 1980s. His work is described as theatrical and he refers to the viewer as 'the actor' for this reason. The effect of a total installation for this 'actor', according to Kabakov should be that she or he is 'submerged' in the work, 'engrossed' by it (qtd. in Bishop, 2010: 14). Similarly, Oliver Grau provides an overview, from the cave art of ancient times to computer-generated virtual environments of the present, of the sensually playful illusions of 'virtual art', highlighting the power of 'unconscious illusion' which can be produced by such work (Grau, 2003: 339–40). In such instances the immersive experience arises where medium and message are fused, resulting in the 'totalisation' of the artwork. This ludically subverts aesthetic and critical distance, placing the perceiver of the art *within* the art. In these situations, according to Grau the artwork becomes Dionysian (see Grau, 2003), moving beyond the visual affects of illusion to become wholly affective, possibly overwhelming and/or intoxicating.

Many one-to-one performances are framed as 'live art', blurring boundaries of theatre and visual art. They may be programmed in galleries or performance space according to the history and discipline from which the artist's work has evolved and been situated. One-to-one performance is created for an audience of one only and is usually brief in terms of duration. Rachel Zerihan provides a historical overview and analysis of this work (see Zerihan et al., 2009) highlighting how it draws on a live art aesthetic with an idiosyncratic potential for the 'spectator' to 'immerse' her or himself in the 'performance framework' and

> to collaborate (to greater or lesser degrees) with the performer so that the two people create a shared experience – responsive and dialectic as opposed to imposed and prescribed. Participation in the perfor-mance event often triggers spontaneity, improvisation and risk – in both parties – and requires trust, commitment and a willingness to partake in the encounter.
>
> (Zerihan, 2009: 3)

A great deal of immersive theatre, whether one-to-one or large-scale, taps into the 'total installation' aesthetic where the scenographic experience offered 'not only physically immerses the viewer in three-dimensional space', it 'is *psychologically* absorptive too' (Bishop, 2010: 14; emphasis original). A 'total installation' aesthetic is clear to see in the work of dreamthinkspeak, Lundahl & Seitl, Mercuriali, Nimble Fish, Punchdrunk and WildWorks in particular.[10] Immersive theatre plays with the forms of installation art yet in addition to the audience–actor's engulfment and interaction with/in the space, there is usually some kind of artist/audience-participant interaction designed to accentuate the sensual involvement and psychological engrossment within the performance.

Immersive technologies, sensual technologies

Explorations in installation art brings me to the more recent influence of 'immersive technologies', which straddle the innovations of the late twentieth century to the present. The definition of immersion taken from Games Studies provided in Chapter 1 go some way to highlighting the immersive aspects of gaming, virtual reality and immersive technologies. In relation to Performance Studies attention is focused in this respect on the *actual* involvement of the audience and performer, sometimes the audience *as* performer in such worlds.

Chris Salter helps to clarify how interdisciplinary immersive practice mixes 'human and technical presences' (Salter, 2010: 349) and, 'consciously and intentionally' entangle technologies making them 'inseparable from the form and operation of the work' in a 'polyphony of practices' (2010: xxxv–xxxvi). From early mechanical technologies to current digital practice the interdisciplinary arts have seen fusions between architecture, performance, scenography and robotic chore-ography, thereby shifting attitudes, experiences and 'interactions' in the parameters of arts practice and blurring the relationship between producer and audience. Salter identifies a lineage that has produced current experimentation that is both steeped in and inspired by our expanding technoculture:

> [A]rtists in the late 1980s and 1990s who were encouraged by the rapid developments in real-time graphics and interface technologies focused increasingly on the mechanics of interaction – how a new kind of unprecedented relationship could be instantiated between human users and machines.
>
> (2010: 321)

The influence of Artaud is clear in the visceral deployment of technology in artistic practice that seeks to connect humans with lived experience in unusual and immediate ways. In immersive practice any use of technology seeks to foreground the sensuous matter of the human body, employed by artists to recover and unleash *felt* experience via mechanical and digital means.

Virtual art as documented by Grau can be seen to exploit the sensual potential of digital technologies to a great degree: the more intimately manipulated the technology the more embodied the experience is perceived to be. In particular, Grau cites the work of Charlotte Davies who uses haptic technologies, wearable sensors, to create physical sensation within artistic events (see Grau, 2003: 198–202).[11] In such artistically fashioned virtual realities, 'the interface is key to the media artwork and defines the character of interaction and perception' resulting in 'a profound feeling of embodied presence', where the 'physically intimate design of the human-machine interface gives rise to such immersive experiences' that the work can reaffirm the 'participant's corporeality' (see Grau, 2003: 198–9). This is relevant not only in relation to the innovation in art practice, but in art *reception* as the human body is addressed 'polysensually', where 'full-body inclusion' demands that the observer 'relinquish distant and reserved experience' and embrace 'mind expanding' or 'mind assailing' perception fused with a holistically sensual apprehension/comprehension of the work (see Grau, 2003: 200); this is crucial to hold onto in terms of the ways in which referenced practice that employs technologies aids the immersive experience.

Immersive technologies which seek to heighten sensual experience include, haptic technologies, holography, surround-sound and head-mounted display or audio features. Such equipment is referred to in the conversations of Part Two by Barrett, Higgin, Gladwin, Lundahl and Seitl, Mercuriali, Morris and Stevens, illustrating a range of theatrical investigations employing sensual technologies. Immersive practice foregrounds a continuing relationship between technological systems and the body where the utilisation of technologies is concerned with artistic control and an *experiential* intent at the heart of the work, as exposed in the current experimentation of Back to Back Theatre, Coney, Lundahl & Seitl, Mercuriali and Punchdrunk. Such explorations in immersive practice go some way to enabling us to acknowledge and understand further the 'human' in our everyday interaction in these technocultural times. Barrett and Stevens each discuss the opportunities transmedia explorations offer theatre practice yet highlight certain limitations of digital realms in regards to the sensual involvement of the interactive participant. In this regard, the works considered in Part Two focus on those practitioners who employ such technologies in order to extend the sensual involvement from individual audience members.

Intimacy, involvement and communitas[12]

Progressive developments in architectural installation can be seen to have some bearing on Joan Littlewood's plans for 'Community Architecture Art' or the 'Fun Palace' (see Littlewood, 1995). It is important to acknowledge Littlewood's 'fun palaces' in terms of rethinking *communitas* inspired by artistic events and involving a more democratic landscape for theatre. Littlewood's vision saw place/space/art in architecture as living experience, 'a way of life', where divisions between everyday leisure activity, art installation and performance are blurred:

> where everybody might learn and play; where there could be every kind of entertainment, classical and ad lib, arty and scientific; where you could dabble in paint or clay; attend scientific lectures and demonstrations; argue; show off; or watch the world go by. It should be by a river. We need the ebb and flow of water to keep us in time.
>
> (1995: 628)

Littlewood's plans, drawn up and made architecturally plausible by Cedric Price, were, short-sightedly, never realised in Britain. Despite this, her ideas provide a cultural manifesto for immersive enrichment (see Littlewood, 1995: 702–8; and Stanley Mathews, 2005). Space, community and 'cultural production', involving ideas around enrichment, empowerment and education, arose out of and were fundamental to this artistic and municipal pursuit. These ideas for civic engagement find some affinity with the philosophies of such companies as Living Theatre and the democratic ideals of the Happenings and include the potentially egalitarian nature of virtual engagement, as highlighted by Stevens in Part Two. Although Littlewood's ideas were never fully realised, her vision for a Fun Palace points towards the potential power of interactive, immersive practice on communities as much as individuals. In particular, her utopian dream indicates the way in which all-encompassing immersive practice can inspire individuals and communities via the creation of experiential worlds where there is a fusion between communal recreation, egalitarian artistic experiences and imaginative fantasy.

In regard to important thinking around *communitas* and the role, responsibility and experience of the individual and collective audience in situations outside of theatre venues, Grotowski's 'paratheatre' is also of some relevance here. Grotowski's extensive research into the training of the performer and the direct connection with the audience led to his realisation that the audience was inevitably passive. Consequently, his theatrical explorations up until his death led him to examine the creativity of the spectator. His experimentations with the fusion of art and the active interiority of humans via these paratheatrical experiments grew into the 'theatre of sources' and 'art as vehicle' investigations still being run in his name after his death in 1999. These were and are civic, cultural and environmental in concept in an attempt to create genuine encounters between individuals and their location, with the self and an immediate community, through a ritualised, artistic coming together.

Today, ideals around the creativity of/from *communitas*, cultural experiences and imaginative fantasy are demonstrated in the immersive practice of Coney, Nimble Fish, Punchdrunk's Enrichment Projects and the intensive creative collaboration with local communities in the work of Wilson and WildWorks. Here space, architectural design and immersive environments are central to the community engagement and experience at the heart of the work. These projects defamiliarise the familiar to transcend experience and empower the individual participants within these events.[13]

Immersive theatres: immediacy and intimacy today

Out of this lineage, it is possible to identify specific strands of practice that are present in immersive theatre today. Modernist theatre practice, especially Artaud's 'total theatre', has influenced consequent performance theory and practice, certainly in terms of scenographic design, actor–audience relationships and highly physical performance styles. It directly influenced the experimentation with art/theatre/life crossovers of the 1960s and to the present. Happenings and Environmental

Theatre, with their open quality in composition, involving impulse and immediacy in execution and appreciation, required that the audience member become active within the event. They embraced general and specific meaning-making opportunities in response to the action, where intellectual interpretation arises from the instinctive experience of the work. Duration was central to these events allowing qualities of time *to be perceived* that ranged across the temporal, sensual and conceptual; with a shared mission that each event could never be repeated. The impact of duration alongside the focus on space and human interrelationships within that space established an environmental sensibility that allowed wider ecological concerns to exist within the very form of the work. All of these features are fundamental principles of much immersive theatre, as demonstrated in the work of Coney, dreamthinkspeak, Punchdrunk, WildWorks and Wilson.

The intimate aesthetic and participatory relationships of current immersive theatre experiences owe much to the installation and live art practice of the 1960s. These played with aesthetic distance, placing the perceiver of the art *within* the art or *as* the art, ensuring critical distance was subverted. Installation work that was placed in everyday spaces heightened the experience of 'real life'. Total installation was inherently interdisciplinary; where technologies were involved these fused the human and the technical to foreground embodied presence, thus reaffirming, rather than alienating, corporeality. The legacy of such an approach is clear in a range of work profiled in Part Two, including that produced by Artangel and especially in the work of Howells, Lundahl & Seitl and Mercuriali. It also underlines how definitions of immersive practice – as installation art, performance or something other – have as much to do with framing, programming and the publications in which work is reviewed as they do to the artist's background and training. This is touched upon in the conversation in Part Two with Lundahl & Seitl.

Communitas inspired by artistic events involved a range of more democratic processes within the theatrical experience. Here place/space/art as living experience fuses communal recreation, egalitarian artistic experiences and imaginative fantasy. The role of the individual and collective audience in situations outside of theatre venues demands risk-taking and investment, alongside sensual and intellectual involvement, from all participants in the event. The ideals of *communitas* and empowerment through immersive practice are clearly present in the practice of Back to Back Theatre, Coney, Howells, Nimble Fish, Punchdrunk Enrichment, WildWorks and Wilson. Happenings, Environmental Theatre and solo live art and installation, like Littlewood's and Grotowski's ideas for practice, explored the edges of experiential boundaries where art and life become fluid. These affinities in form and intent across this immersive inheritance point towards an important connection in outcome, which is to establish an all-encompassing form of experiential performance that requires embodied participation.

As a consequence of a vast array of theatrical antecedents, nowadays, affective qualities exist in a wide variety of theatrical events, the likes of which I have previously considered in *(Syn)aesthetics* (2011). For instance, the performance writing of Caryl Churchill or Sarah Kane is identifiably experiential, comes close to installation and certainly makes direct and unusual contact with the audience. However, such practice falls outside of the remit of this book due to the fact that it does not correspond to many of the criteria listed in the 'scale of immersivity' outlined in Chapter 1. Most significantly, although much theatre work can be described as experiential or visceral, I would not define it as immersive due to the fact that the direct, physical and *actual* immersion of the audience, requiring haptic interaction within the event (involving tactile, kinaesthetic and proprioceptive awareness), is lacking.[14]

Immersion and interaction

This book specifically surveys practice where actual immersion within an experience occurs. Such a relationship ensures the traditional boundaries, roles and definitions shared between performance and audience member are blurred, destroyed, reinvented. Where, in order to address challenges that might exist in the work and to open up the possibilities for involvement, there are 'rules of engagement' that underpin the experience, involving clear, even if tacit, guidelines (written, verbal or unspoken contracts understood) that make the immersive world a safe environment for the participant and embrace the impromptu possibilities proffered by the event itself. Each unique audience relationship foregrounds how sensual interaction in the work is a vital component of the immersive form. Holdsworth in Part Two reflects on the need for such 'contracts' with immersive practice, in order to offer safe spaces or 'get-out clauses' for unwilling audience-participants yet, equally, creating a safety-net for the performers in these enclosed worlds, highlighting the need for 'complicity' within that environment 'in accepting the invisible rules of the space'. All of the contributors refer to some kind of 'contract' or 'caretaking' in this respect.

In regard to this interaction, there is often a 'love it or loathe it' response to such work, as blogs, theatre reviews and anecdotal evidence documents, a large number of individuals dislike this type of practice. Such a reaction goes some way to helping us identify what it is that may be required of us as an audience-participant to help us reach the fullest appreciation of the work. Responses to this work are as diverse as those people who engage in the experience. In some instances there is an unwillingness to let down a guard, to play by the rules, which can prevent a full immersion in the work. I have witnessed an audience-participant refusing to wear a mask at Punchdrunk's *Faust*, her resistance to the form of the work summed up in this action and the remark, 'I know my *Faust*', suggesting there is a way to perform classical works, and this was not it. Along these same lines critics, such as Michael Coveney or Michael Billington, are disparaging of this form, the argument being that this work can lack accomplishment in technique and is without a political and philosophical backbone; that ultimately it cannot compare to the clarity and complexity of ideas expressed through the written play (see Coveney, 2010; Billington 2012). The implication in these responses is that there is a dislike of work that is not driven by linear narrative; that there is a resistance to the perceived 'onus on us' to both create and enjoy the work, an inference that this can be humiliating in practice and inconsequential in effect. Although this book offers an alternative viewpoint to this, I do acknowledge that there is a pleasurable completeness to be had in linear forms of theatre, usually that which has a writer at the centre of the process and where a clear idea or argument is expressed. I also acknowledge that there are those who know that this is the type of theatre for them. However, this is a matter of taste and personal judgement – simply that – and it limits the possibilities of what theatre is to imply that these two strands of theatre practice cannot coexist.

Immersive practice can be faulted, superficial or poorly executed, as can many 'traditional' presentations of plays. Nevertheless, there *is* great artistic and philosophical rigour to be had in immersive practice, as the analysis of Part One documents and the conversations in Part Two demonstrate. As Morris articulates early on in his discussion, a theatrical experience that is driven by the point at which text, image, action and sound 'meet afresh as equals' and where the writer is not the starting point, for the performance has its own power and authority within the discipline of theatre. Here there is a greater complexity to the ways in which a central idea, or combination of thematic ideas emerge and are expressed. Indeed, often the form itself is the thematic idea.

As this indicates, the immersive form requires care in its execution. Where this is lacking, people can become angry at the demands placed on them and thus choose not to play along. There were instances of this with Badac Theatre's 2008 immersive production of *The Factory*, which, although for many brave and committed in its aim to communicate the experience of Jews going to their death in Auschwitz, was flawed in delivery. Consequently, it received a general wave of pejorative reviews related to the expectations it placed on its audience (for example, see Brian Logan, 2008). What does become apparent here is that immersive theatre requires much of the individual audience member: the letting down of boundaries, giving in to experience, willingly engaging in a truly embodied fashion, which can be both a positive and negative experience for an individual. Yet even where work is executed with great finesse, there is still the potential for audience dissatisfaction and dislike due to the interaction required. Maxine Doyle, Choreographer and Associate Director for Punchdrunk, explains:

> If you're less confident – we don't know what audience members bring with them to our world, their history or circumstances, but – within that experience you can be overwhelmed, put off by it.
>
> (qtd in Machon, 2011: 90)

Mercuriali comments on the problems of this work for the audience in her conversation in Part Two. She acknowledges how her Autoteatro experiments, such as *Etiquette* or *Wondermart*, have been met with delight yet also disgruntlement, as blogs recount. She herself debates both sides of these challenges in relation to Punchdrunk's *The Masque of the Red Death* (2007–8), feeling foolish because of the particular connotations the mask wearing had for her as a trained physical performer and thus unable to engage fully with the event. Immersive work has to *enable* the audience to be willing participants. Yet, as Doyle's comments and Mercuriali's observations show, even where encouragement is given and enabling techniques are put in place there can still be a dislike of the interactions required for a range of personal reasons. Furthermore, in cases where audience-participants do give themselves willingly to the work, frustrations can still arise from the form preventing the following of a desired course of action. I was trapped in Punchdrunk's *The Masque of the Red Death* (2007) on one side of the building, enjoying myself, taking the time to experience the side events and the details of the rooms and scenes in which I dwelt, but I was also desperately trying to follow a bigger story, to get over to the other side. Eventually I gave up and went to the bar – a liminal space where the rules of the piece are relaxed in that you can remove your mask whilst still being part of the performance itself – only to be drawn through into the crescendo of the 'final' dance in the ballroom. Despite my frustration at having 'missed stuff', as the dance played out and the remaining congregation either joined in or left I realised that three hours had felt like one, had gone without me being in the slightest bit aware of time passing; frustrations and delights all in one experience.

Presence as *praesence*

Bearing in mind the potency of this practice in terms of an individual's experience, a vital component of immersive theatre is the fact that it revels in the liveness and consequent *live(d)ness* of the performance moment. To clarify, whatever forms that the imaginative journey through the event takes – via fusions of scenographic design, sound, digital technologies, physical performers and interactive audience participants – what is clear is that the sensual worlds created exploit the power of live performance. Immersive practice harnesses the lasting ephemerality of performance as an artistic medium of expression. By 'lasting ephemerality' I am highlighting a paradoxical experience that this work can offer in that the live performance of the work is fleeting and only of the moment, never to be repeated in any form, yet it also lasts in the receiver's embodied memory of the event, a pleasurable and/or disquieting impression that remains.

Immersive events enhance the live(d) audience-performer-participant interaction and exchange that occurs within the event. The live experience of immersive performance colludes in a continuing, immediate and interactive exchange of energy and experience between the work and the audience. It accentuates the 'presentness' of human sensory experience, where 'presence', to borrow from Elaine Scarry's explication of the term, directly correlates to its etymological roots; 'from *prae-sens*, that which stands before the senses' (Scarry, 1985: 197; emphasis original). Further to this, the Latin root form of 'present' accounts for a state of *being* or *feeling* and emphasises the tactile proof of this in *praesent*, 'being at hand' (from *praeesse*; *prae*, 'before' and *esse*, 'be'). By emphasising the meanings therein of presence and present; in the immersive context, the state of stirring *praesence* felt by a participating individual in the event refers back to this full meaning and usage.

By employing parenthesis with 'live(d)' I intend to draw attention to the way in which, in immersive performance experiences, the performing bodies and perceiving bodies that undergo the experience within the duration of that event are charged by the sensual aesthetic and the specific energies of the piece in a live and ongoing present, as much as the performance itself communicates lived histories and shared experiences. 'Live(d)' thus embraces the idea of the performing and perceiving body as living, tactile and haptic material. The embodied experience underpinning immersive practice foregrounds this *praesent* exchange within the live performance moment and encompasses the fact that the human body is itself a tangibly 'lived' being (physiological, social, cultural, historical, political and so on). Consequently, this arousing, experiential form works to expose the *lived* nature of the representations. These interacting performing and perceiving bodies establish a constant *praesence* in the live performance moment. Immersive performance events which are stimulated by the potential human bodies have to make and interpret meanings truly expose and exploit this potential for live(d) experience.

The structure of Part One and Part Two

Part One, Chapter 1 begins with a simple table to provide extreme examples of how 'traditional theatres' and 'immersive theatres' differ in approach and outcome. Chapter 1 proceeds to expand on the ideas introduced above and in Table 1. It offers definitions for 'immersion' and 'the immersive' in performance terms, adapting theories from virtual art and Games Studies. Although this digital perspective assists in getting to the heart of what immersive theatre is, the intention is to rework these definitions, adjusting the ideas to that work which exists in the sensual realm of live performance, with human bodies and physical space as its central concern. In light of this, Chapter 1 summarises qualities of immersion to be experienced within such performance events. The chapter closes by raising questions to be considered in Chapter 2 regarding how one might gauge an immersive event by identifying central features and finer details of this theatrical form.

Chapter 2 addresses these questions and focuses in more depth on the central characteristics of immersive practice, its form and potential function. It surveys some useful analytical and practical stances from performance theory to help elucidate the ways in which a piece of theatre can be deemed wholly immersive. In so doing this chapter uses these performance perspectives to set the parameters of the type of immersive practice under scrutiny. Underpinned by illustrations from a range of exponents in the field, prioritising those who contribute to Part Two, Chapter 2 proposes that diverse practice exists under the umbrella term of 'immersive theatre'. Each example employed offers various measures on 'the scale of immersivity' that closes Chapter 2. This scale pinpoints the particular elements that make-up immersive theatres. It does not intend to provide a comparative analysis of the ways the different approaches to immersive experiences might work on an individual by way of judging the success of works cited. Instead, it contemplates the qualitative experience of this work to point towards some general assumptions that might be drawn regarding the impact of this work upon audiences. Further analysis of the affective impact of this type of work is also provided within the interviews in Part Two.

Chapter 3 surveys useful perspectives drawn from a wealth of backgrounds. These theories, taken from the fields of anthropology, architecture, geography, literature, performance, social science and visual art, help to illustrate further the quintessential features of immersive theatres as put forward in Chapter 2. They draw particular attention to the relationship between space, audience and the sensual experience in immersive theatres and help to elucidate the practice of immersion in live performance. The perspectives employed in Chapter 3 identify various elements of the form, function and artistic approach in style and appreciation of 'immersive theatre'. This chapter begins by summarising characteristic features of '(Syn)aesthetics' to show how immersive theatre is a particular strand of (syn)aesthetic practice. To expand on ideas around immersion and sensate involvement, I consider Gilles Deleuze's insight on 'immanence', sense and sensation and the ludic logic of the paradoxical. Alongside this I examine Kathryn Linn Geurts's research into West African expressions of consciousness and embodiment, specifically that of the Anlo-Ewe peoples. In elucidating the *praesence* and pleasures of the audience I then turn to Umberto Eco's 'Open Texts', Jacques Rancière's 'Emancipated Spectator' and the 'Relational Aesthetics' of Nicolas Bourriaud. Perspective then shifts to survey the significance of space via Juhani Pallasmaa's musings on the sensuality of space, Doreen Massey's theories of the inherent politics of space and place and Gaston Bachelard's evocative study of the 'poetics of space'.

Across Part One the critical outlook employed serves to describe the practice as well as to highlight ways of analysing and appreciating the work. It should be clear that the theories explored foreground a predominantly sensual and embodied approach to meaning-making within analysis which I would like to emphasise as crucial to my own philosophical outlook as much as (and therefore) it underpins this particular stance on immersive theatre practice. Additionally, in relation to the fact that immersive practice owes much to intercultural techniques, it is useful to note that it is mainly in Western European and North American theorising that there has been a prioritisation of cerebral thought over embodied knowledge, with a privileging of sight and hearing over the other senses of smell, taste and touch. Significantly, until very recently, Western theory has largely ignored the underlying senses of proprioception and kinaesthetic 'hapticity' (the holistic focus on haptic sensation and perception).

What is important in relation to embodied theorising is the valorisation of the whole body and its capacity for interpreting from holistic experience; a must when appreciating, analysing and evaluating genuinely immersive events. Analysis such as that offered, and drawn upon, in this book draws attention to the fact that sensual perception and expression is not only a natural and fundamental human potential, it is also culturally prescribed. Following this, it is useful to note how non-Western traditions of informal analysis allow access to a coherent and eloquent means of (and vocabulary for) expressing embodied modes of interpretation. These issues and an equivalent analytical approach to interaction and interpretation come up not just in those theories that focus on sensual comprehension, but also those that are primarily concerned with defining and explaining audience relationships in contemporary performance. Immersive theatre has the potential to reawaken holistic powers of cognition and appreciation that celebrate and call into play alternative methods of 'knowing'.

In order to illustrate the ideas presented in Part One of the book, in Part Two I turn to a range of contributors who are producing wholly immersive events, or exploring immersive techniques within their wider work. Part Two provides a space for practitioners to question and debate their own definitions and experiences of this formalistic approach. There are discussions with Michael Morris of Artangel, Felix Barrett of Punchdrunk and Tristan Sharps of dreamthinkspeak, practitioners whose works have been hailed as exemplary of the immersive form. Conversations also cover a particular immersive strand of practice that 'collaborates' with landscape, specifically with Louise Ann Wilson and with Bill Mitchell and Sue Hill of WildWorks. There are interviews with Adrian Howells, Christer Lundahl and Martina Seitl and Silvia Mercuriali, all of whom offer unique experimentation within the field of one-to-one and intimate, immersive performance. Bruce Gladwin of Back to Back Theatre provides interesting reflections on the role of audio technologies and the proximity of performers in space to draw an audience into the intimacies of an immersive experience. There is also a focus on those companies who expose the power that the immersive form has within applied practice and 'cultural production', as discussed by Tassos Stevens of Coney, Samantha Holdsworth of Nimble Fish and Pete Higgin, Punchdrunk's Director of Enrichment, alongside fellow members of the creative team, reflecting on Punchdrunk's *The Uncommercial Traveller*.

A focus in this book is on theatre that employs technologies within its practice to heighten the live(d), sensual performance experience. Part Two draws attention to those companies who are experimenting with immersive technologies, audio, video and haptic, in order to deepen democratic and sensual access to the work as with Back to Back Theatre or Coney's work. The sensuality of technology is central to the playful explorations of Mercuriali in her theatrical collaborations. Barrett highlights Punchdrunk's ongoing experiments to plunder the possibilities existing at the interstices of immersive technology and immersive theatre to experiential ends. The discussion across Parts 1 and 2 aims to show how the presence of technology can be a fundamental element within an immersive event, encouraging greater access to a sensual and *felt* response from the individual audience member and opening up ideas within and around creative space, encompassing the internal human capacity of imaginative space as much as designed rooms, architecture and geographical location.

The central aspect of 'audience' is addressed throughout this book, textured by my own response to the works under scrutiny, which is woven throughout the analysis and underpins the questioning within the interviews in Part Two. As regards the interviews that make up Part Two, as I stated above the intention here is to provide a creative space where practitioners reflect on their own practice. Primarily these conversations provide first-hand observations from immersive theatre practitioners in which they reflect on their intentions, processes and methodologies for practice, in order that the reader may reach a clearer understanding of what immersive theatre is. These discussions focus on form and how this communicates the concept, themes and narratives of the work. Each provides a space for practitioners to ruminate on the intention for and impact of their work, all of which are generous and self-reflexive in this respect.

Part One interrogates this illustrative practice, with direct reference to these interview reflections and the works under observation, interweaving this with the terms of my own analysis to foreshadow ideas presented in these interviews in Part Two. The combination of academic enquiry and practitioner reflections is intended to help the reader to get to grips with that practice which provides a model for producing immersive theatre. My aim is to make this analysis as open and reflective as possible and to contextualise this practice via an 'objective–subjective' critical perspective. As Part One highlights, immersive practice is a form and process that is applicable across the arts. As you read, I would hope that the critical theories and illustrative examples allow you to draw connections with your own immersive experiences, from whatever discipline this may be.

Part One

Defining Immersive Theatres

I Definitions and Details

Illustration 3 dreamthinkspeak's *Don't Look Back* (2004)
[Photo credit: Gideon Mendel. Image courtesy of dreamthinkspeak]

Definitions

The act of defining is both a pleasurable and problematic pursuit. As Jubb highlights:

> [T]he challenge with this debate, as with all of its kind, is how you define your terms. Are we all going to be speaking about the same thing? Terms such as immersive, intimate, epic, can all be slippery in the context of trying to find common ground or some kind of shared truth.
>
> (2010: n. pag.)

Table 1 'Traditional Theatre' vs. Immersive Theatre

A 'traditional' theatre experience	An immersive theatre experience
You will hear about the performance via the venue's programme or through mainstream adverts and regular marketing strategies. You will buy your ticket from the box office in advance or on the door.	You may hear about the event as part of the venue's programming. The event may be part of a festival of similar events. Or you may *only* have heard about this via word of mouth and online sources such as Twitter or Facebook. You will be aware that the marketing language used is evocative of the mystery surrounding the event, perhaps similar to that of secret societies. You may buy your ticket via a box office or only through online channels.
You will enter the theatre from the street, usually via the main doors of the theatre building. You will show your tickets and be directed by front of house staff to your seat in the auditorium. You will sit and wait for the event to begin.	You may have an extended or intriguing journey to get to the location. This journey itself makes you aware that you are being taken out of your comfort zone. You may remain outside for most or all of the event. If the piece is housed in a theatre it is likely to be one that supports innovative practice. If this is the case, when you arrive you will be directed to a location that is not in the auditorium. You are unlikely to be seated. If you are seated this act in itself feels unusual.
If you are with friends or family you will be chatting about everyday matters, waiting for the lights to go down. A programme may provide information about the performers, the production, the creative team. You are you. You are here to watch a piece of theatre. You are waiting for it to begin.	You have been placed in a context where the performance has already begun. You don't know what's the performance space and what's the everyday space. You are excited and a bit scared. You have little or no idea what you are about to experience. You may have been separated from your friends as part of the journey within the space, as part of the rules of the experience. You may have been partnered with a stranger who you will rely on to work with you through the experience. You may be on your own.

You are reminded to switch off your mobile.
The lights dim, you become quiet.
The curtain and/or the lights are raised revealing another world.

Performers perform on the stage in front of you, technical details add to the impact. You observe, spectate, listen to the unfolding narrative.
You may be present in this space through laughter and intellectual attention, other than that the performance is completed with little or no reference to you being there.
You may have had an interval at some point between acts.

There is a curtain call bow.
You applaud.
You leave the auditorium.

You leave the theatre through the foyer.
The performance was good or it was bad.
You know you have seen a piece of theatre.

You are physically surrounded by another world. You are intensely aware of your habitat and the details of the space. You may be required to use your mobile as part of the performance. You may still be you but you have become a sensitised you. Or you are aware that you have taken on a character, you are playing out a role.

You are in a different world that has its own rules; that is intimate, epic. You are upright, active, engaged in action with the artist with whom you share the space, or working your way through rooms, corridors, across fields, down narrow streets. You are finding a narrative, following performers. You feel like you are responsible for the secrets you uncover and performances you find.

There is no bow. Where the event is a one-on-one you have taken your leave of the artist with whom you have shared the moment. If large-scale you may feel that there is no ending, that a party has begun in the bar. There is a very strong sense of community and shared experience as people chat over drinks, mill around or head to public transport together.

You leave the space and are aware that time has condensed or elongated over the duration of the event. The experience bleeds into the real world, you are aware of attending to detail, sensation being heightened as you wend your way home. You are exhilarated, disturbed, perhaps tired. You are unsure whether that was theatre, art, festival, gig, game, party, therapy. You know you want to do it again. Or you know it demanded too much of you and you will never do it again.

In attempting to define this nebulous form, it is important to reiterate that a great deal of contemporary theatre practice can envelop the audience member in 'the world of the performance' and affect the receiver of the work in an experiential way, regardless of whether or not its form is immersive. As examples I would include the sensual, interdisciplinary practice of Pina Bausch or Robert Lepage and the uncannily condensed writings of Churchill. All of these require embodied attention in interpretation as much as they inspire an unusual and lasting intellectual engagement.

The experiential quality of these performance works thus moves beyond 'conventional' theatre:

> The conventional relationship in theatre (i.e. a non-immersed audience) often seeks to make us forget our physical existence, wrapping us up in the onstage action. Where it is keen to remind us of our presence, it engages with us not as physical bodies, but as a conscious presence. It reminds us that we are watching, before it reminds us that we are sitting here watching. The act of perception is more important than the (passive) act of attending.
>
> (Trueman, 2011: n. pag.)

Leslie Hill similarly notes, '[t]hough conventional theatre-going is a real-time, real-space experience and thus has the potential to be sensually immersive, it is more often than not an audio-visual experience that offers little to the other three senses' (2006: 48). With these observations in mind, the example practice of Bausch, Churchill or Lepage is *not* conventional; each has an experiential essence and 'total theatre' aesthetic that engages a wholly embodied response and points towards an immersive quality within the work. However, the work of these practitioners, although markedly sensual and (syn)aesthetic in form, does not meet the criteria for full immersive practice provided in the 'scale of immersivity' at the end of this chapter. This is primarily due to the fact that the realisation of this work and all productions to date have been presented within more traditional conventions of theatre, where the audience remain physically separate to the action, seated in an auditorium or a cordoned viewing area, attending (albeit corporeally) in this spectatorial fashion. Morris and I discuss this in Part Two. He highlights how the film *Pina* (2011), the Wim Wenders homage to Bausch, in 3-D, conveyed a sense of being on the stage with the dancers. What is striking here is that this illustration accentuates how wholly immersive practice *actually allows* you to be 'on the stage' with the dancers, touching, smelling, feeling the heat and energy coming off their bodies, physically interacting with them, as is the case in Punchdrunk's large-scale work. This indicates that the physical insertion and direct participation of the audience member in the work *must* be a vital component and is a defining feature of this particular strand of visceral practice. Here the audience member, as an interactive agent in the performance, is absolutely central to the movement/physicality and sensual design of the event.

It is also true to say that any (good) performance establishes its own world, creates a sense that performers and design combine to summon up an imagined world for which the audience suspends its disbelief for a given period of time. However, this 'world' has a different connotation to the 'in-its-own-world-ness' of immersive theatre. Of course, it is possible that a company could realise Churchill's plays, say *The Skriker* (1994), *Far Away* (2000) or *Love and Information* (2012), in an immersive setting; the possibilities for these plays and immersive practice are vast and open to experimentation. That aside, the aim of this book is to get to the heart of what it is that makes a piece of theatre *fully* immersive; how we might identify immersive traits and elements being manipulated within a production without it being a wholly immersive event. Equally, to work out the ways in which a performance piece might be inappropriately defining itself as 'immersive' simply because it happens to involve a sequence of audience participation at some point in its proceedings, or because the design begins outside of the stage space in the foyer, or because it is a site-specific, promenade piece. Although these can be important elements of an immersive experience, on their own or handled in an unskilled way, they are not intrinsically immersive. As a way into the definitions and details of what immersive theatre is, it might be useful to summarise how an immersive theatre experience differs, in generalised terms, from what has been referred to as 'traditional' or 'conventional' theatre. Table 1 (see above) provides extreme examples to assist in the act of defining and to encourage debate regarding the type of theatre work visited, qualities of experience had and levels of immersion undergone.

Defining immersiveness, immersion, immersivity

It is difficult to ascertain exactly when 'immersion' first began to be used to describe an all-encompassing artistic experience and even more so to pinpoint exactly when 'immersive' was first applied to theatre practice. 'Immersive', as both noun and verb, was initially assigned to and theorised around computer technologies and telematic environments in the 1980s. Additionally, developments in 'Immersive Theaters' (sic), domed constructions involving multi-media technologies, surround sound and video, designed to create extravaganzas for performance events, large-scale exhibitions, marketing, cinema and entertainment events have been moving forward since the late 1980s. What was the London Planetarium, now the Tussaud's Marvel Hero 4-D Spectacular is a perfect example of this. One need only conduct a search on the internet under 'immersive theaters' to see the range of companies that exist and the facilities available to produce such 3-D and 4-D spectacles.

A number of the practitioners in Part Two discuss the fusion of technical elements as integral to the immersive experience, Gladwin provides particular detail about the significance of sound in Back to Back Theatre events, as do Lundahl & Seitl and Mercuriali to their work. Barrett identifies early on the equal authority of all of the elements of performance in Punchdrunk's practice. Morris asserts that, as a consequence of 'surround-sound', it is possible to play with the directionality of sound and surrounding experiences within more conventional theatre set-ups. Consequently, these technological progressions add to the immersive qualities present in traditional theatre performances. This indicates a possible reason for the overuse of the term 'immersive' to describe such productions, as the technical details are able to draw us more deeply in to the action and emotion on stage. With this in mind, it is important to hold onto where the word is appropriate as an adjective, but may be misleading if applied as a defining category of theatre. As the term has been so closely associated with advances in digital technologies and due to the playful connections that can be drawn between gaming and certain immersive theatre experiences, especially in relation to Coney's practice, it is useful to look to definitions of immersion in Games Studies to help come closer to a definition of what immersivity in theatre might be.

Immersion, involvement and presence: Gaming Theory

In digital disciplines 'immersive' is used as an adjective to describe those computer displays or systems that generate a three-dimensional image that appears to surround the user. It is also understood more generally as pertaining to digital technology or images that deeply involve one's senses and/or may create an altered mental state. In light of current developments in digital technologies in the arts, Grau further elucidates:

> Immersion arises when the artwork and technical apparatus, the message and medium of perception, converge into an inseparable whole ... [T]he principle of immersion is used to withdraw the apparatus of the medium of illusion from the perception of the observers to maximise the intensity of the message being transported.
>
> (2003: 348–9)

Gordon Calleja (2011) provides an informative analysis that interrogates ideas around presence, immersion and incorporation in the digital gaming world. He points out that the term has to be understood under the very specific contexts in which it is used. In this respect, he shows how definitions of 'immersion' in Gaming Theory and Games Studies vary, often used interchangeably with 'presence'. Its use thereby results in confusing meanings when applied generally, particularly because it is also applied in differing ways across varied media including cinema, painting, literature; forms of engagement which are markedly different to those of game practice (see Calleja, 2011: 17–18). This corresponds to the potential confusion that may arise in regards to how 'immersive' is currently employed in marketing language, arts criticism and performance studies. Bearing this in mind, 'Immersive Theatre', as scrutinised here, must be understood as an immersive practice in and of itself, not one that must defer to technological practice nor any other artistic media, but rather, an immersive experience that coexists with these alternative media.

With any analytical process, it is important to acknowledge that words have particular meanings according to the discourse in which they are employed. As Calleja foregrounds in relation to games theories, we need to be mindful of the implications and assumptions that underpin any metaphors and definitions that are used in order that we accurately describe and analyse a practice and experience. A number of the questions that Calleja poses directly relate to the knotty problem of defining exactly what 'immersion' is in the theatre world, and the ways in which the term should be understood if used as a generic metaphor as opposed to being applied to specific forms and experiences. Calleja summarises distinct areas that are useful to consider in relation to what the term immersion defines in Theatre Studies. These include, in brief: a need to qualify the parameters of the term's use – 'immersion as absorption vs. immersion as transportation' or the oscillation between the two; the need to acknowledge the specificities of the medium to which the term is applied and; 'monolithic perspectives on immersion', acknowledging the multiple and varied experiences of immersion in differing everyday and/or artistic contexts (see Calleja, 2011: 32–3).

Calleja surveys presence theories across literature, art and gaming to demonstrate how, whatever the circumstances, a sense of presence is always related to form. He points out that, in Games Studies, 'presence' and 'immersion' can be used interchangeably or may be given very specific and complementary or even contradictory meanings, ranging across player involvement in the narrative of the game to the extent to which computer displays and feedback are capable of creating an inclusive, surround experience for the operator. The latter is achieved via audio, video and haptic means, which influences embodied sensations, establishing a perceived inclusion in an environment (see Calleja, 2011: 20–2).[1]

Following this, in digital gaming, 'immersion' can refer to a range of experiences including 'general engagement, perceptions of realism, addiction, suspension of disbelief and identification with games characters' as much as it is used 'as a promotional adjective to market games', i.e. immersion = good (see Calleja, 2011: 25). This latter point is interesting as 'immersive' is now commonly used, often inappropriately in my view, to market theatre experiences which happen to play a little with site, design and/or audience participation, but to non-experiential (and thus non-immersive) ends. In gaming, this generic overuse of the term in marketing points towards a desire on behalf of the consumer/player to delve 'into a virtual reality that replaces the realm of physical existence' (Calleja, 2011: 25). Arguably, then, in theatre it points towards the fact that there is a bandwagon being jumped on that is exploiting an increasing desire amongst non-mainstream theatre audiences to delve into a reality that both replaces and accentuates the live(d) existence of the everyday, actual world. As the term and elements of the form are appropriated and overused in this way, then there is a subsequent push into, and appropriation by, the mainstream.

Calleja's descriptions of immersion and presence lend clarification to the ways in which immersive theatre establishes a special kind of presence – visceral in every respect, being both embodied and noetic.[2] In the realm of theatre, it can be understood that this feeling of 'being there' is a fact; the audience-participant *is actually there*, physically inhabiting the fantasy world created. This live(d) experience of physical *praesence*, the participant's physical body responding within an imaginative, sensual environment, is a tangible fact and a pivotal element of the immersive experience. In regards to this, audio, visual and haptic feedback is also an actuality rather than a manipulated technical effect. In some instances, such as in the work of Il Pixel Rosso, the interplay of audio, video and haptic technologies in the live experience is activated within a visceral rather than a virtual world. Furthermore, in *And the Birds Fell From the Sky...* or *The Great Spavaldos*, the audience-participant-performer is directly interacting with actual props and the physical guidance of a human performer. This accentuates sensual involvement and plays games with visceral-virtual perception.

Gaming deals in various levels of involvement; kinaesthetic, spatial, shared, narrative, affective and ludic (Calleja, 2011: 4). Players are anchored in the game-world via an avatar, which allows gaming to transcend the levels of engagement experienced in other forms of media, specifically literature and cinema. This

> fundamentally alters how the player perceives herself within the world, and is not present in literature, films or personal imagining. When we identify with a character in a movie or a book, or imagine we are in the same room as the protagonist, we have no way of altering the course of events, no way of exerting agency. Likewise the environments and characters represented in these media have no way of reacting to our presence.
>
> (Calleja, 2011: 23)

It is clear to see how immersive theatre surpasses this virtual quality of engagement and allows for agency and interaction. In immersive theatre the audience-participant-performer-player is anchored and involved in the creative world via her or his own imagination, fused with her actual presence, fused with her bodily interaction with the physical (and sometimes virtual) environments and other human performers. As examples, Blast Theory has been playing with the nature and tools of such involvement in a live manner since the mid-1990s; Coney exploit digital communication to their own, idiosyncratic ends; Punchdrunk are collaborating with MIT using online interaction to explore the potential for virtual engagement with the visceral world of the New York production of *Sleep No More* (2011–).

Calleja refers to the 'processual' nature of certain game enactment, which highlights the variation in the experience that occurs due to player decision-making. Here games are 'processes that create carefully designed, unpredictable interpretations' where 'both the game practice and the meaning it generates are subject to change' (Calleja, 2011: 10–11). This idea of a processual interaction through and within the experience can be directly applied beyond these aforementioned virtual experiments to the structure of Punchdrunk's epic events such as *The Masque of the Red Death*. Here audience-participant-performer interactions, although carefully shaped and in many ways predetermined, allow diverse decisions to be taken and thus invite an exciting variety of interpretations to be made. As this suggests, affiliations between gaming practice and immersive theatre on a grand scale can be clearly drawn in Punchdrunks' work. Coney's *The Gold-bug* explicitly combined the practice of pervasive gaming and immersive theatre. It is clear to see then how concepts and techniques of immersion in gaming relate to the processual nature of certain immersive theatres. Adapting further ideas from Calleja's reading of Game Theory (see Calleja, 2011: 26–32), the following categories can be applicable as definitions of 'immersion' within the immersive theatre experience:

1 **Immersion as absorption**. The theatre event is able to engage the participant fully in terms of concentration, imagination, action and interest; a total engagement in an activity that engrosses (and may equally entertain) the participant within its very form. This is applicable to large-scale immersive events and intimate one-on-one encounters, including those designed within a wider immersive experience.

2 **Immersion as transportation**. Where the audience-participant is imaginatively and scenographically reoriented in another place, an otherworldly-world that requires navigation according to its own rules of logic. Whereas in games practice this occurs in a conceptual space, in immersive theatre a central feature of the experience is that this otherworldly-world is *both* a conceptual, imaginative space *and* an inhabited, physical space. Where 'game environments afford extranoetic habitation by recognising and reacting to the presence of the player' (Calleja, 2011: 29) immersive theatre worlds afford *actual*, physical cohabitation and contact between human bodies, thereby fusing imagination, interpretation and interaction. This otherworldliness, outside of the everyday, can be established within minimalist one-on-one moments just as it can with elaborately designed large-scale events.

3 **Total immersion**. Involving both of the above and leading to an uncanny recognition of the audience-participant's own *praesence* within the experience. Where total immersion occurs, there is always the experience of formalistic transformation in that the audience-participant is able to fashion her own 'narrative' and journey. Certain events may enable emotional or existential transformation to occur due to the ideas and practice shared.

All immersive performance events exist at some point between these three criteria, total immersion being the most intense state experienced.

Immersion, involvement and praesence: *defining immersive theatre*

The first use of the term 'immersive' in relation to visceral and physically inhabited (non-telematic) theatre lacks an incontestable source. From my research for this book, the earliest claimed usage is attributable to Artangel; Morris recalls using 'immersive' and 'enveloping' as adjectives to describe the visceral-visual, physical theatre of La Fura Dels Baus at the Royal Victoria Docks in 1983. Subsequently, Morris and Lingwood explicitly used the term in relation to *H.G.*, a performance installation created by Robert Wilson and Hans Peter Kuhn and produced by Artangel (1995). In this respect, shades of 'the immersive'

have described interdisciplinary, sensory and participatory performance work occurring in places outside of traditional theatre venues
for a good while. The work of Welfare State (1968–2006), of which
Hill of WildWorks was a member, displayed many immersive features;
it actually blurred the boundaries between life and art in the ritual
ceremonies of namings, weddings and funerals that it undertook.[3]
Like the Happenings and environmental practice highlighted in the
Introduction, one need only look to archives of the work of Welfare
State to note the descriptions and analysis that indicate the immersive
nature of the practice, yet the term itself was not applied to the work.

Oily Cart, cited by Higgin as an influence, has been working with
immersive forms since 1981, with audience-participants primarily
made up of children and young people with complex disabilities. Oily
Cart's multi-sensory, interactive practice over the years has employed
various approaches to experience in alternative mediums, such as actual
immersion in water in hydrotherapy pools or airborne activity, using
trampolines, involving states of suspension and upward momentum.
Oily Cart's sensory explorations also prioritise smell and touch through
the use of aromatherapy and physical contact with performers, puppets
and other sensory stimulation. Deborah Warner's *St Pancras Project* (1994)
was an immersive experience for sure, as Barrett indicates in Part Two;
similarly, Pilgrim's work, cited as influential by Barrett and Holdsworth,
falls between theatre and art installation. As these examples suggest,
although the term 'immersive' may not have been applied as a noun,
such practice has employed the language of theatrical immersion within
its forms since inception.

Descriptions of immersion have been used in conjunction with
certain digital performance practice since the early 1990s, due in most
part to this work employing immersive technologies; 'immersion'
and 'presence' related to the multimedia and gaming devices utilised.
These technologies served to enhance the performance experience
in a ludic fashion, sometimes to sensual ends, through the fusion of
the digital and the live at the heart of the work.[4] 'Immersive environments', 'immersive interfaces' and 'immersion' were terms ascribed to
the experimental work of Blast Theory from the mid-1990s, specifically
in relation to the computer technologies and processes the company
explored, and the consequent audience experiences to be had in *Kidnap*
(1998) and *Desert Rain* (2000).[5] Yet 'immersive' is now explicitly used

beyond digital and live-art practices and is more widely applied within a completely different performance context; one which arises from the physical and visual theatres of the 1980s, and is attributable to a diverse range of companies such as De La Guarda, dreamthinkspeak, Punchdrunk, Royale De Luxe, Shunt, Sound & Fury or WildWorks. This immersive practice owes more to landscape as location, architectural inspiration, installation art (in visual, sculptural and sonic fields) and festival environments than it does to digital practice. Prior to 'immersive theatre' being bandied about, names such as Site-specific, Landscape or Sensory theatre were applied to, and embraced by, a range of companies exploring immersive techniques. Holdsworth opens her conversation in Part Two by listing the different terms that have been applied to this type of work and she goes on to consider how other forms and definitions, such as Physical Theatre and Community Theatre, share an inheritance and might be included within its constructs. The roots of all of these descriptions of practice aim to identify the forms at the heart of the work, many of which find sympathetic overlaps with what immersive theatre is understood to be today.

In terms of Performance Studies, Baz Kershaw provides an early and explicit use of 'immersion' and 'immersive' to describe a style of practice and quality of experience in the final chapter of *The Radical in Performance* (1999). He specifically refers to 'an *aesthetics of total immersion*' (194, emphasis original) and points towards the potential this form has for a visceral interrogation of ecological politics, an 'ecology of immersion', and simultaneously positioning such practice as a dynamic force for exploring 'community', 'agency', 'coercion, control, cohesion and collective power' via 'immersive participation' (Kershaw, 1999: 194–9). He argues:

> [T]he history of totally immersive events in Western experimental performance since the 1960s is somewhat fragmentary, partly because some of the early experiments were greeted with bafflement and outrage by established theatre critics.
>
> (Kershaw, 1999: 194)

'Immersive theatre', to describe a particular movement in live performance practice, appears to have entered common parlance within academic and artistic circles from around 2004 and archive research of reviews suggests it entered the lexicon of theatre criticism *circa* 2007. At a similar time this was a term being used to describe 'immersive experiences' in museums and heritage sites; interactive artistic events that included elements of immersive practice where visitor participation, with live performers and various media, was encouraged as part of an 'authentic' connection with the displays. Such theatrical events were intended to bring exhibitions and spaces to life. They can be recognised as part of a continuum of immersive practice that engages the audience within an event in an experiential manner.[6] It is interesting to note how the work of Lundahl & Seitl might find affinities with such practice, certainly in regard to *Symphony of a Missing Room* (2009–11), yet also moves beyond this due to its unusual and intimate experimentation between performer and 'visitor' in museum and gallery spaces.

From 2005 to 2010, the use of the term begins to fix the practice as a 'genre', for want of a better word. This is illustrated by its use in broadsheet criticism, online blogs, across the internet, Twitter and Facebook and, more recently, in the programming, marketing and company mission statements in certain areas of the theatre world. Today 'immersive' is used with impunity to describe a movement that is occurring in contemporary performance practice towards a visceral and participatory audience experience with an all-encompassing, sensual style of production aesthetic. For this reason, 'immersive' is now assigned, often inappropriately, as a defining term for all kinds of theatres that occur in non-traditional venues and/or that include audience interaction. It can be used to describe studio-based works that involve a level of audience participation before the audience are seated in an auditorium. It is sometimes used synonymously with visual and physical theatres and interdisciplinary practice. Consequently, there is a danger that it is becoming a catch-all term for any work that occurs outside of the conventional, spectatorial theatre set-up and/or involves a degree of interdisciplinary practice, which is misleading to say the least. Although these may produce exciting and affective performances, this does not necessarily mean that the audience is involved in a wholly immersive fashion. This imprecision of application emphasises how, when it comes to applying the term in a specific analytical context, there is a need to gauge exactly how the term is being used and to what ends.

Gauging an immersive event

To draw together the concepts surveyed in this chapter, it is clear that 'immersive' as a term used to define work (rather than describe it) has to be understood under the very specific contexts in which it is used. It is important to be wary of where it is used as an umbrella term for any interdisciplinary, site-specific or promenade work. In these instances the word may serve to describe certain qualities in the work, but can be misleading if applied as a defining category of theatre. In this respect, it is in the intention and framing of the event, where it is the artists' ability to succeed in this intention that underpins whether or not an experience is both 'immersive' *and* 'theatre'.

Immersive theatre is discernible as that practice which actually allows you to be in 'the playing area' with the performers, physically interacting with them. This can extend to sensual engagement via a clever use of intimate sound in headphones, despite the action being geographically separate to you. The direct participation of the audience member in the work ensures she or he *inhabits* the immersive world created. This live(d), *praesent* experience, the participant's physical body

Illustration 4   WildWorks' *A Very Old Man with Enormous Wings***. Hayle, Cornwall. Performer Paul Portelli**

[Photo credit: Steve Tanner. Image courtesy of WildWorks and Steve Tanner]

responding within an imaginative environment, is a pivotal element of an immersive experience and a defining feature of immersive theatre. Where virtual or mediated technologies are employed these accentuate sensual involvement and playfully manipulate a visceral–virtual perception. This creative agency, involving processual inter-action through the experience, shapes the unique journey for each participating individual. These decision-making processes also result in a variety of interpretations during and following the event, which underlines the uniqueness of each experience for every individual. All immersive theatres exist on the continuum between 'immersion as absorption' and 'immersion as transportation', with 'total immersion' being the most intense affect/effect at the heart of the experience.

In deliberating over the term's first application to theatre and in debating what definitions might exist therein, a question worth consid-ering is: is there a hierarchy of immersion in diverse contemporary 'performance' experiences? If so, by what criteria is this comparison gauged? Can we compare immersive theatre practices, say, Punchdrunk Travel with 'Murder-Mystery Weekends'; Punchdrunk's bar experiences in *The Masque of the Red Death* with an Essence Communications' Belle Époque Party; or the historically authentic resonance of Punchdrunk's *The Uncommercial Traveller* with the Hampton Court Tudor Kitchen Experience, where one can observe performers dressed in the costume of the Tudor period engaging in the everyday bustle of life in the palace kitchen? Similarly, how comparable are WildWorks' collaborative community events with battle re-enactment societies' monthly activ-ities, where the latter involves a genuine commitment to 'reliving' the attitudes and actions of the particular armies of concern?

Most appreciators of the immersive form would probably accept that there are some shared qualities of experience and mutual aims in mind in terms of the experiential, live(d)ness of these events. Yet it is in the *intention* and *framing* of the particular acts of immersive theatre where the definitions may lie. Murder-Mystery Weekends are fun, themed stays-away where people can drop in and out of role whilst entering into the spirit of a party game of Cluedo. Events such as the Belle Époque Party are simply themed fancy-dress shindigs with expensive drinks and cabaret acts that fit the period of the night. The Hampton Court experience intends to be a spectatorial, educational event where visitors have a live rendering of historical role-play; even in those instances where the visitors themselves are dressed in some aspect of the costume of the day. Battle re-enactment falls between community activity, historical documentation, carnival, theme park, sporting event and charity jamboree. In these events there is always a clear dividing line between fact and fiction, between spectator and event. Whereas Punchdrunk Travel and Enrichment projects or WildWorks collaborations are *intended to be* wholly immersive, wholly artistic events, which aim to blur the boundaries between life and art, and are carefully constructed as such. Quite simply, they are conceived, designed and executed as experientially immersive works of art that have a lasting, emotional and intellectual impact. Howells, in Part Two, draws attention to the ways in which the intention of a piece of theatre defines its role and function as a piece of art for each and any audience-participant. It is this aspect of intention, alongside *the artists' ability to succeed in this intention* that is useful to hold onto when examining what makes an experience both 'immersive' *and* 'theatre'.

In order to expose the quintessential 'immersivity' of immersive theatre, it is useful to address what it is in relation to form and aesthetic that defines this particular performance practice and sets it apart from the conventions of traditional, spectatorial theatre and other forms of affective performance. The proceeding consideration of central features of immersive practice and the 'scale of immersivity' outlines the finer details of immersive techniques that go some way to defining the parameters of the form. With this immersive gauge, I hope to lead the reader to see that an array of performance work might exploit various combinations of these features to a greater or lesser degree and thus to greater or lesser effect. This has some bearing on whether or not the final production is successful in its aim to be an immersive event, however grand or minimal its production values. This scale of immersivity, alongside the illustrative works referenced in Part Two, should help to identify where a total immersive experience exists according to the artists' intentions, performance values and audience response to the work.

2 Features and Finer Details: A Scale of Immersivity

It is, of course, a value judgement to suggest that there is a hierarchy of live, immersive experiences. That said, and bearing in mind the diversity of practice that can exist under this banner, it is useful to discern an immersive performance scale by which we might measure the level of immersion and its consequent affects and effects. Across this scale, we can acknowledge a continuum of responses required from an audience member that are attributable to the ways in which an event exploits sensory elements or incorporates corporeal aspects in the design and 'delivery' of the work.

Central features of immersive practice...

This chapter expands on central features of immersive practice. These are, firstly, the involvement of the audience, ensuring that the function and experience of the audience evolves according to the methodologies of immersive practice. Secondly, within the experience, there is a prioritisation of the sensual world that is unique to each immersive event. Thirdly, the significance of space and place is a key concern of such practice. This includes the specific venue used as the inspiration for the work, its architectural details and design as well as landscapes that are the site for work. It can also incorporate a focus on geographical location, community and local culture, history and politics. In this way the site and wider location can work as the source of the material for the event as much as its physical frame.

...Audience involvement, audience evolvement

As Susan Bennett has argued, 'the involvement of the audience in the theatrical event is undoubtedly complex' (2003: 204), which is especially true of the role and presence of the audience in immersive

Illustration 5   Mercuriali's *Wondermart* (2009)
[Photo credit: Ant Hampton. Image courtesy of Silvia Mercuriali]

work. In immersive theatres there are diverse ranges of ways in which the audience are involved in the work.[1] Bishop summarises how the threefold agenda of 'activation; authorship; community' attached to participatory and interactive artistic practice from the 1960s onwards can be allied to one or all of the following aims:

[1. T]he desire to create an active subject, one who will be empowered by the experience of physical or symbolic participation. An aesthetic of participation therefore derives legitimacy from a (desired) casual relationship between the experience of a work of art and individual/ collective agency...[2]. [C]eding some or all authorial control is conventionally regarded as more egalitarian and democratic then the creation of a work by a single artist.... Collaborative creativity is therefore understood both to emerge from, and to produce, a more positive and non-hierarchical social model...[3. A] restoration of the social bond through a collective elaboration of meaning.

(Bishop, 2006: 12)[2]

Although context and forms may change from one immersive performance experience to another, a constant feature of the audience involvement that remains and defines the experience as totally immersive is the fact that the audience are integral to the *experiential* heart of the work and central to the form and aesthetic of the event:

> [I]mmersive theatre...marks a piece of theatre *experienced from within* rather than as an outside observer.... You are part of it, rather than looking on fundamentally distinct.
>
> (Trueman, 2011: n.pag., emphasis added)

In this way the audience in immersive theatre practice enters the realm of *'viveur* (one who lives)' (Bishop after Guy Debord, 2006: 13). Mike Pearson offers valuable insight into the ways in which site-specific performance 'involves an *activity*, an *audience* and a *place'*, which takes the particular process and relationship that occurs between work as a whole (including space/place and performer) and audience member to 'more creative articulations of *us, them* and *there'* (Pearson, 2011: 19, emphasis original). Pearson also refers to the audience member as participant and *percipient*, the latter term taken from Misha Myers, which foregrounds the sentience of the participant 'whose active, skillful, embodied and sensorial engagement alters and determines a process and its outcomes' (Myers qtd in Pearson, 2011: 178). Following this, an important consideration is why current audiences might be turning to immersive practice. Morris surmises in Part Two that audiences today are keen for visceral experiences as more people spend time online. He suggests that this type of work can remind an individual what it is to feel alive. Barrett, Mercuriali, Lundahl and Seitl draw similar conclusions in their conversations.

Bourriaud comes up with some useful observations in this respect. He posits, due to the mechanisations of everyday social functions that are 'reducing our everyday relational space', machines such as Superloos and ATMs 'now perform tasks that once represented so many opportunities for exchanges, pleasure or conflict' (Bourriaud, 2006: 162). Accepting that, as Bourriaud claims, '[a]rt is a state of encounter' (2006: 162), immersive practice creates a space for reinvigorating human interaction and exchange, however 'fictionalised' the encounter might be. At the very least it causes an audience member to attend to the interaction and exchange occurring in the moment, whether or not she or he is 'enjoying' it. Such work negotiates open relations where the status of the individual experiencing the work 'alternates between that of a passive consumer, and that of witness, an associate, a client, a guest, a co-producer and a protagonist' (see Bourriaud, 2006: 168). The latter, audience member as protagonist, is especially true of one-on-one performance. Barrett in Part Two reflects upon his early experience of Wilson and Kuhn's *H.G.*, during which he realised his desire to reinvent the audience presence within an immersive experience; 'to remove the other audience *being audience* from the picture', as he felt this was detrimental to an individual's connections with and interpretation of the work. Punchdrunk's mission to place the audience at the epicentre of the experience repositions these individuals as creative 'comrades' in the processual interaction and, simultaneously through the masks, they become 'ethereal beings' that haunt the event, part of the scenographic design. Punchdrunk has, accordingly, evolved an audience that has a unique artistic agency within the work.

In light of this, immersive events have seen to an evolution or *evolvement through involvement* of a particular kind of audience – or perhaps a particular kind of audience has caused the evolution of immersive practice. Either way, what is clear is that in live, immersive events there is a fusion between Alison Oddey and Christine Whites's inter-audience-spectator-watcher (see Oddey and White, 2009: 12–14), evolving the idea and the *practice* of audience or spectator beyond the conventional attitude and action between one or other of each of these terms and into that of a decision-making participant in the work. As such, the audience member in immersive theatre maintains the skills and desires of the audience-spectator, yet additionally takes on the responsibility of direct involvement, closer to performer-collaborator. Here, it is embodied engagement from the audience member in the same space where there is a sensual involvement of both performer and the space that finds some sympathy with the notion of the audience *percipient* (Myers in Pearson, 2011: 178). As Mitchell puts it, a WildWorks audience member gently transforms into percipient, becoming:

> more alert, looking for clues. They are insecure, unsure of what might happen next. Their senses are heightened. They are more aware

of each other and become a temporary community experiencing something new together.

(in Savine Raynaud, 2008, 13–14)

Consequently, the immersive work under examination here requires various definitions of the audience member in the event, which includes audience-spectator-watcher-protagonist-percipient. If doing justice to the experience requires a definition that includes the etymological root for all the activity that might be encompassed within her or his involvement with the immersive event, then the naming of this activity, and any individuals involved in this activity, could take a long time.

The practitioners featured in Part Two provide alternative attitudes to, and thus names for, audience members such as 'visitors', 'audience-participants', 'playing-audience' and 'guest performers'. What becomes clear throughout this book is the fact that it is difficult to come up with a term to describe the particular nature of audience involvement with this work as it ranges from performance to performance, and across the different types of immersive works under scrutiny. Defining the audience as 'immersants' or 'immersees' in the event might be an appropriate term, but arguably should then also be assigned to any performers and other human bodies within the work, and so differentiation between these cohabitants in the immersive world becomes blurred (which can be fitting in certain productions).[3] 'Immersee' could also suggest passive immersion, lying back and letting it happen to you with little or no navigation of the work nor decision-making occurring on your part. Perhaps it is best for any individual participant in the work to define her or his role in the experience as a whole for themselves, related to how far and in what ways they felt involved and according to the quality of experience they had. For this reason, I have chosen to range across varied terms for the audience member. In many cases I hold on to the word 'audience' in order to refer to what most of us understand as, more-often-than-not, the ticket-buying-participant experiencing the event. The use of this term also accepts that, for many of us, 'audience' has moved beyond the auditory role indicated by the etymology of the word and become a generic word for the receiver/interpreter of an event, including where that relationship involves active participation in collaborative reception. The particular term used at any given time is also intended to draw attention to the type of involvement activated corresponding to the particular work/s under scrutiny in the given example. What you will notice is that I move from one expression to another according to what seems most fitting in relation to the idea and action under scrutiny.

In certain immersive theatre pieces, audience involvement is accentuated or guided by immersive technologies; usually audio, video or haptic, as is illustrated in Part Two in the conversations with Gladwin of Back to Back Theatre, Mercuriali and Lundahl and Seitl. Here audio and video technologies enhance and direct the imaginative journey through the work. In these instances the technologies are used in an endeavour to accentuate the sensual involvement of the audience-spectator-participant. Acknowledging how everyday technology use can serve to distance human interaction and destroy a sense of personal connection, Mercuriali argues that immersive practice can employ technology to return the user 'to the personal relationship that is much more precious than anything'. Whatever the involvement in the action of the immersive event, a central feature of the audience participation, and a particular detail related to any corporeal memory that may remain with an individual subsequent to the experience, is related to the sensual construction of the worlds in which the participant is immersed.

... Sensual worlds: immediacy, intimacy and sensuality

Awakening and engaging the fullness and diversity of sensory awareness is a central feature of immersive practice. This may include the Artaudian idea of the senses being assaulted, invigorated, via what Morris refers to as the 'bombardment' of an extreme visceral experience. Alternatively, it can be a subtle awakening of the senses across the duration of the encounter. Crucial to immersive practice is the fact that there is no focus on one particular sense but rather a play within the realm of the senses combined in an acknowledgement, manipulation and celebration of the power, promise and potential attributable only to live performance. This is true even where that performance employs pre-recorded digital worlds. Il Pixel Rosso's *And the Birds Fell From the Sky...* plays with this feature in that the disorientating effects of the work, in which you engage via video goggles, is sensually 'validated' by the ways in which the participant is haptically manipulated through actual and imagined locomotion – you are transported in a wheelchair, forced into a vibrating car seat, whilst the visual imagery suggests you are being kidnapped, driven through a nightmarish town inhabited by the Faruk, a lawbreaking, clown tribe – as well as through all of the other senses; alcohol is sprayed onto you, the touch of your partner and guest-performer's thigh against yours as you are crushed together in the car seat, the breeze against your face as you are suddenly in a wide, open space, green and vast, where a bird has fallen from the sky and the message it carries attached to its foot falls into your outstretched hand before the goggles are removed.

The olfactory experience becomes heightened in immersive theatre. Sometimes this is accentuated by the 'aroma design' of the performance, a theatrical construct highlighted by Sally Banes (see 2007: 29–37). Here the aroma becomes part of the design, so scents are added to the space and become an interactive feature within the space, as with Punchdrunk's intricate scenographic design; the bottled perfumes on dressing tables in *The Masque of the Red Death*, the odour of chemicals in Faust's laboratory, contrasted with the scent of fir trees in the forest outside in *Faust* (2006–7), or the gloopy aroma of soup in *The Uncommercial Traveller*'s 'self-supporting cooking depot' (2011c). Similarly, the scent of candles, rose petals and freshly laundered towels in Howells's *The Pleasure of Being: Washing, Feeding, Holding* (2011) adds to the experience of *being* in another world. Equally, in immersive practice, because all of one's senses are heightened, it is difficult not to become acutely aware of the natural aromas of the space, of polished wood floorboards, of dank cellars, of earthy green woods.

Banes details a taxonomy of odour in performance of which there are six categories:

(1) to illustrate words, characters, places and actions; (2) to evoke a mood or ambience; (3) to complement or contrast with aural/visual signs; (4) to summon specific memories; (5) to frame the performance as ritual; and (6) to serve as a distancing device.

(2007: 30–1)

In immersive performance the olfactory design is often a combination of several of these categories, going way beyond a device for surface illustration to be a key to full sensual immersion within the themes and narratives of the work. Bond, co-creator of *You Me Bum Bum Train*, refers to the obsessive 'smell-checks' she completes to ensure the authenticity of the olfactory immersive experience in the event (in Sarah Hemming, 2012). Here olfactory persuasion not only indicates and tells sensual stories, it has the power to vividly 'summon up memories' (Banes, 2007: 32) which go some way to fusing past and present in time, to connect lived experience with the live(d) performing moment. Smell is the sense that is most closely connected to memory in the brain and it this that has the capacity to invoke a whole repertoire of emotions allowing audience-immersants to understand themes and narratives in a direct and affective manner.[4] The olfactory also activates the gustatory sense; in some instances involuntarily where we might taste the dankness of an underground cavern as we smell it at the back of our throats; in other instances where the practitioners themselves accentuate this, the offering of food or drink as gift, as with the handing out of chocolates in Wilson's *Fissure*, or as further sensual immersion in the narratives and experience of that world, such as the sharing of short supplies of water surrounded by the odorous, confined atmosphere in the Nimble Fish production of Clare Bayley's *The Container*.

Haptic perception (incorporating tactile touch – skin to surface, skin against skin – *and* kinaesthetics and proprioception) is often crucial to the immersive performance experience; whether via direct interaction and sensual involvement with the bodies and spaces of the work or via the sensation of haptic vision that can come about through the sensual aesthetic of the immersive world and is brought to bear by the nature of an individual's participation within it (even where direct and reciprocal tactile interaction with performers or objects is not a feature of the work). Haptic perception is a whole-body experience, as Rosalyn Driscoll clarifies:

> [H]aptic sense … is the oldest, most comprehensive and complex of the senses, with receptors embedded throughout the body from the skin down into the joints and muscles … a deep well of sensory input.
>
> (2011: 108)

Gianna Bouchard (2009), Laura Marks (2000, 2002) and Rebecca Schneider (1997) provide useful analysis regarding haptic touch and haptic vision that helps to clarify this idea. Considering the way in which the 'spectator' engages with the disciplines of the visual arts (performance, film and digital technologies), each of these theorists show how sight can become tactile through looking *and looking again* at the sensual aesthetic of a work, which activates a sensory involvement akin to touch within this act of looking alone. In the case of immersive performance, this is of course embellished by opportunities to *actually* touch and interact with space, objects and performers. Where the sensuality of performing bodies and architectural or natural spaces are emphasised, Schneider's arguments for 'sensate involvement' enhanced by 'eyes which touch' come to the forefront (Schneider, 1997: 32). As the discussion with Howells in Part Two clarifies, in the heightened moment of an immersive experience, observing itself becomes experiential. This encourages 'embodied vision' which, drawing on proprioceptive human capabilities, is able to see 'beyond the visible' (Schneider, 1997: 22–36). Similarly, for Marks, eyes can 'function like organs of touch' (2000: 162) which expands on the multi-sensory, reciprocal interaction between perceiver-participant and the mediatised work of art in contemporary practice (see Marks, 2002).

Marks's ideas support my argument that performance experiences that incorporate immersive technologies such as the video goggles in Il Pixel Rosso's *And the Birds Fell From the Sky...* or *The Great Spalvados* (Mercuriali, 2012) or the audio technologies heightening imagination and perception in Mercuriali's Autoteatro collaborations, *Etiquette* and *Wondermart*; Back to Back Theatre's *Small Metal Objects* or *Tour Guide* (2009–); Lundahl & Seitl's *Rotating in a Room of Images* or *Symphony of a Missing Room* and the haptic technologies employed by Extant Theatre Company in its exploratory project *The Question* (2010a, 2010b). In Part Two, Barrett draws attention to the importance of touch in Punchdrunk's work arguing that in the sensual worlds the company creates, involving a haptic fusion of scenographic design and interacting performing/ perceiving bodies, 'touch is the most pure and potent sense'. In this way he underlines how, within any artistic experience but particularly with immersive practice:

Touching grounds the aesthetic experienced in the body – in muscle and bone, gut and heart. Touching is the body asking questions and

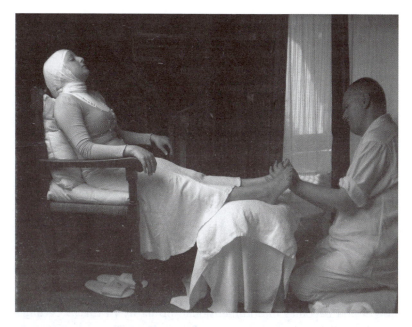

Illustration 6   Howells's *Foot Washing for the Sole*. Attic room in Arab guest house, Nazareth, Israel, October 2008
[Photo credit: Hisham Suliman. Image courtesy of Adrian Howells]

> finding answers ... not a bloodless, intellectual exercise but a somatic, sensory knowing by the body-mind .... The participation of the body in exploring art expands the possible sources of meaning.
>
> (Driscoll, 2011: 111)

Bouchard argues that 'touch is an integral part of the dynamics of corporeal intervention' and certain artistic representations and methods approximate the sensation of haptic vision, allowing 'a slide to occur between vision and touch' (Bouchard, 2009: 165). Such sensory elision directly impacts on the nature of perception and the embodied memory that one has of the work in any subsequent processes of recall, including re-imagining, analysing and interpreting, attached to that work. The conversations with each of the practitioners in Part Two 'touch' on this, especially in the discussion with Lundahl and Seitl in relation to *Symphony in A Missing Room*.

Traditionally, as highlighted in Chapter 1, theatre has prioritised the aural and visual. Often the endeavour is to draw the individual audience member into the process of becoming aware of the full scope of the senses, and certainly the prioritisation of alternative senses (such as touch, hapticity and smell), in the process of narrative construction and thematic interpretation that is both vital in this work and a primary concern of the artists producing the work. As Stephen Di Benedetto suggests, it is 'by exploring the role of sensorial perception and stimulation that we can broaden our understanding of the capabilities and possibilities of nonverbal expression in the performing arts' (2007: 125). The prioritisation of all the human senses, not just sight and hearing, opens up (and requires) a new taxonomy for holistic appreciation in immersive theatres. Within immersive practice, sound and vision are accentuated in ways that reach beyond traditional theatre scenarios. Each of the conversations in Part Two highlight differing approaches to re-imagining the aural and visual experience for an audience-immersant in an event. For instance, Gladwin clarifies how sound becomes multidimensional, primarily in that it becomes 'the defining physical space' in any Back to Back Theatre production; the aural encounter being central to reorienting an individual's sensory experience with that of others within the event. Such play with the multidimensional and holistic capacity of the full human sensorium allows for a new protocol of interaction and exchange to establish itself, reconnecting an individual with her or his own body as much as connecting an individual with other bodies.

This is articulated by Lundahl and Seitl in Part Two, who also refer to their interest in the instinctive sentience that humans are capable of, the enigmatic 'sixth sense'. This draws on an unusual feeling of 'knowing' and loosely connects with what I have previously referred to in relation to experiential performance as a '(syn)aesthetic sense' (Machon, 2011: 20), where the fusion of cerebral and corporeal cognition encourages the full sentience of the human body, drawing on intuition, to make sense/*sense* of the unarticulable. Such a special perception taps into primordial or instinctive bodily receptors and is unusual due to the unsettling/exhilarating nature of *the process of becoming aware* of this holistic fusion of the senses within interpretation. This causes the audience-immersant to *feel* the ideas and states of the performance *in the moment*. The effect of such a response can ensure that the individual holds onto the moment they have experienced and remembers this feeling corporeally in any subsequent interpretation of the work where the fusion of the 'felt' and the 'understood' is responsible for making sense/*sense* of intangible, inarticulable ideas (see Machon, 2011: 13–24). I discuss this notion further in Chapter 3.

Practitioners who experiment with taking sight away completely, as in Lundahl & Seitl's *Symphony of a Missing Room* and *The Infinite Conversation* (2011; ongoing), or Extant Theatre Company's explorations in *The Question?* (2010) or *Sheer* (2012), and Sound & Fury's early experiments as part of the BAC 'Playing in the Dark' Season (1998) to its wholly immersive *Kursk* (2009) and *Going Dark* (2012), illustrate the shifting of perception that occurs when sight is removed and space is reconfigured, forcing an audience member to attend by using the full sensorium in experiencing the work. This serves to accentuate embodied perception by heightening holistic sensory awareness.

Extant Theatre is experimenting with immersive technologies, prioritising haptic engagement that locates the 'drama' within an audience-participant rather than outside of her or him, to be heard or 'seen'. Maria Oshodi, Extant's Artistic Director, who is visually impaired, highlights how sighted people can become lazy in their approach to looking at and fully experiencing an event.[5] *The Question?* employs a lotus-shaped device that audience-participants hold in their hands, which opens when getting close to action and closes when not, to navigate their way around a darkened playing space and interact with performers. Through this, Extant is examining the ways in which a performance is *actually located within* the audience participant's body and imagination. This illustrates the interactive relationship required in the practice and makes tangible the notion of audience-participant as 'site/cite' of performance. A key aspect of this exploration was the removal of sight. Oshodi clarifies:

> when things are mediated through sight, there can be a remoteness because your vision is usually working at long distance. Whereas often my awareness is brought much closer to hand, where my body can reach, at the end of my hands. I was interested in translating that to a wider audience, an audience that was sighted or visually impaired.
>
> (in Oshodi and Machon, 2011: n. pag.)

A number of the practitioners profiled in Part Two manipulate sight within the immersive event in order to reinvigorate the other human senses, playing with what is and is not perceived visually, as with the goggles or manipulation of total blackouts in Lundahl & Seitl's work or the video goggles within Il Pixel Rosso's *And the Birds Fell From the Sky...* or *The Great Spalvados*. Many of the practitioners profiled in Part Two heighten those senses that are usually deemed as secondary – smell, taste, hapticity. Dimming light to focus these other senses more sharply, as much as to accentuate the mysterious atmosphere within the worlds they create, ensures that the experience is holistic, that you are sensually and *sentiently* engaged with the world. With each of these companies, at the points at which you are sighted, you are encouraged to look and look again, to look with your whole body, to attend to (as in to be truly *praesent* in giving attention to) the situations, narratives and ideas all around you.

Correspondingly, practitioners may also carefully direct the audience-participant's gaze in order to foreground the otherworldliness that exists within the everyday, as Mercuriali colourfully clarifies in her discussion of *Pinocchio* (2007). In this piece, performed for an audience of three for the duration of a short but bizarre car journey, the sound-track and unusual performances within the enclosed world of the car and the window onto the outside world are made strange through the lens of the (wind)screen and the world established by the performance that is internal, even when external, to the car.[6] Together, these foci manipulate the immediacy of the gaze and the heightened experience of the participants engulfed in this world, which then ensures every-thing that is perceived within this space and time becomes unusual, dreamlike. Similarly Hill and Mitchell highlight in Part Two how, by directing focus in an almost cinematic way when immersing the audience in the landscape of/as the performance event, WildWorks make the everyday become remarkable and allows the inborn awe evoked by the natural world to be fully appreciated. Wilson provides similar illustration of how audience-participants re-imagine and deeply connect with 'place' during, and as a consequence of, her work.

Different modes of sensory perception need to take priority in any given immersive performance event according to the senses foregrounded in that particular piece. This play of the senses, the reawakening of the holistic sentience of the human body allows for an immediate and intimate interaction within the performance event.[7] It also gives credence to rethinking the ways in which humans 'think', the ways in which we are able to experience and interpret a work of art. Specifically, it lends authority to the *a priori* knowing that humans are capable of. Immersive practice is and *must be*, an embodied event:

> Immersive theatre makes one's physical presence inescapable. With no distance between oneself and the work, the edge of one's body is the beginning of the work's sphere. An awareness of the work, involves an awareness of one's body. We perceive it not just through the eyes and ears, but through our whole body, whether by touch or movement, smell or taste... [I]mmersive work makes us bristle in a way that traditional theatre, watched from afar, does not.
>
> (Trueman, 2011: n. pag.)

It is the process of becoming aware of one's sensual responses that makes an individual aware of *being in the moment* and highlights her or his *praesence* within the sensuality of the immersive event. In this way the visceral design and impact of immersive theatre further accentuates, and often activates, the special relationship between audience-participant and performance that is brought about in such practice. Following Di Benedetto, here the audience member becomes 'attendant', 'implying presence and participation' (2007: 126) and a reciprocal, sensual relationship being established between the self, the space and other bodies in that space (whether performing or audience participants) and to the performance event itself.

This idea of total attendance and sensual engagement with the work has some bearing on the various ways in which certain practitioners describe the audience/participants in their work and helps to define the particular interaction of creator and receiver of the work within the process of production. Here 'attendant' should be understood in terms of 'attending to', giving embodied attention to the ways in which perception comes to bear, the ways in which one is experiencing the work; of being aware of one's presence and participation in the moment rather than simply 'in attendance' as in 'in servitude' to the work. This is accentuated by the ways in which many of these companies institute preparation techniques to gently immerse you in the world: pre-performance rituals and framings to acclimatise the guest participant within the work; antechambers where you are masked, introduced to characters or guides who will take you through the world; or settings which steep you in the outlandish environment as with the work of dreamthinkspeak, Il Pixel Rosso or Punchdrunk. Sometimes the contract of participation is made clear beforehand as part of this process, whether written for or told to you, as in Howells's work, or verbally guided through audio instruction as with Back to Back Theatre or Lundahl & Seitl's practice. Alternatively, sensory awareness may be gently suffused into and drawn out of you as you embark on the physical journey to the event as is the case with WildWorks' productions. A number of practitioners blend a balance of the two, such as Wilson, who presents clear written guidelines related to the requirements of the event prior to and during one's individual journey to the work and an immersion of the individual into the piece once the collective journey is begun with the other participants in the event. Her description in Part Two of the initial train journey for *Fissure* resonates in this respect.

With these acts of preparation the sensory awareness of an individual's relationship to space, to others in that space is activated in a heightened manner. In this way these initial activities can become highly ritualised, akin to the experience of a rite of passage. In the conversations in Part Two, Hill and Mitchell refer to leading WildWorks' audience-participants in *Souterrain* to a point of 'being in the moment' and intuitively receptive to the work. Hill clarifies that it is due to the strength of the worlds created that audience-participants are enabled to inhabit it fully and consequently volunteer themselves instinctively for the action within it. Lundahl and Seitl also highlight the preparation their visitors are taken through in order to embody the experience. In each example there is a sense that the audience-participant's imagination and proprioceptive senses are being nurtured in order to facilitate an act of 'intuiting' her or his way through the event. This involves mutual trust as is illustrated by Hill and Mitchells' example of the moment in which the audience write their memories in *Souterrain* (see Image 22), or Lundahl and Seitl's reference to *The Infinite Conversation* and the tangible intimacy forged by the stories shared. This idea is also taken up by Mercuriali in Part Two, particularly in her consideration of *Etiquette* and *Wondermart*. All of these examples demonstrate how:

> Artists who harness more than our eyes and ears encourage us to wake up, to be alert to the world around us, and to interact actively with the objects and creatures around us. It is an invitation to live, to feel, and to be part of a larger community.
>
> (Di Benedetto, 2007: 134)

In this way immersive practice can encourage individuals to invest in each other as much as in the work. This can lead to a palpable sense of *communitas* in the moment and sometimes, as is documented below and in the conversations with Punchdrunk Enrichment, WildWorks or Wilson, in a legacy that remains as a consequence of that event.

... Space, place and praesence: site-inspired practice

The significance of space; landscape, architecture and the detail of the design within this is crucial to the immersive impact of this work. Chapter 3 surveys critical perspectives on experiencing space, drawn from philosophies of architecture, art and geography in specific theoretical depth and detail. By way of foreshadowing this, it is useful to consider a practical outlook from scenographic and site-specific analysis of space as presented in performance theory, to understand the way in which immersive theatre embraces and attends to location.[8] All of the artist contributors to Part Two articulate how site inspires their work and is a performance in and of itself. Dorita Hannah elucidates:

> *Space* – whether a suspended pause, a blank area, an empty room or a limitless cosmos – *performs* ... it is the fundamental immaterial-material utilized by designers creating sites for theatrical performance. Space is the stuff of architects (who construct it) and scenographers (who abstract it); experienced by inhabitants (immersed within it).
>
> (2011: 54, emphasis original)

With the unadorned starting point of space and audience, a democratic landscape for shared experience is roused from the outset in immersive theatre. Hill and Mitchell of WildWorks make this vibrantly clear in

Illustration 7 Back to Back Theatre's 'Stem Cells', *Soft* (2002)

[Photo credit: Jeff Busby. Image courtesy of Back to Back Theatre]

their discussion in Part Two. They detail the transformative effects that immersive practice has upon the space and subsequently the audience when experiencing the work, as much as acknowledging the crucial influence of landscape upon WildWorks' immersive aesthetic. Sharps highlights how respect for location, in relation to the shaping of how the audience-immersant might experience that space, is an overriding feature of dreamthinkspeak's practice.

Scott Palmer suggests, in addition to the 'radical alternative' afforded by immersive environments, specific spaces and places introduce further qualities to the experience that are triggered and made sense of via an embodied response:

Often it is precisely the richness of this phenomenological, multi-sensory experience of place that makes the event so memorable, as visual, aural, olfactory and tactile elements become an integral and often heightened part of the audience experience. ... Space is felt kinaesthetically through multiple senses – it dictates how we feel and how we relate to others.

(2011a: 78–82)

In Punchdrunk's work the scenographic design within a space is not only manipulated to reveal narratives and to expose themes and ideas at the heart of the work, the site also has its own rules and regulations (sometimes explicit with the presence of masked attendants denying access or ensuring safety; sometimes implicit, enter, search the drawers, read the documents, play, be *praesent*). The space is always inhabited and has its own stories to tell. Here, then, the design inspired by the architectural setting is central to the immersive experience. Nimble Fish and Punchdrunk's Enrichment projects take this idea further to enable students to perceive spaces within schools as deregulated, reconditioned with new 'rules' of engagement and imagination. Higgin clarifies, referring to *Under The Eiderdown* (2011d):

> The idea is to identify what makes this space different from the classroom, the staffroom, walking into any other room in the school; that's where the work we do in schools draws really heavily on the techniques that we use within bigger installations and in terms of the worlds that we've created in our main artistic bodies of work. So you get that sense that you're somewhere completely different, that the space tells a story as well. The sense that the room can hold your attention; if there was no performer in there you would still be in a performance, within a world, within a storytelling environment.

(Higgin and Machon, 2011: n. pag.)

For Higgin, in such instances the immersive experience is made more intense because the storytelling environment established 'bleeds into the real world', is ignited by the durational life of the event, whilst also lasting beyond within the imagination and body of the pupils; 'the *feeling* you create within the school goes out of that shop and the pupils are in that world. They're *in* this story and this idea and this fiction. Once they've been in the shop they're in that state of mind' (in Higgin and Machon: 2011: n. pag., emphasis original).[9] Here the immersive experience *enriches*; fuels the imagination of young minds, enabling individual children to embody the experience to the extent that the immersive environment is alive and charged *within* the child, beyond the scenographically heightened space.

Holdsworth describes a similar approach with Nimble Fish's work in schools in her conversation in Part Two. She highlights the ways in which Nimble Fish collaborate with communities and encourage them to find an artistic access to their local environment thereby reigniting residents' relationships with their community as a consequence. Holdsworth also points out, connecting closely with Punchdrunk Enrichment, WildWorks and Wilson's techniques for the development of a work, how a two-way immersive 'world' is experienced where Nimble Fish immerses itself within the locations and histories of the local community, in order to create sensually-imaginative work with and for them in a meaningful and reciprocal manner.

With immersive practice, the traditional confines and use of studio space moves beyond the conventional deployment of such staging to become the world of that performance. Coney's play with BAC studio-space with *A Small Town Anywhere*, Howells's work *The Garden of Adrian* (2009), Punchdrunk's overhaul of BAC with *The Masque of the Red Death*, Lundahl & Seitl's *Symphony of a Missing Room* or Il Pixel Rosso's *And the Birds Fell From the Sky*...; with each example the studio-ness of the studio space is imaginatively dislocated from its actual surroundings. In different ways in each of these works, dimension is distorted; the space as a whole is upturned within your imagination and disoriented through the play with the haptic sensation of the immersive experience, whether resulting from the play of the scenography or relayed through video goggles and other forms of technologically enhanced sensory stimulation, alongside a carefully controlled interaction with the performers and other participants within that design. With these productions, due to the immersive aesthetic and the relationship between the audience-participant and the event, the studio becomes something other for that brief moment in time. Usually, it is the case that this sensual siting of the work leads to a 'citing' of the work corporeally within the participant's embodied memory of the piece.

... Immersive worlds: immersive environments and the environment

With the crucial element of space/place and audience at its core, immersive practice often lends itself to an exploration of environmental concerns and ecological interests, as is exemplified in the work of Wilson and WildWorks. Pearson points out how 'environmental awareness and growing concerns over degradation and climate change' inevitably has some impact on any site-specific practice (see Pearson, 2011: 100–4). Furthermore, where the scenographic re-imagining of site occurs in collaboration with its local community, as with Nimble Fish's work, there is often a focus on artistically recycling materials from the surrounding environment. This practice was exemplified in Lotos Collective's *The Trial of the Mariner*, at Hoxton Hall, London (2011), which was a site-responsive, immersive event, incorporating dance, surreal animation, large-scale puppetry, circus arts and live music by The Junk Orchestra.[10] Plastic consumption, the destruction of the oceans and the consequences of this to climate change was at the heart of its scenographic and thematic experimentation. Local families were engaged in *art and recycling* through this activity; all feeding back into the experiential and political concerns and outcomes of the piece.

Roth provides a clear argument for the ways in which sensually proactive, immersive practice has a special capacity for communicating, in an embodied, non-judgmental way, the environmental politics that are at the forefront of socio-geographical thinking. The power of sensorial worlds where the engaging of the audience has a particular power due to the 'embodied sentient consciousness' that can be raised during, and as a consequence of, the work can have a lasting influence (see Roth, 2007: 157). Kershaw asserts:

> [T]he dynamics of an aesthetics of total immersion in performance, through which spectators become wholly engaged in an event which they...inherit as a complete environment...can somehow create access to new sources of collective empowerment...they may indicate the potential for a radical response to the ecological nightmare promised by the post-modern world.
>
> (Kershaw, 1999: 194)

Illustration 8 *Jack Scout* **by Louise Ann Wilson Company and Sap Dance. Performer: Natasha Fewings**

[Photo credit: Nicola Tarr. Image courtesy of Louise Ann Wilson Company and Sap Dance]

Here 'an ecology of performance' is established quite straightforwardly through the 'exploration of the relationships between humans and the environment' (Kershaw, 1999: 214). This can occur in immersive practice in both a conceptual and a physically engaged manner, as illustrated by Wilson's *Jack Scout* (2010; see Illustration 8) or *Fissure* (see Illustration 21). As she explains, the 'form shape and content ... respond to the physical nature of the landscape of a place', 'its geology, topography, geography, history and archaeology' (Wilson, 2011a: 73).

> Within this dynamic environment, the audience can re-imagine the everyday and see the familiar afresh. My concern is to create relationships between space, performer and audiences and to find new ways of revealing, re-showing and re-enchanting a place by saying: 'Look anew at what is here; witness the surface of things, and then look again and you will see something more profound about *this* place and perhaps about the world, and how we experience it, and our place within it.
>
> (Wilson, 2011: 65, emphasis original)

As Wilson's approach makes clear, the environmental themes in the work emerge as a direct correlation of the artist working so closely with a landscape and its indigenous community. In these instances the local experiences of the environment merge with wider ecological arguments pertaining to the natural world and human interaction with it. Wilson's discussion in Part Two, alongside that of Hill and Mitchell of WildWorks, demonstrates the ways in which the environment both shapes the event and becomes an underlying concern within the work due to the complex histories and sensualities of the topography, out of which the performance arises and in which it is performed. Further to this Hill, Mitchell and Wilson all highlight how the weather within these specific geographical locations collaborates with the event and influences the experience of that work.

The prioritisation of proprioception through the haptic and tactile – the focus on the moving performers' bodies fused with the audience-participants' moving bodies – alongside the accentuation of the olfactory and the aural within space cultivates 'a sentient consciousness where feeling and thought join', where the senses combine with the politics of the work and carry the performance as 'embodied ecological metaphors' that are, by their embodied nature, automatically capable of 'awakening holistic perspectives' (Roth, 2007: 163). Here it is the very form that allows interactive encounters within and between space, which has the potential to heighten 'corporeal presencing' and to foster 'integrative perceptions of self and the world' (Roth, 2007: 163).

In worlds that are sensually active, requiring that the guest-participant is sensorially responsive, kinaesthetic sensitivity is accented and the 'dynamic role of space itself in performance and lived experience' becomes paramount; space becomes the primary 'organizing element' for the themes and ideas (see Roth, 2007: 158–9). Seitl is particularly eloquent regarding notions of hapticity and *praesence* within the kinesphere of space in her reflections on Lundahl & Seitl's practice in Part Two. The rhythm and flow of audience-participants and performers through a site as illustrated by Barrett, Hill and Mitchell, and Holdsworth and Gladwin, endow space with 'energy flows, making it feel alive rather than neutral, casting it as organic rather than empty', defining it as 'shared', 'continuous and tactile', where the movement of one person impacts on others' experiences (see Roth, 2007: 159). Roberto Sanchez-Camus of Lotos Collective, artistic director of *The Trial of The Mariner*, draws a perceptive observation regarding the movement of the audience during this production:

A really good analogy that I have for one of the methods of audience deployment is as a breath; to create moments of assembly and then moments of individual chaos where the audience can choose what to do…you deploy for moments of exploration and then come together for collective moments, deploy and come together, deploy and come together and so on. I see it like a breath. You exhale and the audience goes out and you inhale and they come together for a singular moment and then chaos again. It gives the piece a very good rhythm and flow.

(Sanchez-Camus and Machon, 2011: n. pag.)

Immersive practice that concerns itself with the environment is capable of locating the individual organically within *and* as a continuum of the wider environment, physically and politically.

The scale of immersivity

With these central features and illustrations in mind I will close this chapter by pinpointing the specific elements that are identifiable within any immersive experience. The extent to which each element is present within a work goes some way to gauging how immersive an event is. Various combinations of the following criteria may be identified and experienced to a greater or lesser degree dependent on the individual work in question:

'In-its-own world'. From the outset the immersive world should exist on its own terms and will be created from all or any of the criteria given below according to the parameters of its own existence. Here the *feeling* of being submerged in another medium – as with immersion in water – is established from the outset. The world operates both within and outside of the time-frame, rules and relationships of the 'everyday' world. These are places that have their own rhythm and choreography. It is its own unique environment and its own unique ways of '*being*-within' that environment for performers and participants alike. As the conversations in Part Two all point out, the 'in-its-own-worldness' is an artistic intention as well as a strangely elusive charm of the experience. The special quality of the world encountered is attributable to the idiosyncratic ways in which the following elements are put together.

Space. A central feature of immersive and intimate performance is an exceptional awareness of *space* and *place*; a sensitivity explored by the practitioner in the creation of the work and the audience-immersant experiencing that world. The specific location and/or the 'transformation' of that space according to the aesthetic of the event is vital. The space, and the journey within that space, has to contain the 'in-its-own-worldness' of the event. The experience of the space is also reliant on the specific audience relationship within the event. The focus on space within this practice highlights a crossing of boundaries in the creation of increasingly unusual and sophisticated hybrids. The practitioners accentuate the immersivity of a given location; harnessing the natural power of landscape and/or exposing the experiential qualities of dimension and design. Lundahl and Seitl provide diverse examples of this from their work. Gladwin notes Back to Back Theatre's interest in exploring architectural or geographical space in relation to how it empowers the performer and thus shapes the production. The discussions around Punchdrunk's practice demonstrate how vital design is to the immersive power of any event. Hill and Mitchell of WildWorks and Mercuriali all identify how the focusing of the surrounding environment within the world of the event causes a (re)cognition of space and place within the audience-immersant. In these instances the 'outside world' becomes part of the world-of-the-event, a factor that has its own unusual, sometimes transcendental, effect that adds to the immediate experience and subsequent memory of the production as a result. Where natural landscape is the site, the climate and elemental forces come into play and are key features that inspire the sensual response of the audience. Wilson along with Hill and Mitchell provide vivid illustration of this. A dominant feature in those immersive theatres that embrace landscape as site is the potential for harnessing the histories and inherent politics of 'place'. The practice of Wilson, WildWorks and Nimble Fish highlights the potent possibilities for *communitas* that come into effect when working in this way. Site-specific and promenade events do not automatically become immersive events; the response to the space and the journey through that space has to accord with all other factors listed in this scale for the event to be wholly immersive.

Scenography. The scenography in external locations will be tailored to draw attention to the topography and will embrace elemental forces and natural light across the duration of the work as Hill, Mitchell and Wilson describe in Part Two. Scenography in architectural settings will underscore the existing features and ambient qualities of the space, as Holdsworth and Howells highlight. The attention to detail in all of dreamthinkspeak's work or Punchdrunk's lavish design for a smaller scale Enrichment project, such as *The Uncommercial Traveller*, as much as one of the company's grand masked productions, involves a sensitivity to the stories that reside within the history, atmosphere and dimensions of a space whilst simultaneously adding to this with a powerfully 'in-its-own-world' aesthetic. Costume design becomes an extension of the scenographic aesthetic of the work and is influenced by the landscape or architecture as much as the bodies of the performers and the actions they execute. However flamboyant or minimal it may be, design is key to the experience of the space and to the otherworldliness created.

Sound. Sound is a vital component of the experience as many of the conversations in Part Two identify, including where the experience plays with 'silence' and the ambient sounds already present within the chosen environment. Designed, composed and naturally occurring sound is important, in equal measures; whether the hushed sound of an enclosed space, such as the ritualised experience of a one-on-one in Howells's work; the natural sounds in the corridors that can punctuate the sound installations within the epic events of Punchdrunk's practice; or human dialogue designed as affective sound, snatches of overheard conversation or private mutterings rather than explicit speech as in certain dreamthinkspeak productions. In these contiguous spaces (such as peripheral corridors and stairwells) where a designed soundscape is absent, one becomes bristlingly aware of the sounds of others' footsteps, of the intrinsic smells of the environment, of the strangeness of inhabiting the wider space. Rather than drawing you out of the experience, it engages you further within it, even if only in your desperation to 'get back in to where it's all happening'. Similarly, the natural sounds of the landscape that accommodate the work of Wilson or WildWorks coexist with the designed soundscapes of the event, one serving to enhance and feed into the other. Higgin, Gladwin, Lundahl and Seitl, Mercuriali and Morris provide eloquent accounts of the differing ways in which audio-enhanced immersive experiences can define the world that you exist within for the time-frame of that experience. They can be vital to the intimate, individual experience, as with Lundahl & Seitl's work, or a collective quality of experience, as with Back to Back Theatre's *Small Metal Objects*. Mercuriali's *Etiquette*, *Wondermart*, and *And the Birds Fell From the Sky...* are interesting in this respect. Her discussion in Part Two clarifies how the audio experience establishes both the intimacy of an individual experience *and* a sense of complicity with one or more people around you, whether they are knowingly involved in the experience (*Etiquette* and *And the Birds Fell From the Sky...*) or not (*Wondermart*). The audio-journeys taken in these diverse events are essential in inspiring the imagination that underpins that world.

Duration/al. 'Durational' implies that time is treated as an organic and important experiential element of the event. Duration is not simply 'how long it lasts', the running time of the performance from start to finish, but holds a greater significance in regard to the inter-active relationship established between the audience-participants and the event within the timescales set. Whether intensely concen-trated to minutes or spanning days, months or beyond, the length of time spent within the world impacts on the experience of the work according to the parameters of the event. Duration may be specific and prescribed, just a few minutes with the artist as with many one-on-ones, or an event that is durational may invite the audience-participants to enter and leave the world as they choose. Each approach has consequences in relation to the interpretations placed on the experiences and narratives encountered according to the time spent engaging with the experience, dwelling in that world. Specific timings for an entrance to and immersion in the event – which can include the journey to and discovery of the given location, as with Coney, Nimble Fish, Punchdrunk or Wilsons' work – is often a fascinating facet of the wider experience. These timings, whilst practical in nature, also allude to the contract into which you are entering, the exclusive and ludic society which you agree to join, the secret invitation by which you might pass into the 'otherworldliness' of this particular domain. The play with time within immersive events heightens a carnivalesque and kaleidoscopic turn within that world, which accentuates the visceral quality of the event and can serve to elongate, contract or coil time into a helix; temporality itself becomes experiential. This *felt* sense of time-play is illustrated in particular through the discussion of Howells, Punchdrunk and Lundahl & Seitl's work.

The specifics of a given date and time for a particular immersive event, as with Coney's *The Loveliness Principle* (2011, 2012; ongoing), WildWorks' *The Passion* or Wilson's *Fissure,* can also emphasise the ephemeral nature of such work where a particular piece only occurs that once; however epic in scale and lasting in its impact, it is also frustratingly fleeting, literally 'of the moment', utterly experiential in the 'you had to be there' sense. Works such as these are rare and one-offs and accentuate the unusual way in which immersive practice is always exceptional, individual and transient in experience, yet also has a 'life beyond' the specific occurrence. This life beyond, or lasting ephemerality, exists in an individual's embodied memory of the piece. The discussion with Wilson concludes with the way in which the embodied memory of walking sites and cites both inform the physical impact of *Fissure* as well as the ideas traversed. Furthermore, certain events can establish a practical legacy as a consequence of the one-off performance. The discussions around the work of Coney, Nimble Fish, Punchdrunk, Punchdrunk Enrichment projects, WildWorks and Wilson provide clear examples of this.

Interdisciplinary/hybridised practice. Immersive theatres are always interdisciplinary, blurring boundaries between installation, performance, private and public ritual, underground gigs and open-air festivals. Often, these works incorporate elements from varied disciplines including architecture, improvisation, storytelling, spoken and/or physical performance, dance, circus skills, aerial arts, puppetry, sculpture, digital or mechanical animation, gaming, sound, film, video, audio and/or haptic technologies. Whatever the disciplines incorporated, these events can involve a range of imaginative staging techniques. The presence of text is often explored via non-verbal means in this work; speech may be entirely absent or present in poetic and/or whispered contexts. It will be interwoven with dance and other elements within the production. Often, it is made otherworldly in the clandestine nature of verbal exchanges within intimate encounters. Written text may be incorporated into the scenographic design, inscribed via the action of the performers.

In all instances words becoming a textured layer in the sensual world of the event. Where immersive work employs technologies, this is to heighten the sensual experience of the work and thereby increase the human sharing of embodied experience, rather than technology employed to distance the participant from the work. Technologies in immersive practice are used with dexterity to ignite the imagination; to offer clues and set experiences in place; to give a carnivalesque logic to the illogical, as is the case with Coney's *A Small Town Anywhere* or any of Rabbit's interventions, or Mercuriali's practice, especially *Pinocchio, And the Birds Fell From the Sky...* or *The Great Il Spalvados*. All of the conversations of Part Two provide discerning illustration of the varied ways in which practitioners are experimenting with interdisciplinary practice in order to accentuate the immersed, embodied experience of the performer and audience participant in the event.

Bodies.   There is a focus on the body in the performance itself and in the audience's immediate and subsequent appreciation of the event. In this way bodies can become simultaneously sight, site and cite of the performance. Referring back to the interdisciplinary nature of such practice, highly trained performing bodies are often key to this experience, such as with the work of Punchdrunk, Lundahl & Seitl and Wilson. Equally, in the more minimalist one-on-one pieces, where disciplines involved are reduced to a minimal aesthetic, bodies here are accentuated in the shared experience of the moment, as with Howells's carefully choreographed and acutely ritualised pieces, *Foot Washing for the Sole* or *The Pleasures of Being: Washing, Feeding, Holding* or *Lifeguard* (2012). In such intimate instances, as the conversations with Howells and Lundahl and Seitl illustrate, the interacting body of the audience member is as vital to the performance as that of the performer. As Howells observes, the audience-participant's body 'co-authors' the work with the artist.

Audience.   A pivotal criterion: the direct, actual, physical insertion of an individual audience member within the world of the event, into the performance itself, is paramount and absolute. Where an event is wholly immersive the audience-immersant is *always* fundamentally complicit within the concept, content and form of the work. As a consequence, throughout this book and in a number of the interviews in Part Two, you will note that the naming of 'the audience' as such becomes a vexed term in itself. All of the contributors highlight the special and active exchange that occurs between the performance and the audience member, illustrating the breakdown of division between audience and creative crew. Hill and Mitchell illustrate this continuum of interaction that occurs in WildWorks' productions and describe how the audience becomes the 'camera' in terms of locating the image to focus in on and then follow, in order to experience the event in full. As previously mentioned, a number of the contributors find their own informal names for the relationship established. These include Barrett's 'comrades', Howells's 'audience-participant', Lundahl and Seitl's 'visitors', Holdsworth's 'co-creators', Mercuriali's 'guest-performers', Stevens's 'playing-audience' or Wilson's '"attendant" audience'. These demonstrate how the idea and *praesence* of 'audience' is evolved according to an interdisciplinary attitude; Stevens nods to game-play in its widest context; Lundahl and Seitl's term 'visitor' owes as much to the visual arts (visitors to exhibitions) as it does to performance and suggests an active invitee who will be taken care of and be treated as a willing guest within the event. These assorted terms also acknowledge how the relationship with the audience in immersive events moves way beyond traditional passive performance/audience relationships. In immersive theatres audience members become active participants, collaborators and co-creators, moving into the realm of audience-adventurers.

The nature of audience interaction in the work always requires some level of participation and involves some experience of immediacy and/or intimacy as a consequence. However, it should be stressed that, although all immersive experiences involve some degree of participation and may involve an experience of intimacy, not all participatory theatre nor all one-on-one performance is immersive according to the experiences detailed above. As all of the conversations of Part Two highlight, the relationship with the audience within immersive practice is unique to each production and shaped carefully in order to establish the parameters of the world as well as to ensure a safe yet playful environment in which the experiences of that world can exist. Consequently, you will note how each conversation refers to a 'contract' that is shared between audience member and artist.

A 'contract for participation'. In all instances where an immersive world is established there will be a commitment to taking care of the audience within the event. This is identified by practitioners in Part Two as a 'contract' that is formed in the creation and execution of the work. This may be explicit in the form of written or spoken guidelines and agreements shared prior to entering the space. It may be implicit within the structures of the immersive world and therefore become clear to you in tacit fashion as you make your journey through the event. These 'contracts' are central to the safety of both the audience-participant and the artists during the event. They invite varying levels of agency and participation, according to how far the audience-participant is prepared to go. Each of the conversations foregrounds the idea of immersive practice giving audience-participants permission to behave in an active and sentient manner within these worlds, in a way that more conventional theatre productions – even those that are experiential in form – do not.

Finally there are two essentials that can be considered as elements in their own right but should also be augmented as addenda to each of the elements outlined above. Somewhat more abstract in definition these are, in short:

Intention. Is the event framed as an artistic experience, does it *intend* to work as a sensual and intellectual, immersive artistic product? Is there a strong degree of critical engagement with the immersive form in order to explore and express the depth of feeling and thinking that exists in the conceptual, thematic and narrative ideas underpinning the work?

If so, is this intention underpinned by;

Expertise. If the intention is there and elements given above are employed, has the artist or the company an authoritative grasp of the artistic potential and creative constraints of the form and of the 'contract of participation' in order to enable the participant in the event to have a full, undeniable immersive experience?

If the answer to both of these final criteria is 'yes', then it is likely that you have experienced a piece of immersive theatre. What becomes clear from all of the conversations in Part Two of this book is that audience and space are often the starting point for each event. All of the interviews illustrate how a careful fusion and intricate layering of each of these elements (or various combinations therein) is vital.

There are a number of performances that explore immersive techniques to a certain degree, to add an experiential quality to a particular event, without being wholly 'immersive'. Headlong Theatre's *Decade* (2011) described itself as an immersive event due to the fact that the production had been housed outside of the National Theatre's building in a former trading hall in St. Katherine's Docks, London, close to the City and formerly London's World Trade Centre. The design within this location had sought to recreate an authentic set of the Restaurant at the Top of World, New York's World Trade Centre, and as you entered the event, there was a basic degree of audience participation to suggest that we were going through security checks. However, once inside the lavish set, the performance was executed according to the traditions of spectatorial theatre: we (the audience) watched them (the performers), sometimes in different spots around the venue, always as stationary, only intellectually engaged, observers. As Gardner points out, referring to *The Pillowman*, Martin McDonagh's play at The Curve (Leicester, 2009), though such entrances may invite you to be mindful of the fact that you are entering the world of the play, this is 'just an add-on' (Gardner and Machon, 2011: n. pag.). These exercises allow some degree of entering into the 'feel' of the themes and narratives of the production, yet do not a wholly immersive performance make. Works such as this may invite participation or demand a degree of relational interaction, may add texture to the aesthetic; however, the event in full is not a wholly experiential and immersive event.

This scale of immersivity, alongside the works referenced in Part Two, should help to identify where a complete immersive experience exists according to the intentions, performance values and audience response to the work. In terms of grand and minimalist production values, the scale of immersivity also seeks to highlight the differences and similarities between large-scale immersive practice and one-to-one experiences (bearing in mind that there are a diversity of ways in which these 'two' approaches might be executed and achieved). The interviews in Part Two illustrate the affinities and distinctions between these forms. A number of the contributors refer to other companies when describing the extents of their own practice or in identifying and establishing where they have had immersive experiences as audience members. The work of the practitioners outlined in Part Two examines the intimate and immediate power of immersive practice and highlights how these experiences produce *shared qualities of experience* which engender the epic in the intimate and uncover the intimate in the epic.

To support the basic principles that clarify what defines immersive practice, as presented in the scale of immersivity, it is useful to turn to sympathetic perspectives that help to elucidate the ways in which such work can be seen to be distinctively and unquestionably immersive. The following chapter surveys theories from a range of disciplines that serve to identify and interrogate various elements of the form, function and artistic approach in style and appreciation of immersive practice. My intention with Chapter 3 is to clarify further the relationships and ideas that underpin immersive theatres. In so doing, these perspectives further elucidate the act of 'total immersion' in performance terms.

3   Immersive Perspectives

Illustration 9   Lundahl & Seitl's *Symphony of a Missing Room*, National Museum Stockholm, 2010

[Photo credit: Andreas Karperyd. Image courtesy of Lundahl & Seitl]

Immersive perspectives: *feeling*, form and function

This chapter surveys a range of theories drawn from varied disciplines across anthropology, architecture, geography, literature, performance, philosophy and visual art, all of which offer approaches to embodied meaning-making. These critical perspectives help to identify various elements of form, function and artistic approach in immersive theatres and point towards the ways in which such practice can be experienced and analysed in order to appreciate the art form fully. Combined, they help to construe and define what makes immersive practice genuinely, whether wholly or in parts, immersive within the contexts put forward in Chapters 1 and 2. I begin this chapter by summarising characteristic features of my own theory of (syn)aesthetics to show how immersive theatre is a particular strand of (syn)aesthetic practice. In form, approach and outcome immersive theatre exemplifies (syn)aesthetic approaches to practice and analysis.

Immersive practice and experiential form: (syn)aesthetics

(Syn)aesthetics derives from 'synaesthesia' (the Greek *syn* meaning 'together' and *aisthesis*, meaning 'sensation' or 'perception'). Synaesthesia is also a medical term to define a neurological condition where a fusing of sensations occurs when one sense is stimulated, which automatically and simultaneously causes a stimulation in another of the senses; an individual may perceive scents or words for certain colours, or a word as a particular smell or experience tastes as tangible shapes. So in terms of this neurocognitive condition, synaesthesia is defined as the production of a sensation in one part of the body resulting from a stimulus applied to, or perceived by, another part.[1] This appropriation of certain features of the scientific analysis of synaesthesia is intended to emphasise the human capacity for perception, which shifts between realms: between the sensual and intellectual; between the literal and lateral. These realms are defined by their outcomes for each individual, distinguishable by a *felt* appreciation of 'making sense' in a semantic and cerebral fashion and '*sense*-making', understanding through somatic, embodied perception via *feeling* (both sensory and emotional) created in performance. In (syn)aesthetic practice the process is often fused as a making-sense/*sense*-making experience.[2]

In addition to the neurological delineations, within the term '(syn)aesthetics', I also include the definition of 'aesthetics' as the subjective creation, experience and criticism of artistic practice. (Syn)aesthetics, as a defining style and sympathetic analytical discourse, fuses ideas held within the medical term with those surrounding the aesthetics of performance practice. Bearing this in mind, my reworking of '(syn)aesthetics', with a playful use of parenthesis, encompasses both a fused sensory perceptual experience and a fused and sensate approach to artistic practice and analysis. The parenthesis is also intended to distinguish (syn)aesthetics from the neurological condition from which it adopts certain features, whilst simultaneously foregrounding the 'syn' to emphasise various notions of 'fusing together' in arts practice and analysis.

(Syn)aesthetic performance practice is always imaginative in form and usually interdisciplinary in execution (see Machon, 2011: 54–81). Immersive theatre is exemplary of the style. It fuses various disciplines to create its own hybridised language that ensures the work produced is multidimensional and layered in form, inviting the audience to become active, sentient participants in the work. When an audience is encouraged to experience the layers of 'meaning' in the work by becoming part of the ludic play at the heart of the form itself, a dynamic curiosity is ignited; a curiosity that may seek to unearth narratives, themes or to just *be* within the work.

As a strategy of analysis (syn)aesthetics prioritises individual, immediate and innate processes of recall and interpretation. Integral to this is 'corporeal memory' and 'embodied knowledge'. These describe an intuitive knowledge that refers human perception back to its primordial impulses, which encompass the emotional *and* the physiological capabilities of the physical body. This allows for a slippage between our human faculties of intellectual and instinctive perception; a factor alone that can affect a certain disturbance in the processes of production and appreciation. Each of the conversations of Part Two document the (syn)aesthetic nature of immersive practice, particularly in relation to the way in which intuition and instinct are central to the audience-participant's navigation and appreciation of the work.

Wrapped up in a (syn)aesthetic response is the notion that the body is the sentient conduit for the appreciation of artistic work in general, and immersive performance in particular. To experience (syn)-aesthetically means to perceive the details corporeally. Fundamental to (syn)aesthetic interpretation is the fact that the original, visceral experience remains affective in any subsequent recall within the embodied memory of the work. Following this, any cerebral analysis that transpires is influenced by this affective state; the analysis and articulation of that analysis is invested with that rich and *felt* quality of experience. Rational reflection becomes part of, or is secondary to, the visceral experience. Often, this results in a comprehension of the work that does not engage logical sense, but instead *understands* the work on a deeper level without necessarily being able to describe or explain this. (Syn)aesthetic work, as exemplified in immersive practice (and articulated in the conversations in Part Two), activates the 'thinking body', the aspect of the human body which is capable of communicating *and* interpreting in the live performance moment; a sensory intellect which exists within the body and follows its own rules of logic that are both separate from *and often intrinsic to* cerebral intellect; think about the human 'fright, flight or fight' instinct here or 'gut reactions' and the idea is immediately clear. This helps explain the '(syn)aesthetic-sense', where the intellectual understanding of the work can come close to a feeling of transcendence in much the same way that occurs in meditative or dream consciousness.

In light of this, in (syn)aesthetic practice and appreciation there is a breaking down of the boundary between the real and the imaginary to provide a perception of hidden states, of the ineffable. The dream-worlds created in immersive practice provide abundant illustration here: the blurring of art and life in Coney's practice; the ritualised havens of Howells's intimate encounters; the highly charged visions of Il Pixel Rosso's fantasies; the ornate playgrounds of Punchdrunk dominions. Here dramatic techniques express ideas, thoughts, emotional experience, psychological states and so on that are beyond the bounds of conventional communication, making the intangible lucidly tangible. This can affect an unsettling and/or exhilarating *process of becoming aware* of the fusion of senses within interpretation. Cognitive processes are disturbed, which causes the individual to experience the ideas and states of the performance *in the moment*. This can ensure that the audience-participant in the work holds onto that moment and recalls this feeling corporeally in any subsequent interpretation of the work. It is this fusion of the *felt* and the 'understood' in making sense/*sense* of intangible, inarticulable ideas that is crucial to (syn)aesthetic appreciation. Put simply, we *feel* the performance in the moment and recall these feelings in subsequent interpretation.

(Syn)aesthetics embraces performance work which constantly resists and explodes established forms and concepts, of which immersive theatre is paradigmatic, and is open to developments in contemporary practice and analysis. Immersive practice shifts between artistic forms and performance disciplines, just as it shifts between the sensual and intellectual, the somatic and the semantic, and it foregrounds the unique potential held in the 'liveness' of the live moment.

Immersive theatre accentuates the 'presentness' of the performing moment as a lasting-ephemerality through the *'praesentness'* of human sensory perception. It is quintessentially (syn)aesthetic in that it manipulates the explicit recreation of sensation through visual, physical, verbal, aural, tactile, haptic and olfactory means. Here I do not simply refer to the mere description of a sensual experience, but sensation itself being transmitted to the audience-participant. This can occur *actually* within the real-time, locational experience of the event (scents, textures, sounds and physical proximity in the space). These features can then be accentuated and made doubly experiential via an individual's corporeal memory which may trigger and/or charge the moment via the traces of an equivalent lived, sensate experience within the perceiving individual (the memory of childhood-bathtimes-flannel-on-skin, the redolent scent of dressing-room lipstick and powder, the sensation of being drunk through audio distortion). Whatever the intense sensual experience, it must always be coupled with careful discipline in form to avoid any unnecessary over-indulgence in sensuality 'for the sake of it', which ensures that a measured reflection on the work is possible. The live(d) experience of immersive performance colludes in a continuing, immediate and interactive exchange of energy and experience between the work and the audience.

Immersive perspectives: making-sense/*sense*-making

To elucidate further ideas around immersion and sensate involvement, I will now consider three sets of 'immersive perspectives', sympathetic theories which I have drawn together here to help colour and clarify what makes a performance event total in its immersivity. The first perspectives expand on ideas around comprehending and articulating the particular sensual exchange of immersive practice and the consequent capacity for making-sense/*sense*-making that is activated in individual participants in this work. Deleuze's insight on 'immanence', sense and sensation and the ludic logic of the paradoxical; and Geurts's consideration of West African expressions of consciousness and embodiment, specifically that articulated by Anlo-Ewe peoples through '*seselelame*' (Geurts, 2006) prove useful in this respect. The second collected perspectives help to elucidate the *praesence* and pleasures of the audience, turning to Eco's 'Open Works'; Rancière's 'Emancipated Spectator'; and examines further the 'Relational Aesthetics' of Bourriaud. Perspective then shifts to survey the significance of space via Pallasmaa's musings on the sensuality of space; Massey's theories of the inherent politics of space/place; and Bachelard's 'poetics of space'.

Gilles Deleuze: 'immanence' and the ludic logic of sense

Deleuze (1925–1995) was a French theorist writing across the disciplines of philosophy, literature, film and fine art. His thinking around immanence identifies that there is a fusion between 'immanence', a state of being, existing or operating within the material or physical qualities of human experience, and equally in the experience of transcendence. Transcendence is a state of suppressing the materially 'immanent' and entering into an esoteric or otherworldly state, beyond the physical qualities of human experience; usually an ineffable experience by its very nature (see Deleuze, 2001). Here, '[t]ranscendence is always a product of immanence', engaged in the process of becoming, of actualisation (Deleuze, 2001: 31). This in-between state is most acutely called into play by an individual when confronted by particular works of art (in the sources cited he refers to the sensually affective theatres and poetry of Artaud and Samuel Beckett, the visceral-visual art of Francis Bacon and the literary illogicality of Lewis Carroll). Such artworks can take us both into and outside of our bodies. They resonate and allow us to engage with 'an ineffable essence' (Deleuze, 2004: 68) within the experiences and the ideas that the artwork explores. This directly connects with (syn)aesthetic work, which articulates this same quality of experience triggered especially by wholly immersive practice. John Rajchman summarises how Deleuze 'elaborated a new conception of sense' in relation to challenging meaning-making processes where '[s]ensation has a peculiar role in it' and, in the case of works of art, sensation is synthesised according to a peculiar logic – a logic of multi-plicity' (2001: 8–10). Mercuriali illustrates this point in her reflections on the ludic interplay of the visual experience through the goggles juxtaposed with the wider sensual experience, including the kinaes-thetic play, in Il Pixel Rosso's work. These (syn)aesthetically pull the audience-immersant between the plausible and implausible. As Mercuriali puts it in Part Two, this affects a 'dangerous' play that instils 'the doubt of what is and isn't real'. Such an engagement with a work of art ensures that '[t]he work of art leaves the domain of representation to become "experience"' (Deleuze qtd in Rajchman, 2001: 16).

In terms of the inherent logic of sensation, Deleuze echoes Artaud's theories for theatre and highlights how, in the moment of appreci-ation of an artwork, the work itself 'acts immediately upon the nervous system, which is of the flesh...reaching the unity of the sensing and the sensed...sensation is in the body and not in the air' (Deleuze, 2004: 34–5). In this respect, Deleuze argues that 'artworks just *are* sensation' (Rajchman, 2001: 9) and, as with immersive practice, they can make us aware of, and allow us to enter into, a paradoxical 'pure presence' (Deleuze, 2004: 52). Deleuze refers to this as 'a pure plane of immanence' (2010: 26) which connects with the *praesent* quality of experience in the live moment of the (syn)aesthetic performance event and points towards the live(d)ness of immersive arts practice. This is an 'absolute' experience where the feeling of being 'in the moment', a constant *praesence*, ascribes the full force of the experience to the moment of being in the event itself; 'it is only when immanence is no longer immanence to anything other than itself that we can speak of a plane of immanence' where 'an absolute immediate consciousness' is activated (Deleuze, 2001: 27). The affective potential of a truly immersive experience can bring about such a feeling and consciousness in an individual where the sense of 'between-times, between-moments' (Deleuze, 2001: 29) comes about due to the *felt*, live(d) quality of every second of the duration of the piece. Seitl illustrates this beautifully in Part Two in her reference to 'choreo-graphing absence', where the audience-immersant becomes part of the composition of the piece. Seitl's methodology for interactive movement between performer-immersant and audience-immersant involves the most delicate experience of touch and guidance, where you actually feel the sensation of floating in the space. This quality of movement plays with immanence, waiting for the next physical interaction by *attending to the waiting* rather than anticipating the movement (see Illustration 9). For Seitl, the timeless quality of these moments accentuates the ongoing present, plays with anticipation, encourages that individual to experience *being*. Similarly, Sharps illustrates this concept in his reflections on dreamthinkspeak's *Don't Look Back* (2004). Here immanence as *timelessness* is made tangible via the suspended action of sleeping undertakers and the final image, the unbearably slowed-down retreat of Eurydice; both unsettling and breathtaking.

As these examples suggest, wholly immersive theatre experiences bring about the feeling of the 'pure place of immanence' or 'absolute immanence', which is firmly located in the body and in 'absolute, immediate consciousness' (Deleuze, 2010: 26–7). For Deleuze, 'that which is most profound is the immediate (2010: 11). Immediacy allows for an encounter with, even an entering into, a state of transcendence. Pure immanence in this respect connects with ideas around being *praesent*, intensely 'in the moment'. This is illustrated by blogs and reviews responding to Howells's highly ritualised and beautifully intimate works such as *Foot Washing for the Sole* (see Illustration 6) and *The Pleasure of Being: Washing, Feeding, Holding* (see Illustration 12). In Part Two, Howells describes his highly attuned approach to '*really being*' within the process and attending to a given action. His work is a paradigm for intimate, immersive practice that taps into this fused state of immanence; being within and between his own body, another's body and the artistic experience.

Kathryn Linn Geurts: embodied feeling, embodied knowing: 'Seselelame'

Geurts is an anthropologist whose consideration of West African expressions of consciousness and embodiment, specifically that articulated by Anlo-Ewe peoples through '*seselelame*', is useful in understanding how immersive practice has the potential to reawaken embodied consciousness and cognition for which, in certain non-Western cultures, there already exists an accepted and expressive vocabulary (see Geurts, 2003, 2006).[3] Geurts defines '*sensing*' as 'bodily ways of gathering information' and argues that it is 'profoundly involved with a society's epistemology, the development of its cultural identity, and its forms of being-in-the-world' (2003: 3; emphasis original). She highlights the limitations in mainstream North American, European and British thinking and teaching around the senses and perception, in order to show how this has some bearing on how social and cultural experience and interpretation is bound up in the sensory order that is established from early education, rather than being a physiological fact:

> A culture's sensory order is one of the first and most basic elements of *making ourselves human*. I define *sensory order* (or *sensorium*) as a pattern of relative importance and differential elaboration of the various senses, through which children learn to perceive and to experience the world and in which pattern they develop their abilities…. The sensory order…of a cultural group forms the basis of the sensibilities that are exhibited by the people who grew up in that tradition. Such sensibilities…become fundamental to an expectation of what it is to be a person in a given time and place.
>
> (Geurts, 2003: 5; emphasis original)[4]

Following this, the accepted sensorium of a given culture influences and inhibits embodied interaction and analysis in everyday, as much as artistic, experience. For Geurts, despite overturning the Cartesian split, much Western aesthetic, phenomenological and neuroscientific theorising around emotion and bodily feeling in consciousness is culture-bound, which she summarises specifically in relation to Antonio Damasio's theories (see Geurts, 2006: 164–6, 169–71). Geurts uses her anthropological perspective, focusing on the West African Anlo-Ewe people's communicative powers, to demonstrate how consciousness and 'knowing' embrace a panoply of inner states and embodied involvement, incorporating emotion, sensation, perception and cognition, and is articulated via the concept of *'seselelame'*, most closely translated as 'perceive-perceive-at-flesh-inside' (Geurts, 2006: 165). She draws parallels between this accepted, everyday approach to acknowledging and articulating experience and Damasio's theories around the 'feeling of knowing' within human consciousness (see Damasio, 2000). According to Geurts, the Anlo sensory order does not divide itself across the Western five-senses model (sight, hearing, taste, smell, touch), but instead *seselelame* is a generalised feeling within the body 'that includes both internal senses (such as balance and proprioception) and external senses, as well as other perceptual, emotional, and intuitive dimensions of experience' (2006: 166). In this respect *seselelame* is understood as a specific sense as well as serving as a descriptor for human sentience in general.[5]

Following Thomas Csordas, Geurts clarifies that *seselelame* is best understood in relation to 'somatic modes of attention' (Csordas qtd in Geurts, 2006: 166) that acknowledge the shared milieu of subjectivities of sensory engagement within and between our own individual body and the bodies of others directly around us. *Seselelame* illustrates a culturally specific form in which Anlo people 'attend to and interpret their own bodies while simultaneously orienting themselves to the bodies of those around them', which creates links across sensation, perception, emotion and moral reasoning (Geurts, 2006: 167). This is a holistic sensual awareness and expression, 'attuned to introspectively oriented bodily feeling' (Geurts, 2006: 174). It emphasises and fuses inner and outer senses, tangible and intangible feeling, thereby acknowledging the combination of sensation and sentience that impacts on cognition, proprioception and kinaesthesia. All of the five senses are accepted as being interconnected 'affairs of the whole body' rather than discrete experiences of either the nose, the ear, the tongue, the hands or the eyes (Geurts, 2006: 169). By acknowledging this interplay of sensation, interpreting and acting upon these feelings and instincts, *seselelame* is a useful concept for supporting and explaining the embodied sentience innate in all humans, which exists in everyday pursuits and can be activated by carefully crafted immersive events.

Bearing this in mind (and body), it is important to acknowledge that the quality of holistic appreciation and subsequent analysis that is brought about by immersive practice is an active, everyday quality of experience from which Western, technologically driven, lives have become alienated. This is relevant in regards to why the immediate and intimate practice of immersive theatres has become more prominent and popular in British theatre experiences by way of addressing this lack and allowing a feeling of 'aliveness' to enter back into the perceptive faculties, in the way a good walk or beautiful sunset can. Rather than appropriating this Anlo term as a theoretical concept and academic jargon within this book, my intention is to show how Geurts's study is useful to prioritising embodied knowledge; the senses within sense within human processes of interpretation.

Geurts's studies document how other ways of knowing are valued, taken as commonplace in societies and cultures where the body, mind

and spirit are not divorced from one another. It demonstrates recognised approaches to being and perceiving in the world, whether in
the everyday or artistic (accepting that the artistic is a heightened
expression of the otherworldly within the everyday) which, in general,
a Westernised intellect is often at odds with. This way of articulating
experience and *being* describes and helps us to understand the ways
in which intimate and epic immersive theatre practices can work on
an audience-participant. Immersive work can activate the full range
of the human sensorium within and across perceptual, emotional and
intuitive dimensions of experience and interpretation. Accordingly,
this concept of *seselelame* connects with (syn)aesthetic analysis and
helps us to describe and better understand the fused embodied ways
in which we undergo and make sense/*sense* of this work, both in the
moment of the encounter and subsequent to the event.

Immersive perspectives: the pleasures of the audience

In elucidating further the *praesence* and pleasures of the audience, where
the powers of immanence and the pleasures of making sense from/of/
within *sense* find their beginning, I will now turn to Eco's 'open' works,
Rancière's 'emancipated spectator' and the 'relational aesthetics' of
Bourriaud.

Umberto Eco and open works

Eco, an Italian semiotician and author, put forward invaluable theories
related to the audience of contemporary artistic works, specifically
music, literature and the visual arts. Like Roland Barthes, working in
the literary realm at the same time on the pleasures of the writerly text
which saw to the 'death of the author' and the 'birth of the reader'
(see Barthes, 1987), Eco's perspectives celebrate the active judgment
of the audience member when interpreting and experiencing
modern artistic works (see Eco, 1989). It takes into consideration the
individual and innate potential of a singular person to engage with
a work, which has some impact on the unique quality of experience
to be had by any one audience member, supporting ideas developed
in (syn)aesthetic analysis. In so doing, it also accentuates the idea

that contemporary arts practice explores ambiguity, suggestivity and problematic constructs because such is the actual experience of modern living. Art can only represent and express the experience of human existence by employing equally open and complex forms (see Eco, 2006: 32–5).

Where works are designed to be open, within the composition of the piece there is a degree to which the performer is invited to be autonomous in her or his interpretation of the work; to 'impose his judgment on the form of the piece' which formulates 'a fresh dialectics between the work of art and its performer' (Eco, 2006: 20–2). Here 'openness' relates to '"indefiniteness" of communication, "infinite" possibilities of form, and complete freedom of reception' (2006: 25). The open nature of immersive practice invites the audience to be an active collaborator in the work, resulting in an outcome where the work is in constant formalistic and interpretative movement; the artists and audience 'make the work together' (2006: 37).

This 'openness' of form becomes active in the exchange between performer, performance and audience member and directly relates to the manner in which the work is then received and interpreted. Here an event is arranged as

> a sequence of communicative effects in such a way that each individual addressee can refashion the original composition devised by its author. The addressee is bound to enter into an interplay of stimulus and response which depends in his unique capacity for sensitive reception of the piece.
>
> (Eco, 2006: 22)

The very form of the artwork gains an 'aesthetic validity precisely in proportion to the number of different perspectives from which it can be viewed and understood' (2006: 22). As this would suggest, such multi-layered work, by embracing multi-perspectival shifts in apprehension and appreciation, consequently takes on 'a wealth of different resonances and echoes' through these multiple interpretations, without impairing the artwork's original essence 2006: 22).

In these cases, each and every experience of an artistic event is 'both an *interpretation* and a *performance* of it' because each situation relies on the individual's unique reception of the work which 'takes on a fresh perspective for itself (Eco, 2006: 22; emphasis original). Consequently, the open form of immersive practice offers a vast array of possibilities for interpretation 'within a given *field of relations*', where the work is to be 'completed' by the audience-participant according to their individual experience of it (2006: 36; emphasis original).

Eco acknowledges that any work of art 'demands a free, inventive response' (2006: 23), but asserts that it is a perspective that has come from contemporary theory and practice, it was not an approach taken in work prior to the twentieth century (despite the fact that such an approach and theoretical perspective can now be applied to many works produced before the twentieth century). He highlights how the 'force of the subjective element in the interpretation of a work of art (any interpretation implies an interplay between the addressee and the work as an objective fact) was noticed by classical writers' such as Plato, particularly in relation to the figurative arts and the way in which the 'scientific and practical development of the technique of perspective bears witness to the gradual maturation of this awareness of an interpretative subjectivity pitted against the work of art'. However, he goes on to say that this 'awareness has led to a tendency to operate against the "openness" of the work, to favour its "closing out"' by way of looking at the work 'in *the only possibly right way* – that is, the way the author of the work had prescribed' (2006: 23; emphasis original). For Eco the mutual interrelationship of open performance/interpretation specifically describes any work where the artist has *intentionally* taken such an approach and is aware of the implications that exist therein:

> rather than submit to the 'openness' as an inescapable element of artistic interpretation, [the artist] subsumes it into a positive aspect of his production, recasting the work so as to expose it to the maximum possible 'opening'.
>
> (2006: 23)

Eco highlights how, in some instances, rather than being indefinite and infinite in its possibilities for form, 'openness' actually involves rigorous rules that allow this diversity of interpretative solutions. The suggestion of total freedom in appreciation, despite the fact that it might seem this way in some instances to the receiver of the work, is *designed* within the careful construction and execution of the work. Alternatively, the form of the work puts forward 'infinite suggestive possibilities' which can be performed with 'the full emotional and imaginative resources of the interpreter' (2006: 27). Work such as the large-scale Punchdrunk productions *Faust, The Masque of the Red Death* or *Sleep No More* (see Illustration 1) are open and ludic in their form. Consequently, the way these works invite the audience-immersant to participate are rich and vast. This ensures that the work itself, whatever the source material that inspired it, is 'open to new configurations and probabilities of interpretation' whist still remaining true to the essence and spirit of the original texts (see Eco, 2006: 29). It also heralds the idea of the 'processual' attitude in engaging with such work, where variation in the experience occurs due to the audience-participant's decision-making, following carefully constructed processes that are put in place to encourage unpredictable and transformative interpretations.

Arguably, one of the reasons why immersive practice has taken such a hold of audiences and infiltrated the mainstream is because it invites a vitality of form which *cannot* be replicated or fixed (in the manner of a formulaic musical franchise, for example), fundamentally because it relies on the active participation, which leads to the unique response of each individual audience member in order to 'complete' the experience.[6] This points towards an ongoing movement in this type of practice, which celebrates

> a new cycle of relations between the artist and his audience, a new mechanics of aesthetic perception, a different status for the artistic product in contemporary society. ... [A] new relationship between the *contemplation* and the *utilization* of a work of art.
>
> (Eco, 2006: 39; emphasis original)

Eco's thinking is useful in validating and celebrating the role of individual interpretation in an artistic experience, foreshadowing that aspect which is integral to (syn)aesthetic appreciation. It also highlights how clear codes and rules make up such practice in order to allow the experience to *feel* free and liberating and thus lead to creative agency; a feature identified by each of the contributors to Part Two.

Jacques Rancière's 'emancipated spectator'

Rancière is a French philosopher who theorises the relationship between aesthetics and politics. His perspective is central to the collaborative nature of all immersive events, particularly because he confronts the ways in which effective participatory theatre is the place where the challenges of the form meet a depth of artistic thought and critical engagement to powerful effect. He emphasises the potential of a democratic and active community within such experience. Like Eco, he points out that it is the receiver of the work who activates the artistic experience and is the person 'engaged with decisions about how to act', charged with seeking out the meaning in collaboration with the performance itself, exchanging the position of 'passive spectator for that of scientific investigator or experimenter' (Rancière, 2009: 4). This is true of the wild and fast-moving experiences of Punchdrunk or WildWorks' practice and, equally, of the more contemplative interactive decisions taken between creator and audience-participants in the gentle movement of Wilson's work or in the quiet intimacy of Howells's encounters, the playful interaction of the performer-participant in Mercuriali's work or the visitor in Lundahl & Seitl's immersive experiences.

Rancière also refers back to Plato, and highlights how Plato had posed the need for a 'choreographic community' where everyone moves in accordance with 'the community rhythm' (2009: 5). For Rancière, active participation as audience/community allows for intellectual, autonomous emancipation. Here emancipation means 'the blurring of the boundary between those who act and those who look; between individuals and members of a collective body' (2009: 19). Emancipated audience activity has the potential to move across the continuum of theatrical mediation proffered by Brecht and Artaud, where 'the Brechtian paradigm…makes them conscious of the social situation that gives rise to it and desirous of acting in order to transform it' and Artaud's arguments require that the audience is surrounded by the performance, which causes them to 'abandon their position as spectators' to be 'drawn into the circle of action that restores collective energy' (2009: 8). Rancière affirms that in any theatre, 'viewing' has to be understood as an 'action' where the audience member 'observes, selects, compares, interprets' placing her or his own interpretation on the work according to her or his own history and reflective approach as an 'active spectator' (2009: 13). This 'detective' work is apparent across all the conversations of Part Two and exemplified in Coney's work.

Acknowledging Wagner's *Gesamtkunstwerk*, Rancière points out that contemporary theatre practice crosses boundaries, blurs roles and mixes genres, inspiring a range of interactive relationships within performance that seeks to 'relaunch' the 'form of the total artwork' (2009: 21). However, he suggests that rather than undertaking this with the intention of creating the 'apotheosis of art and life', such theatrical experimentation is often merely egotistical play and produced to appease a 'consumerist hyper-activism'. For Rancière, this is particularly the case where an over-indulgent use of technologies are involved, which can lead to a 'confusion of roles' that simply enhances the effects of the performance 'without questioning its principles' (2009: 21). It is likely that many of us have had some experience of work such as this, where the total theatre experience is merely style over content, playing with formalistic trends to superficial ends, without depth of thought, sometimes without careful discipline. In such instances the artists involved are simply using 'this form of hyper-theatre to optimize the spectacle rather than to celebrate the revolutionary identity of art and life' (Rancière, 2009: 63). This is not to say that spectacle for its own sake is not a pleasurable experience, but that the fun and fantasy of it is all there is. Interestingly, Hill draws attention to the joys and disappointments of such spectacle for its own sake in the WildWorks conversation in Part Two. This superficial approach to form refers back to the 'intention and expertise' criteria in the scale of immersivity.

To concur with Rancière's thinking, truly immersive practice which demonstrates this depth of thought and control of form requires that spectators 'become active participants as opposed to passive voyeurs' (Rancière, 2009: 3). Here participation and interactivity between the work and the immersants empowers the audience through a playful and/or probing questioning of 'the cause-effect relationship itself' in order to 'conceive it as a new scene of equality where heterogeneous performances are translated into one another' (2009: 22). This involves, to some extent, a critique of spectacle-for-its-own sake in order that the immersive effects of the work serve to 'work for a society where everybody should be active' and pertains to 'the alpha and omega of the "politics of art"' (2009: 63). Here the inherent politics of any worth-while performance event can be understood as

> a shift from a given sensible world to another sensible world that defines different capacities and incapacities...processes of dissociation; a break in the relationship between sense and sense...what is seen and what is thought, what is thought and what is felt.
>
> (Rancière, 2009: 75)

Politics in these instances have as much to do with reconnecting the perceiver with their affective selves as with sharing an ideological perspective. The inherent communal politics that arise from this can be as subtle as a reawakening of a sense of 'being', as is triggered by Coney or Howells's work, which causes an individual to channel positive thought and action in subsequent activity. Equally, it can manifest itself as live(d) response to socio-political situations in the performing moment which activates an ideologically and/or community concerned politicised response as a consequence.[7] The latter is demonstrated in the work of Back To Back Theatre, Coney, Nimble Fish, Punchdrunk Enrichment, WildWorks and Wilson. These practitioners display a desire to explore with their audience-participants the link between 'what one knows with what one does not know' (as Stevens puts it, the 'what is' and 'what if'), which requires a constant and energised exchange between practitioner and audience member; the latter playing the role of 'active interpreters who develop their own translation in order to appropriate the "story" and make it their own story'. Here the 'emancipated community' offers a dynamic interchange between 'narrators and translators' (Rancière, 2009: 22).

Of great importance here is the idea that the sensual/communal link between the artwork, the practitioner and the audience-participants holds its own unique political interaction involving a 'complex set of connections and disconnections':

> Human beings are tied together by a certain sensory fabric, a certain distribution of the sensible, which defines their way of being together; and politics is about the transformation of the sensory fabric of 'being together'.... The solitude of the artwork is a false solitude: it is an intertwining or twisting together of sensations...a human

collective is an intertwining and twisting together of sensations in the same way.

(Rancière, 2009: 56)

The conversations with Stevens of Coney, Holdsworth of Nimble Fish and Hill and Mitchell of WildWorks provide eloquent illustration of this in practice. In these instances, corporeal experience allows for 'transformed "sensation"' where the artist has woven together 'a new sensory fabric by wresting precepts and affects from the perceptions and affection that make up the fabric of ordinary experience' (Rancière, 2009: 56).

Rancière's call for an emancipated spectator who becomes an active participant in the work of art is modelled in genuinely immersive theatre practice. The creative agency experienced within the artwork of the audience-participant has the potential to lead to a political agency on an individual or collective level. The inherent politics of the work, as brought about by the democratic practice of shared experience, demonstrates the profound potential of this artistic form.

Nicolas Bourriaud and relational aesthetics

Bourriaud is a French art critic and curator. His idea of 'art as a state of encounter' (Bourriaud, 2002: 18) is significant in helping to define the form and the experience of immersive theatre. Bourriaud surveys a breadth of visual and conceptual arts practices from across the twentieth and into the twenty-first century in identifying a 'relational aesthetics' and a range of critical ideas and approaches including those from Rancière (see Bourriaud, 2002, 2006). Bourriaud asserts that relational aesthetics 'does not represent a theory of art...but a theory of form' and it is this factor that is pertinent to immersive practice in general as, for Bourriaud, it is the relational *form* that can account for a 'lasting encounter' with the themes, concepts and content of any work (2002: 19). Such form, because its very nature of interaction and its acceptance that the beholder of the work is key to the meaning that derives from it, is open to continual development and change. Embracing the 'ambivalent and supple' critical and aesthetic stance of Felix Guattari, Bourriaud identifies that artists who explore relational form create work which cannot be fixed, is always in a state of becoming, due to its need for a live interaction with its receiver/participant. Here 'the beholder is the joint creator of the work' (Bourriaud, 2002: 99).[8]

It is the idea of *encounter* that is important. The various interrelationships within and between the work and the receiver/participant are the foundation of the work *and* any subsequent analysis of that work. This allows for, in fact invites, a plurality of experiences and responses to the work, helping to emancipate the receiver-participant within the process. It ensures that meaning is elaborated collectively, both amongst a community of participants in the event and between the performance itself and the participant/s. Bourriaud highlights how various practices of interactive art are linked by a system of 'intensive encounters' where the 'substrate is formed by intersubjectivity, and which takes being-together as a central theme' (Bourriaud, 2002: 15). Here it is the artistic event and the beholder or participant in that event that are conjoined in a 'collective elaboration of meaning' (Bourriaud, 2002: 15). This notion of 'being-together' is central to the shared experiences (whether at the same time in collective events or in terms of having 'shared' an experience of a one-on-one) of immersive practice. Evans and Savoy, performers in *The Uncommercial Traveller* both alight on the experiential 'sharing' as a quintessential difference between traditional performance and immersive practice. As Evans explains in Part Two:

> [Y]ou're taking people into the world that you're *in*; you're *in* this world aren't you and then you've got the audience, three participants in our case, and you can make them come in with you so that you're all sharing. If you're successful, then we all believe that we've been there.

Creative agency is thus experienced by performer-participant and audience-participant alike. The example of *The Uncommercial Traveller*, alongside the work of Coney, Howells, Nimble Fish, WildWorks and Wilson, proves Bourriaud's theory that relational artistic activity can become a democratic means for positive societal and communal interaction. Bourriaud foreshadows the observations of many of the contributors to Part Two, who identify the ongoing demand for immersive practice as an antidote to the alienating experiences of globalisation and virtual socialising and networking (see Bourriaud, 2002: 60–1, 65–78).

Immersive events are forms of artistic work that create locational and durational conditions 'whose rhythms are not the same as those that organize everyday life' and that 'encourage an inter-human intercourse which is different to the "zones of communication" that are forced upon us' in the everyday (Bourriaud following Karl Marx, 2006: 161). Bourriaud draws attention to notions of contract and duration that enter into the frame with such practice where 'the work prompts meetings and invites appointments, managing its own temporal structure' (2002: 29).

Works created around 'the sphere of inter-human relations' involve 'methods of social exchanges, interactivity...within the aesthetic experience being offered to him/her' it is this alongside diverse means of playing with 'communication processes' in the event that work together as 'tangible tools serving to link individuals and human groups together' (Bourriaud, 2002: 43). Such artistic practice offers 'spaces where we can elaborate alternative forms of sociability, critical models and moments of constructed conviviality' (see Bourriaud, 2006: 166). According to Bourriaud, participatory events since the 1960s have seen a 'constitution of convivial relations' (2002: 30); note Jubb's reiteration of this in relation to immersive practice as cited in the Introduction. Immersive events can encourage a way of being with strangers that falls back on this constitution, allowing social relationships that happily embrace a level of interaction with strangers similar to those of going for a meal, entertaining friends, hosting a party, sharing intimacies, establishing a connection with those with whom you share the encounter, whether that be on a one-to-one or with a greater number.

Immersive events allow an emphasis on contact, tactility and immediacy (see Bourriaud, 2006: 165). In terms of immersive theatre's attention to space and duration, the inherent relational aesthetics of such practice ensures that its audience-participants 'envisage the relations between space and time in a different way' (Bourriaud, 2002: 48). Much immersive theatre, and particularly that which is under-pinned by community enrichment and cultural production as discussed in the Coney, Punchdrunk Enrichment, Nimble Fish and WildWorks' conversations, can be understood as artworks, which

function as interstices, as space-times governed by an economy that goes beyond the prevailing rules for the management of the public... inspired by a concern for democracy. For art does not transcend our day-to-day preoccupations; it brings us face to face with reality through the singularity of a relationship with the world, through a fiction.

(Bourriaud, 2006: 167–8)

The intention, form and impact of immersive theatre connects ideas around audience with ideas around space. In particular, the notion of encounter allows for an experiential interrogation of environmental concerns through performance across landscape where an ecological sensibility exists within the very form of this work. Consequently, the immersive form can be seen to provide a bridge that links relational aesthetics with spatial aesthetics. To demonstrate this further, I will now survey the significance of space in immersive theatre events via Pallasmaa's musings on the sensuality of space, Massey's theories of the inherent politics of space and place, concluding with Bachelard's philosophy on the 'poetics of space'.

Immersive perspectives: the significance of space

Space is vital to the immersive experience. Each of the conversations of Part Two demonstrate diverse ways in which space is considered, manipulated and integral to the immersive process from start to 'finish', for practitioners and audience alike. The combined perspectives proffered by Pallasmaa, Massey and Bachelard eloquently assist in reinforcing and clarifying the significance of space to immersive practice.

Juhani Pallasmaa: the sensuality of space

Pallasmaa is a leading Finnish architect and architectural theorist. His outlook on space proffers inspiring analysis on the significance of embodied imagining and haptic involvement in *all* aspects of aesthetic appreciation, particularly in regards to the sensual qualities of architecture. Pallasmaa's writings make the reader think about experiential perception *in general* as much as in direct relation to spatial awareness and architectural framings. Most importantly, Pallasmaa demonstrates through his reflections on architecture how space activates body memory and both encourages and requires methods of interpretation that simultaneously draw on and acquiesce to this (see Pallasmaa, 2000, 2005, 2009 and 2011). His theories demonstrate how physical space should only be apprehended through all of the human senses, including kinaesthetics and proprioception. He provides a discourse for buildings that, in immersive practice, are found or wrought in such a way as to make the inhabitants acutely aware of the affective quality of that space to the experience as a whole. He is especially persuasive regarding the fundamental significance of haptic perception and appreciation which is key to the visceral power of much immersive practice (see Pallasmaa, 2005, 2009).

Pallasmaa pinpoints how physical architecture accentuates an individual's *praesence*:

> Architecture frames, structures, re-orients, scales, refocuses and slows down our experience of the world and makes it an ingredient of the embodied sense of our own being; it always has a mediating role instead of being the end itself.
>
> (2011: 100)

Mercuriali illustrates this concept in Part Two in her discussion of *Pinocchio*; how she and Brockis worked '*with* the architecture of the public space in order to attract attention to the lines of that space'. Arguably, any practitioners who explore immersive practice exploit the narratives and sensual aspects of a space to these ends. In particular, designers working with the space accustomise themselves to the 'enveloping spatiality, interiority and hapticity' of space, honouring it – whether architecture or landscape – in accordance with the powers of peripheral vision. This centres the inhabitant within the space, which returns us to a 'preconscious perceptual realm…experienced outside the sphere of focused vision' (Pallasmaa, 2005: 13). Hill and Mitchell of WildWorks and Wilson provide fitting illustration of the immersive power of honouring natural space in this way.

Accordingly, when working within architectural space it is clear that immersive work, such as that of Punchdrunk, owes much to its scenographers for allowing the peripheral experience of the space to fuse with the sharp, focused vision of *the detail* in space. Here attention is drawn to the immediate, localised detail of design, the choreography, the action in the wider space. This is exemplified in the work of Back to Back Theatre, Punchdrunk, WildWorks and Wilson in particular. It is doubly apparent in Sharps intricate play with the details of design-within-the-design in dreamthinkspeak's model versions of the building housing the event, as he illustrates in Part Two. These miniature versions of the space, like architectural models or set-designs, hone in on the intricacies of the world in which the performance dwells, serving to inspire the imagination (see Illustration 10). These constructions also speak to a childlike curiosity about these worlds, and play on the idea of a world within a world that has its own dimensions.

Such ornate play within space accords to Pallasmaa's arguments for a creative interplay of peripheral vision (which requires our haptic, proprioceptive sentient powers), and sharply focused vision (which bows to the tactility of the eyes and the hands). These two forms of perceptual apprehension, combined, automatically ensure a rich, multi-layered quality of comprehension and thus a holistic, sensual experience as a result (see Pallasmaa, 2005: 9–13). This is certainly the case for Punchdrunk, who respond to the peripheral ambience and the wider narratives and textures of a site, whilst equally honing in on the details of the space; its tones, textures and features. The creative team then construct the work and dress the space to accentuate these experiences.[9] So, too, Howells, as his conversation identifies, although on a much sparser scale. Lundahl & Seitl encourage their 'visitors' to the work to take note of the sensuality of the space in which the event occurs in a variety of ways, and in so doing activate the 'interior architecture' of the imagination. Furthermore, Seitl highlights how the interplay of the sensual and choreographic design of *Symphony of a Missing Room* or *Rotating in a Room of Images*, enables the visitor to feel as if they themselves are part of the space; to become aware of the edges of the body fusing with the kinesphere.

Entering a traditional theatre or studio space makes us aware of the separateness of the world presented to us, even when we might be placed in such performance/audience configurations as 'in-the-round' or traverse staging, there is still a distancing that occurs through the rules of engagement, the conventions by which we enter and inhabit that space and the visual/aural/technical formation of that space itself; the auditorium, the focus of the gaze, lighting configurations, exits and so on, all direct us to experience the space as that in which a performance

Illustration 10   dreamthinkspeak's *Before I Sleep* (2010). The doll's house in the 'Cherry Orchard House' in the Co-operative Building, Brighton

[Photo credit: Jim Stephenson. Image courtesy of dreamthinkspeak]

occurs. By focusing on 'the dominance of the eye and then the ear, with a certain suppression of the other senses', the audience are pushed into 'detachment, isolation and exteriority' (Pallasmaa, 2005: 19). In this way the 'fourth wall' set-up of the proscenium arch and many traditional theatre experiences frame the event in the same manner to make it an 'art of the eye' rather than facilitating a haptic sense of human rootedness in the [imaginative] world' (Pallasmaa, 2005: 19).[10] This thinking extends the comparisons made in Table 1.

Whereas in site-responsive immersive practice, the space is integral to the experience of the work, we are not separated from it but *in* it, of it, surrounded by it, dwelling in it, travelling through it; the space is thus integrated within and as the world in which the audience-participants are immersed which ensures this sense of 'rootedness' in the world of the event is actively *felt*. By embracing the sensuality of the exteriority of these worlds and the place that you take within it, it also accentuates the individual interiority of that experience fusing external and internal sensations throughout the event. Some works are only ever created for one place and are never repeated, as with the full range of Wilson's work, others may be toured and thus redesigned, reworked, however subtly or extremely, according to the specific locations at which the piece is sited, the immersive practitioner being attuned to responding to the specifics of the new environment. This is illustrated in Howells's discussion of *The Pleasure of Being: Washing, Feeding, Holding* or Hill and Mitchell's discussion of WildWorks' *The Very Old Man With Enormous Wings* and *Souterrain*. An intriguing take on this is dreamthinkspeak's *The Rest is Silence*, for which a vast container to site and tour the immersive experience was designed. At the time of the discussion, as the piece premiered across England, Sharps himself wondered how this would resonate according to the sites in which it was located; how those sites would influence the ending of each production. At The Riverside Studios in London, the final sequence lifted blinds to reveal the storage space of the studios, heightening the thematic concerns with notions of theatre and artifice that existed in this interpretation of *Hamlet*, bringing the audience back to our physical locale, so different to the concentrated installation world that the container space had established.

Pallasmaa highlights how, 'the tendency of technological culture to standardize environmental conditions and make the environment entirely predictable is causing a serious sensory impoverishment' and weakens the opportunity for haptic sensation and embodied involvement (see Pallasmaa, 2000, 2005: 12–13; and 2009: 95–100). He argues that an 'uncritical application of technologies' divorces us from textured sensual and individual experiences (see 2011: 20). It is important to stress that with affective immersive practice, such as dreamthinkspeak's productions, technology *serves* the sensual; adds to the 'opacity and depth, sensory invitation and discovery, mystery and shadow' inherent in a site and in the immersive experience itself (Pallasmaa, 2000).

Pallasmaa emphasises the multi-sensual nature of space and, thus the fact that multi-sensory methods of appreciation are required in the experience of space. This is certainly true of immersive experiences. Pallasmaa's discussion of 'acoustic intimacy' in space adds to the 'experience of interiority' where '[h]earing structures and articulates the experience and understanding of space' (2005: 49). Sound in space is central to the immersive experience, as the interviews in Part Two indicate. Sound in space is often the key to unlocking an audience-participant's imagination. This is also true of audio-described experiences *through space*, which can both defamiliarise and heighten the individual response to the surroundings; sharply focusing the journey within that world in a (syn)aesthetic manner, allowing sound and vision to become tactile and haptic.[11] In immersive practice that exploits headphone experiences to play within and against the haptic and visual aspects of the particular world, the intimacy of this sound in/as space becomes integral in/as experience and accentuates the (con)fusion of interiority and exteriority within the experience. As the conversations in Part Two highlight, in the work of Back to Back Theatre, Lundahl & Seitl and Mercuriali in particular, sound in space becomes a playful entity which often guides and wreaks mischief upon an audience member in her or his journey through the work.[12] Here the ludic play of the aural adds to the whole experience as the audience-participants' senses are manipulated in order to overturn expectation; to surprise, delight and disturb.

Pallasmaa's writings illustrate how experiences that immerse the participant in space stimulate the whole human sensorium, demanding that all of the senses take an equal role in the affective comprehension of that site. In so doing, the individual within the world is made acutely aware of her or his *praesence* in that space ensuring that the space itself is encountered as an 'architecture of the senses' (Pallasmaa, 2005: 70) where individual participants *dwell*, utterly alive to it. By attuning to space, Pallasmaa highlights how the 'dweller' therein becomes aware of how space can resonate with the temporal domain; the sensual dimensions of space and time impacts on the experience and makes the perceiver aware of them. In these experiences it is possible to become acutely aware of dwelling in space and time. This *process of becoming aware* heightens the awareness itself:

> The experience of time and the sense of temporal duration and continuity have a seminal mental importance in architecture; we do not live only in space and place as we also inhabit time.
>
> (Pallasmaa, 2011: 78)

Supporting Bourriaud's thinking, Pallasmaa acknowledges how, 'all the arts deal with and manipulate time' and most significantly he asserts how 'experiential time in the arts can be compacted, accelerated, slowed down, reversed and halted' (2011: 78). This elucidates how time becomes an inhabited force within the immersive experience. Pallasmaa affirms how distinctions can be drawn across architectural structures, a feature that immersive practitioners latch onto, in that certain buildings can 'contain and hold time' whereas others can 'evade or explode time', in this way, as Pallasmaa surmises; '[a]rchitecture is commonly understood as the art form of space but it is equally significantly a means of articulating time' (Pallasmaa, 2011: 78, 109). This becomes particularly noteworthy in conceiving of the fusion of space and time in order to create a world that exists in and of itself in immersive practice. Higgin highlights the 'fusions of time' that become affective in *The Uncommercial Traveller* (2011c) via the scenographic detail, the historical research, the narratives revealed and through the older performing bodies; all variations on embodied time. Sharps provides illustration of this with his reflections on dreamthinkspeak's *Before I Sleep*. With this piece the many layers of architectural interiors served to fuse past, present and future, and make manifest Pallasmaa's notion of time that is at once held, evaded and exploded: the actual walls of the Co-operative building in which the piece was housed, the scenographic design of the Cherry Orchard House within this; the doll's house in the nursery of the Cherry Orchard House; the Wendy House in the department store; underscored by the assorted models of scenarios within various rooms across the floors of the building (see Illustrations 10 and 25). By dwelling within and amongst these intricate layers, it is possible to become palpably aware of the ongoing present that connects past and future, to *feel* the charge of history that inhabits space.

Pallasmaa highlights how space has the ability to activate the imagination (see 2011). Space in immersive practice, both in its 'constant' features and in its 'collaboration' with the artists who have accentuated and embellished these features through sympathetic design, is integral to the experience of being taken into another world as well as being taken into our own imagination. It is the combined imagination of the artists and the audience-participants that creates the immersive world. This fusion of imagination and embodied apprehension reconnects us with our capabilities of total, corporeal comprehension. It allows the pleasurable alleviation of alienation from the imagination and the senses that is a side-effect of modern daily living.

As a consequence immersive practice directly involves us in our own experience of lived, sensual perception (see Pallasmaa, 2009: 150). Following Pallasmaa's theories it is possible to see how immersive practice, where the attention to space and the whole array of human senses perceiving within that space, can return an individual to an experience of her or his *praesence* and an *ongoing present* as it requires that she or he halt, attend and dwell in the moment; moment by moment. Consequently, immersive practice is an artistic form that exposes Deleuzean immanence and encourages the 're-humanised', (re) sensitised, in an individual's experience (see Pallasmaa, 2011: 14–24).

Doreen Massey: the politics of space and place

Massey is a social scientist and geographer. Her writings demonstrate the deeply lived, historicised and political qualities inherent in any geographical place, which are made manifest in the individual and collective experiences of space (see Massey, 2010a, 2010b). Her writings draw attention to the significance of *felt* internal spaces; in particular the spaces of emotion, memory, imagination, thought and instinct, as triggered by a human response to external space. This thinking can be directly applied to corresponding experiences within immersive theatre.

Illustration 11   'Sparky', at *re:bourne*. (2010). Sparky created by Kinetica, operated by Ceem Art Studios practitioners

[Photo credit: Beth Cuenco. Image courtesy of Nimble Fish]

Massey defines how space is beyond the presupposed idea of a geographical or physical context in which events take place. Space is not merely a surface across which one travels and where interrelationships occur but equally *a concept*, an imagined domain, that locates us. Space is 'the product of interrelations' which are 'constituted through interactions, from the immensity of the global to the intimately tiny' (Massey, 2010a: 9). For Massey, space is 'always under construction' because it is 'a product of relations-between', so it is 'always in the process of being made' and thus 'a simultaneity of stories-so-far' (2010a: 9). Barrett, Higgin, Hill and Mitchell, Holdsworth and Sharps all talk in Part Two of listening to spaces, the stories that space has to tell, which are then acted upon in the sensual design and choreography of the work, making Massey's theory immediately tangible.

Due to the open, amorphous potential of space, it is the 'sphere of possibility of the existence of multiplicity in the sense of contemporaneous plurality' in which 'distinct trajectories coexist' (Massey, 2010a: 9). Put another way, what this points towards is that: (i) space is the location where lots of people and things coexist and in/ on which lots of situations occur at the same time; (ii) the historical memory of this simultaneous activity is a constant in that space, that activity lives on, it haunts that space; and (iii) therefore, space makes you aware of the continuing presence of 'the things done in it' and connects past, present and future via location. Immersive theatre actively demonstrates this and makes us aware of these complexities in the live(d) moment. Massey shows how space can be understood to be more abstract than place as 'place is space to which meaning has been ascribed' (see Massey, 2010a: 183):

> [P]laces…necessitate intervention; they pose a challenge. They implicate us, perforce, in the lives of human others, and in relations with nonhumans they ask how we shall respond to our temporary meeting-up with these particular rocks and stones and trees.
>
> (Massey, 2010a: 8, 141)

Bear in mind that I am applying Massey's observations around the geographical consideration of space and place, and 'placing' it, very specifically, in the immediate and local geographic-emotional-artistic space of the immersive event. In doing so, I intend to underscore how space/place within this practice encompasses a variety of spatialities including the geographical, the architectural, the actual versus the virtual, the local and the global, the open and the confined, internal and external. A place can be understood 'as integrations of space and time; *as spatio-temporal events*' (Massey, 2010a: 130; emphasis original). This resonates with the quality of experience that comes about in immersive theatre events where the fusion of space and duration are paramount and take on their own resonance within the affective experience of the work; both during the event and in any subsequent process of recall.

Massey debates on the relational politics of spatial activity, and her ideas around 'throwntogetherness' and 'the politics of the *event* of the place', consider the significance of the inherent politicisation of places (Massey, 2010a: 147–62; emphasis added). Massey's questioning of a 'politics of connectivity' (2010a: 181) if applied to the communal experience of immersive practice highlights how, where individuals are drawn together in a relational way in space and time, the act automatically and implicitly confronts a politics of decision-making and of control. This might exist in and of itself only in that space and time, or can expose the narrative(s) themes and function of an actual political issue related to the wider space/place of society, both inside and outside the event. This occurred with the immersive interpretation of Clare Bayley's *The Container* produced by Nimble Fish, performed in a two-tonne articulated lorry, parked in the street; a space which, as Holdsworth identifies, became politically charged. Similarly, Hill highlights how WildWorks' practice never forces the issues of a place but immerses itself in them so they naturally come to underpin the form and themes of the final event. She stresses that the layering of varied sensual elements within immersive practice, rather than a focus on speech, allows for a more experiential embracing of the political narratives and challenges that are present within the space and thus the work.

The intimate connectivity of one-on-one performance, with its very particular time-space continuum, can focus in a concentrated fashion on the politics of that connectivity – the fact that human interaction and ideas around community, caring and compassion are all too absent from out daily lives in the 'outside' space of the grounded (to use Massey's term) or 'real' world. Thinking in particular of Howells's *The Pleasure of Being: Washing, Feeding, Holding* the question that Massey poses, 'why do we so often and so tightly associate care with proximity?', is apt to this highly ritualised, respectful and concentrated (in space, time and action) work. Furthermore, as Massey continues, perhaps with the ultimate political impact of this piece there is a *felt* realisation (in the moment and subsequent to the experience) of the fact that 'it is not "place" that is missing, but grounded, practical, connectedness' (Massey, 2010a: 186–7). Following Massey, these relationships in a focused space and time automatically raise questions and certainly inspire reflection around 'the spatialities of responsibility, loyalty, care':

> [i]f we take seriously the relational construction of identity (of ourselves, of the everyday, of places), then what is the potential geography of our politics towards those relations?

> (2010a: 189)

In Part Two Gladwin reflects on how Back to Back Theatre's immersive explorations draw attention to the natural action of everyday space and place and thus foreground relational constructions that exist within specific locations. The discussion of Punchdrunk Enrichment's *The Uncommercial Traveller* together with the dialogues with Howells and Hill and Mitchell draw attention to the ways in which this is realised in their particular approaches to immersive practice. Both Holdsworth and Wilson in their conversations demonstrate how, by siting theatre in everyday, 'real' spaces, the audience-participant feels ownership of that location; the site itself is non-exclusive and welcoming – as Wilson puts it, 'I'm a citizen of this place or of this land'. Yet simultaneously the immersive experience designed within and across that space ensures the location, history and interaction of that space/place becomes heightened, epic. In this way the history of everyday activity and social relations, alongside the immediate activity of the audience-participant in that space during the immersive event, is defamiliarised and made special.

Massey, highlights an inherent politicisation that occurs through the drawing together of groups within a specific space/place, even where these are formed from as few as two, where the notion of the political stems from 'a community consciously undergoing the experience of its sharing' (Jean-Luc Nancy qtd in Massey, 2010a: 154). Coney embraces this idea in much of its work and specifically in *A Small Town Anywhere* (2009). In this work a small company of audience-performers are assigned roles via hats and badges as citizens of a small town: the history of the town is revealed and pieced together through the processual choices of the playing-audience; the performance is made in response to these decisions. On a thematic and narrative level, this work explores the edges of *communitas* and solidarity when it is put to the test. It physically manifests the concept via the form itself and the *communitas* that emerges through the audience-performers play.

Massey contemplates the politics of human connectedness in space, recognising that it is the interrelations between space and place, objects and space/place and people in space/place that are central to social, historical and political experience; everything returning to the significance of *space* and/in *place*. Within these interrelations there is a 'positive interconnectivity', where 'any notion of sociability' implies 'a dimension of spatiality' (2010a: 188–9). It is the sense of 'being-together', as put forward by Bourriaud (2002: 15), that occurs and is *felt* in space. For Massey:

> The very acknowledgement of our constitutive interrelatedness implies a spatiality; and that in turn implies that the nature of that spatiality should be a crucial avenue of enquiry and political engagement...this kind of interconnectedness, which stresses the imaginative awareness of others, evokes the outwardlookingness of a spatial imagination.
>
> (2010a: 189)

The discussion of *The Uncommercial Traveller* in Part Two foregrounds the way in which immersive practice can allow a direct and tangible access to the history, politics and social interactivity of a place in the research and development stage of the work. By translating these explorations into immersive theatre, it enables the audience-participant to inhabit this history and make contact with the politics.

Massey highlights important factors attributable to space in allowing, inviting, demanding certain relational politics, which are essentially embodied. Connecting with the arguments above from Bourriaud regarding relational aesthetics, Massey helps to elucidate the importance of space to the experience of connectedness, relatedness, or rejection of this, within immersive practice. These combined perspectives outline the nature of engagement between individuals within a particular time and space, where 'There is...an inherent orientation of joy towards engagement with what lies beyond the self, and hence towards sociability; and there is corresponding orientation of sadness towards disengagement and isolation' (Moira Gatens and Genevieve Lloyd qtd in Massey, 2010a: 188).[13] Importantly, Massey foregrounds Gatens and Lloyds' interpretation of Spinoza's concept of imagination, reinforcing the idea of the 'inseparability of individuality and interdependence' which has 'affective dimensions'; this in turn lends the imagination 'a corporeality' where 'imagination involves awareness of other bodies at the same time as our own'. Massey also highlights the corporeality of connectedness that occurs in spatial relatedness where 'experience' is not only an internalised, haptic activity, but consists of a multiplicity of events and relations that constantly associate and interact (see Massey, 2010a: 188).

These elements are demonstrated in the democratic collaborations of Nimble Fish, which offers a new approach to thinking about the relational politics of the collaborative process. For Nimble Fish, responsibility and interconnectedness within a given space and time (the temporality itself a continuum which extends beyond and prior to the physical collaboration) are genuinely shared and progressively rethought in terms of an immersive, mutual sociability as much as in relation to an immersive artistic process. For Holdsworth, 'immersive theatre is about inclusion'.

Massey's ideas are particularly apposite when thinking of the immersive environmental practice of Wilson, in her respectful and symbiotic relationship with geographical space and her invitation to her audience/partner-walkers/co-collaborators:

> space presents us with the social in the widest sense: the challenge of our constitutive interrelatedness – and thus our collective implication in the outcomes of that interrelatedness; the radical contemporaneity of an ongoing multiplicity of others, human and non-human; and the ongoing and ever-specific project of the practices through which that sociability is configured.
>
> (Massey, 2010a: 195)

Massey highlights how the *felt* internal spaces of emotion, memory, imagination, thought and instinct, are activated by the immediate and wider external space/place that an individual inhabits at any given time. Her thinking here meets Pallasmaa's in pointing toward the way in which embodied space breaks down barriers between the perceived contradictions of the internal/external binary to establish a continuum of *felt* and *thought* experience. These ideas are affectively realised in Wilson's work, as she eloquently articulates in Part Two, which 'metaphorically' *emplaces* 'the "interior landscape" of the human body within the physical landscape'. Following Massey it is possible to understand how space envelops, becomes the envelope, container, casket of the experience. A domain within which we can understand we are genuinely immersed. In this way, Massey's theories meet the aesthetic ideas of Bachelard regarding the visceral poetics of space.

Gaston Bachelard: the poetics of space

Bachelard (1884–1962) was a French philosopher who theorised across science, psychology and poetics. His *Poetics of Space* becomes an elucidation of immersive practice, specifically that which attends to the details and idiosyncrasies of space, whether in its natural form or adorned through design. To apply his thinking to immersive practice is to detail the myriad ways in which space is opened up as a *felt*, lived and imaginative poetic in both an epic and intimate manner; (re)lived again in the action of any subsequent embodied memory of the space that envelops the immersive event. These are spaces within which the audience-immersant is invited to 'inhabit with intensity' (Bachelard, 1994: xxxviii):

> Space that has been seized upon by the imagination cannot remain indifferent space subject to the measure and estimates of the surveyor. It has been lived in, not in its positivity but with all the partiality of the imagination.
>
> (Bachelard, 1994: xxxvi)

Holdsworth echoes this in her conversation in Part Two, reiterating ways in which 'the fiction of space *allows*': allows the imagination to be activated, triggers *felt* experience, gives permission to behave in a way that goes against convention, takes the space and the action within that space outside of the everyday.

As if foreshadowing immersive practice, Bachelard places great emphasis on the way in which imagination works in the spaces we inhabit:

> By the swiftness of its actions the imagination separates us from the past as well as from reality; it faces the future. To the *function of reality*... should be added a *function of unreality*.... If we cannot imagine, we cannot foresee.... [T]he imagination sharpens all of our senses. The imagining attention prepares our attention for instantaneousness,
>
> (Bachelard, 1994: xxxiv, 87; emphasis original)

The imagination thus functions on a Deleuzean 'plane of immanence'. For Bachelard, poetry enables the imagination to take 'its place on the margin, exactly where the function of unreality comes to charm or disturb...the domain of pure sublimation' (1994: xxxv). Therefore poetically manipulated space has the potential to achieve these ends. His musings describe the way in which design within immersive spaces unlocks psychologies and narrative situations that lay dormant within source material, 'a phenomenology of what is hidden' (1994: xxxvii). This is true of dreamthinkspeak's and Punchdrunk's scenography and the way in which its affective and sensual powers have an immediate impact and invoke lasting effects. The design teams for dreamthink-speak and Punchdrunk, inspired by the source material from which they work, can be seen to explore Bachalard's idea of 'topoanalysis' which is 'the systematic psychological study of the sites of our intimate lives' (1994: 8).

Bachelard encapsulates ideas around the power of space, 'housed spaces, as both trigger and holder of the memory, of imagination and of sensual experience. In terms of the sensual experience of space and the way in which that activates a sense memory, this comes about due to the 'passionate liaison of our bodies' with space and the memory of a particular experience that it might hold (see Bachelard, 1994: 15).

dreamthinkpeak and Punchdrunk both play with experiential psychologies through found spaces; carefully exposing the thematic potential and narrative possibilities that already exist within a found space, carefully adding textural detail through design to the spaces. In so doing, they reignite a childlike curiosity, which emphasises the power of the intimate within the wider epic experience; the vast expanse of the whole experience plays on throughout the buildings that they inhabit, whilst individuals play amongst the objects and effects finding their own individual experiences, intricate psychological and sensual detail, that add layer upon layer to the full-scale narrative of the event.[14] In the Punchdrunk Enrichment conversation Evans and Savoy, performers in *The Uncommercial Traveller*, highlight how it was the dressed space that unlocked themes, narratives and individual psychologies for them as performers; as Evans put it, 'the space was directly speaking to all of the characters.' Savoy notes that the scenographic space proved crucial to drawing the audience-participants into the Dickensian world that they inhabited.

Bachelard also indicates the poetic power of space that has been found and reassigned according to the work placed within it. For example, Howells's *The Pleasure of Being: Washing, Feeding, Holding* took possession of an antiquated bathroom of BAC and re-imagined it through the low lighting already present in the space aided by candlelight; a ritualised hush and the intimacy of the exchange that occurred within this surrounding fed off the sounds and textures that already existed within the space, accentuating the safe, womblike qualities of the room to enhance a feeling of 'protected intimacy' (Bachelard, 1994: 3). Within such reawakened space, the actions performed, however small, subtle and intimate, take on epic proportions due to an ongoing sensual, imaginative and actual exchange between the participants in the act, the space, the duration and the event as a whole. The space becomes re-imagined through this act and simple words and gestures take on poetic and deeply ritualised authority. Extreme as it may sound, in such instances perception is enhanced, consciousness is touched and rejuvenated. In a space/time continuum that is heightened, where attention is drawn to detail and to dwelling, *being*, in the moment, a unique interaction occurs.[15] The space frames the event and accentuates the quality of experience occurring within it. It takes everyday activity and defamiliarises it, makes it special, allowing the event that takes place in that space to attain a higher degree of reality, hovering in-between the felt sensation of the 'reality' and unreality of the experience that is generated by the imagination:

> The minute we apply a glimmer of consciousness to a mechanical gesture…we sense new impressions come into being beneath this familiar domestic duty. For consciousness rejuvenates everything, giving a quality of beginning to the most everyday actions.
>
> (Bachelard, 1994: 67)

The immediate and subsequent sensation and expression of Howells's *The Pleasure of Being: Washing, Feeding, Holding* answered the question posed by Bachelard; 'how can secret rooms, rooms that have disappeared, become abodes for an unforgettable past?' (1994: xxxvi). In instances such as this, where the receiver of the work experiences a collision and collusion of poetic space and time, it is possible to become aware of a sensate exchange that occurs between the artful designs of the practitioner and the discipline of the work within which we exist.

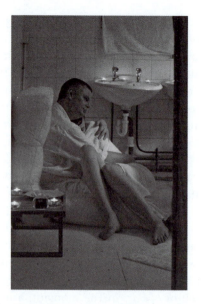

Illustration 12 Howells's *The Pleasure of Being: Washing, Feeding, Holding*. BAC, London, July 2010

[Photo credit: Ed Collier. Image courtesy of Adrian Howells]

The vastness of the ideas that can be engaged with in such instances connect with the idea that 'the impression of immensity is *in us*' as much as it is inspired by the experience (Bachelard, 1994: xxxix; emphasis added).

In immersive worlds such as those created by Howells, WildWorks or Wilson, it is possible to 'sense the concordance of world immensity with intimate depth of being' (Bachelard, 1994: 189). Equally, work that plays within and through the history of a space, such as WildWorks' *The Enchanted Palace* (2010–12), at Kensington Palace, London, or dreamthinkspeak's *Before I Sleep* at the Co-operative Building, Brighton, actually explore the edges and the in-betweens of the 'synthesis of immemorial and recollected' memory and imaginings, allowing the audience participant to experience the space 'in its reality and in its virtuality' (1994: 5). An equivalent sensation occurred within BAC's 2011 One-on-One Festival. The building was taken over by a series of intimate and immersive events that produced an immediate otherworldliness within the confines of the space, where locations within the building were traversed from one experience to the next, creating an internal order and structure to such an extent that the outside, everyday life became separate, unreal for the duration of time that I was in the venue. This impacted on the time it took for my journey home by car, a private space which acted as a decompression chamber to assist my coming out of this domain. In this way, the immediacy of the experience and the particular way in which the space was revitalised demonstrated how it is in the sensual apprehension of concentrated time and space 'in the most restricted intimate space that the dialectics of inside and outside draws its strength' (Bachelard, 1994: 229).

Bachelard provides a lyrical discourse on the way in which certain architectural forms, turrets, attics, vaulted ceilings, corners, passages, each has their own quality which in turn has the potential to elicit an equivalent resonant response in the perceiver's body, imagination and emotional memory. Similarly, furniture such as wardrobes, chests and drawers are emblematic of internal poetic spaces that resonate with their own metaphors and as vessels for curiosity; what lies within? It is no surprise that these effects – doors, chests, drawers and wardrobes – feature heavily throughout a vast range of literary, theatrical and artistic references. This is because these spaces are suggestive of secrecy, hidden spaces, doors to an imagined world, where 'to open it, is to experience an event' (see Bachelard, 1994: 74–89). The immersive aesthetic holds onto the feelings that resonate within the dimensions and textures of such spaces and exploits these effects to its own ends.

Sharps alludes to the power of levels, doors and the imaginative space of buildings in his discussion, and many of the practitioners express the idea of the immersive experience as entering another world via some mysterious portal. Amelia, the 6-year-old comrade who escorted me to Punchdrunk's *The Crash of the Elysium*, pointed out that the immersive experience as a whole is 'a bit like Narnia'. In this way immersive practice understands the potency of imaginative dwelling places to inspire the imagination and evoke poignant and powerful responses in an audience-participant. Here, then, an understanding of the imaginative space internal to the audience-immersant comes to the forefront. Immersive events can reawaken these primitive and poetic experiences of space and place. Consequently, in immersive practice, architectural spaces become 'imbued with dream values' (Bachelard, 1994: 17), the sensual and noetic effects of which last in an affective manner in any subsequent process of recall.

Immersive theatres: audience, space, duration, sensation

The ideas interwoven across these perspectives serve to elucidate central features of immersive theatre. Each of these theories helps to show how immersive theatres directly involve us in our own experience of lived, sensual perception. The experiential nature of immersive practice prioritises embodied knowledge and the making-sense/*sense*-making processes of human perception and interpretation. *Seselelame* is a useful concept for supporting and explaining the embodied sentience innate in all humans, which exists in everyday pursuits and can be activated by carefully crafted immersive events. Here the emotional and intuitive dimensions of perception hold their own weight in meaning-making processes. Similarly, (syn)aesthetic appreciation shifts between realms – between the sensual and intellectual, between the literal and lateral – and relies on perception that comprehends the details of an event corporeally. Participants in the event may be inspired to attend to and interpret their own bodily experience of the work, while simultaneously orienting themselves to the bodies of co-participants in the event. In this way, immersive theatres can establish links across sensation, perception, emotion and moral reasoning in form and content. In immersive theatres sharply focused visual and tactile perception combined with the wider, haptically influenced, peripheral experience of the space ensures the inhabitant attends to the intricate detail of the event and guarantees a rich, multi-layered quality of comprehension. The intimacy of sound in/as space becomes integral in/as experience and accentuates the fusion of interiority and exteriority within the experience. Within immersive worlds inhabitants dwell in time in the space just as they *dwell in the activity* within the duration of the event and equally dwell, attentively, in their own bodies.

Immersive theatres encourage the participant to understand the work on a deep, embodied level without necessarily being able to describe or explain this, both during and following the event. This sensory intellect follows its own rule of logic that is both separate from *and often intrinsic to* cerebral intellect. It can effect an unsettling and/or exhilarating *process of becoming aware* of the fusion of senses within interpretation. The original, visceral experience remains affective in any subsequent recall within the embodied memory of the work.

Individual imagination is key to this sensory intellect. The imagination is manipulated or guided by the poetic (re)inventions with space, time and design within the immersive world created. In immersive theatres, space, combined with carefully executed activity, opens up a *felt*, live(d) poetic in both an epic and intimate manner so that the individual inhabits that world with intensity. Within such reawakened space the actions performed, even where small, subtle and intimate, take on epic proportions due to an ongoing imaginative and physical exchange across and between the participants in the act; the space; the duration; and the event as a whole. Immersive theatres imaginatively combine a range of elements and techniques to heighten experience and defamiliarise everyday action, which establish worlds that hover in-between the felt sensation of the 'reality' and the 'unreality' of the experience.

The *praesent* quality of experience in an immersive performance activates Deleuzean 'immanence', where the feeling of *being in the moment* as a constant *praesence* can engender a palpable feeling of being alive. This supports the idea that immersive theatres have become prominent and popular in British theatre experiences *because* it encourages and celebrates this feeling of 'aliveness'. Immersive theatre is an artistic form that encourages the rehumanised and resensitised in an individual experience. Immersive theatre actively demonstrates how space is the palpable medium where the historical memory of simultaneous activity is a constant *praesence*; it makes the inhabitant aware of the continuing presence of its past activity via topography and dimension; tangible manifestions of the fusion of past, present and future.

Immersive theatres prioritise the *praesence* of the audience through the playfulness of relational aesthetics. Immersive theatres validate and celebrate the role of individual interpretation in the artistic experience;

they transform the sensations and experiences of the everyday, making these special, unusual, in the process. Well-executed immersive theatres are governed by forms and codes of practice that allow the experience to *feel* free and lead to creative agency, enabling artists and audience to make the work together. They invite/require a plurality of experiences and responses which can emancipate the audience-participant within the process. This creative agency has the potential to lead to a political agency on an individual or collective level. The transformative qualities and underlying politics of this work, as brought about by the democratic practice of shared, sensory experience, demonstrates the profound potential of this artistic form.

Varying degrees of shared experience and 'being together' within immersive theatres accentuate feelings of community and conviviality. Space provides the charged medium where people and things coexist in this live(d) manner. Immersive encounters within a location that honours the geography and inherent politics of that place allow for an experiential interrogation of social and environmental concerns. An ecological sensibility can exist within the very form of this work, as it encourages participants to attend to their *praesence* within the space. Immersive events encompass a variety of spatialities, including the geographical, architectural, physical and virtual, local and global, open and confined, internal and external. Embodied space breaks down barriers between the perceived contradictions of the internal/ external binary to establish a continuum of *felt* and *thought* experience. By emphasising contact, tactility and immediacy, immersive theatres re-envisage the relations between people, space and time and mark the event within a participant's embodied space or interior architecture. This interplay of spatialities thus sites/cites the activity of *being* together during and following an immersive event.

These critical perspectives, drawn together here, show how the immersive aesthetic and experience focuses on an individual, immediate and innate response to the event, during each moment and in any subsequent process of recall and interpretation. Part Two now invites you to engage in conversations with immersive theatre practitioners that demonstrate these ideas in practice. These discussions provide illustration of the ideas presented across Part One and offer examples of those forms, techniques and aims pinpointed in the Scale of Immersivity in Chapter 2 and elaborated on in this chapter. The contributors engage in a similar debate to that put forward in Chapter 1 regarding the indefinable, heterogeneous quality of this work, yet they also point towards clear features that are shared across diverse forms of immersive theatre.

Part Two

Immersion, Intimacy and Immediacy in Practice

Introduction

The following conversations with leading exponents of immersive theatres highlight a diversity of outlooks in terms of form, content and methodology. Each discussion also emphasises consistent features of 'immersivity'; primarily the prioritisation of the audience member within an individual and collective, interactive experience; the interdisciplinary nature of immersive practice, which embraces juxtaposition and a more 'open' response to the experience; and a focus on how space and place are vital to the form and choreography of the work.

Bodies are predominant in each discussion; performing bodies and perceiving bodies and the particular affective power for communication that results from the proximity of each combined in space. In this respect the way in which immersive practice answers a desire for shared human contact is repeatedly reflected upon in each discussion. Morris of Artangel talks of this in the opening conversation in his consideration of how immersive theatre events allow a participant to make genuine, human contact; to feel alive. Howells underscores the notion of how immersion implies a deep involvement in the activity within that world in his reflections on *really being* in the moment of the event. He asserts that the intention and expertise that is executed in setting up the conditions for the immersive situation can lead to the individual participant 'being fully alive' in that world. Wilson's discussion of *Fissure* and Hill's reflections on WildWorks' *Souterrain* provides illustration of how an immersive event that explores the complexities of death and grief can enable participants in the work to celebrate living and *attend to being*.

In terms of this embodied experience it is also notable that each conversation refers to respecting the way in which an instinctive response, intuiting through an event, is integral to the form and thus demanded of the immersant in the work. Barrett, Lundahl and Seitl, Holdsworth of Nimble Fish, Hill and Mitchell of WildWorks and Sharps of dreamthinkspeak highlight how this regard for intuition, coupled with the layered, non-linear nature of the work, encourages the audience to become playfully curious. With a shared focus on the potential of the full sensorium of the human body, these conversations demonstrate how immersive theatres give credence to the intellect of the body. Lundahl asserts how it is only through physical investigation and embodied knowledge that challenging intellectual concepts can be fully understood. In this way, these discussions reinforce the fact that embodied analysis has its own authority within a wider field of artistic and critical theory.

With immersive theatres the respect for the audience member as participant and collaborator is central to the process and the 'product'. Many of the discussions talk of a contract that is entered into between audience-participant and artist to ensure a safe (even if it *feels* dangerous) journey through the work. The Coney, Howells, Lundahl & Seitl, Mercuriali, Punchdrunk Enrichment and WildWorks' discussions all touch on this, highlighting the creative control that ensures safety and enables agency for the audience-participant within the work. These contributors also refer to the 'care' for the audience member beginning with 'the preparation'; immersive rituals that these practitioners take their audience-participants through in order to acclimatise them to the world they are about to enter.

All of the contributors share ideas around audience participation and agency, illustrating the ways in which audience members become collaborators and co-creators in the work. Howells talks eloquently about how his audience-participants become 'co-authors' of the work, using their bodies as the source and site of sensual material for the narrative. Mercuriali highlights the ways in which immersive practice requires risk and investment from audience-participants and complicity between these 'guest-performers'. Stevens provides playful illustration of the ways in which individuals are drawn into the blurring of art and life in Coney's adventures. The discussions of Coney, Nimble Fish, Punchdrunk Enrichment, WildWorks and Wilsons' work illustrate the affective potential for empowerment and *communitas* that can evolve in this work which embraces ideas around individual and collective agency and civic responsibility. The discussions of Back to Back Theatre and of Punchdrunk Enrichments' practice also highlight how these forms and techniques offer creative agency to the performers as much as to the audience-participants. Each of these conversations demonstrates various ways in which immersive theatre can be a democratising force.

Wider notions of empowerment and transformation in relation to the role that the audience plays in immersive practice is also made clear. Morris highlights how immersive practice is transformative in form, because the audience-participant refashions and shapes the event according to her or his decision-making and navigation through it. Mitchell of WildWorks echoes this, highlighting how the landscape is an affective aspect within this that enables audience-participants to be curious and 'receptive'. This is true of large-scale works, where space must be covered and levels traversed, and minimalist pieces where the decision-making is more intimate and confined. Seitl refers to the way in which the bodies of their 'visitors' transform as a consequence of sensory interaction with the performer – through touch, the haptic experience of movement and the audio interaction. She clarifies how this process itself leads to a deeper sense of spiritual or imaginative transformation. Lundahl extends this notion by contemplating the ways in which these results are stimulated by sensate triggers that embrace that individual's 'archive of lived experience'. Gladwin begins by asserting Back to Back Theatre's aim to make work that is ideologically transformative, enabling all participants in the event to go to 'a new territory'. Hill of WildWorks and Wilson eloquently draw attention to the way in which immersive forms allow individuals and communities a deeper engagement with a narrative that demonstrates affective transformation. By excavating and embracing experiential narratives immersive theatres offer a catalyst for personal and, consequently, collective change, as noted by Morris and Stevens. Similarly, Howells reflects on the transformational power of his one-to-ones where, in giving time and space to an individual to invest in her or himself, she or he can 'then go back into society and be an effective member of the community'. As this suggests, immersive theatres have the potential to be deeply transformative in many ways ranging from the artistic across the existential to the political, as is illustrated by Hill and Mitchells' discussion of *The Passion*.

The transformative potential of immersive theatre is also illustrated in many of these discussions where encounters with the epic within the intimate is made manifest through the form. In particular the discussion of WildWorks' practice demonstrates this on various levels. Hill clarifies how, for WildWorks, such encounters occur through the use of 'proxies'; individual volunteers from amongst the audience-participants that allow a personal interaction to be palpably felt by the larger group of witnesses. This conversation also reflects, through *Souterrain*, on the way that epic themes, powerful meanings, can be embodied through an individual's intimate and immediate connection with archetypal narratives that are made live(d) through an event. Additionally, this dialogue contemplates the fusion of the epic and the intimate that is stimulated by attention and *praesentness* within an immersive environment; an individual's ability to perceive the vastness of a landscape and to attend to the sensual detail of the immediate space in which she or he is located.

The conversations with Hill and Mitchell, Holdsworth, Sharps and Wilson make clear the ways in which space and place are vital components of each of their methodologies for immersive practice. These conversations highlight how the environment offers a unique layer to the themes and forms of the work. Wilson's reflections show how the act of encouraging individuals to *be* in an environment enables an intuitive and intense connection with that world. These discussions also highlight the socio-economic politics and philosophies that are automatically and tangibly present within immersive practice that respects the place from which it evolves and in which it is produced.

The interdisciplinary nature of immersive practice is central to all of these discussions. All of the artists reflect on the different languages of the performance and highlight how verbal language is always played with in a heightened fashion, whether defamiliarised as shadowy mutterings as in Punchdrunk's epic productions, where dance and design communicate the narratives and themes; interwoven across live and mediated performance in dreamthinkspeak's work; the intense and intimate, clandestine conversations shared with participants in Howells's work; the playful messages inscribed via various media by Coney's comrade, Rabbit; or the fusion of artistic languages in Wilson's or WildWorks' events. The importance of imaginative and sensual scenographic design to immersive practice is made clear across all of the discussions. Wilson, first and foremost a scenographer, draws attention to her ongoing aim for there to be no division between audience, performer and space, and highlights how the fusion of sensual elements within her work, including installation and environment, is central to the aesthetic and thus sculpturally layers the total experience. Her conversation touches on the way in which an audience is enabled to experience themes and ideas on a material level, woven into the fabric of the immersive form itself. Gladwin describes the way in which architectural and scenographic design in Back to Back Theatre's *Soft* had its own choreographic hapticity within the performance. Barrett and Sharps are particularly eloquent on the significance of scenography in the work and, along with Morris, to the equal importance of each interdisciplinary element that is artfully manipulated within the experience. Note how Barrett describes a Punchdrunk audience as becoming part of this scenography. Barrett and Mercuriali draw interesting observations about how immersive practice can expose the ways in which technological communication can both limit and open up the possibilities for human engagement. The discussions with Gladwin, Lundahl and Seitl and Mercuriali illustrate the potential that immersive technologies can play in unlocking the imaginative space of the audience-immersant and, in accentuating a feeling of intimacy within and between the work, the artist and any other co-participants in the space. Gladwin highlights how the use of intimate surround-sound via headphones can be as liberating for the performer as much as it is holistically immersive for the audience member. Gladwin, Higgin, Mercuriali and Morris all point out the affective significance of sound in audio journeys and performances within an immersive experience. These provide intimate verbal narratives, hone in on action and image, heighten the detail of the imagination and of the space and enable a sharing of alternative sensory experiences between individuals within the event. As Gladwin puts it, 'sound has its own theatrical value' and when employed to immersive ends it creates the sensation of 'stepping into' alternative experiences.

As this suggests, there are clear connections and affinities to be drawn across all of the discussions. The titles given to each are intended only to add a flavour of the ensuing conversation in relation to the theorising of Part One. What is evident from each dialogue is the focus on a central edict of immersive practice; that being the creation of otherworldly-worlds in which the audience-participant is completely immersed. Part Two provides a space where these practitioners can examine their own history and practice, and articulate the problems and pleasures of defining what they do. Wilson's reflections, in particular, emphasise how the language used to describe and define the work, during and after the event, is itself often elusive.

Each discussion demonstrates the ways in which these practitioners are evolving a range of methodologies for creating such work. Before reading these conversations it may be useful to return to the introduction to each artist, offered at the start of this book, to (re)familiarise yourself with the background of each practitioner and the work under scrutiny. In transcribing each conversation I have aimed to hold onto the conversational form and flow to convey the personal voices present in each interview and the organic development of each discussion.

Conversations one

Michael Morris of Artangel

Immersive theatres – intimacy, immediacy, transformation

Michael Morris: I've always been resistant to labelling things. At the ICA [Institute of Contemporary Arts] in the early 1980s there was a desire to set what we were doing apart from the mainstream, literary traditions of theatre. The first season that I worked on with Tim Albery was called 'Theatre Not Plays' – a suggestion that theatrical experience need not be driven by linear narrative, but by the point at which text, image, action and sound can meet afresh as equals. This became the ICA's mantra; the idea that the writer was not necessarily the starting point for a project and that text could be integrated into a live experience in a different way. Of course, in 1981, London was not such a crowded field as it is now. The ICA then became home to what John Ashford and I also called Performance Theatre or Performance Work. And later my successor, Lois Keidan, chose to define it as Live Art; all, in a way, variations on the same thing. What is different about that, which this book attempts to pinpoint, is the breaking down of the line between spectator and spectacle so the audience become participants at the centre of an event, which not only lacks linear narrative, it doesn't have a physical boundary either. And of course that was very exciting for everyone gathered in the space. When I first encountered the Catalan group La Fura dels Baus in 1982, I became hooked on being in the midst of a *mise en scène* and also partly being able to influence what happened. Two things were significant and formative for me about experiencing Les Fura Dels Baus at that time, which directly led to the work with Artangel in the following decade; it didn't take place in conventional spaces and that interested me because, by then, even after a couple of years at the ICA, I had become frustrated by the boundaries of the black box. We tried to configure it every which way to ring the changes, but the same dimensions remained for a relatively small audience. The kinds of artists that interested me at the time I felt could be seen in a mainstream context, but in a different way, exploring the potential of non-theatrical spaces and the potential for art, which meant the public became participants, transformative in terms of the control they had over the event and transformative in terms of the effect the work had on them. It was a real experience and, in the case of La Fura dels Baus, a bombardment. It was an alliance of many factors. 'Immersive' was simply a way of describing something that felt new and different in terms of the way they used location, the way in which the audience became active participants, the way in which everything felt integrated and there was no barrier between the auditorium and the stage. It felt like a way of describing something that was taking place; so we used 'immersive' as a handy adjective, amongst many others, rather than as a defining term.

Josephine Machon: *From that experience to the present day, how would you define an immersive event; are there particular features that for you are quintessential?*

MM: For me it's as much to do with space and location as it is to do with form. 'Immersive' implies that something is surrounding you, enveloping you. That's another word we used to describe Les Fura Dels Baus, 'enveloping'; something that you felt consumed by.

JM: *You have also talked abut the significance of Robert Wilson and Hans Peter Kuhn's* H.G. *in terms of Artangel's trajectory and its influence on immersive practice in general, specifically in Felix Barrett's work with Punchdrunk. Would you expand on what you feel the significance of* H.G. *was?*

MM: *H.G.* began with the narrative image of an abandoned dinner party inspired by the first page of H. G. Wells's *The Time Machine*. But the narrative then became much, much looser. The way that the visitors experienced the space was not prescribed or determined; there was no set route to follow and there were no guides. The sense you had was that you were there to explore, following your instincts on a trail marked out by sound and light. The spaces in-between the principle tableaux that Bob [Robert Wilson] had designed were barely illuminated. We wanted the invigilators to be in the shadows and not to intervene unless there was a real necessity to do so; not to warn people of the trip hazards because we felt people were grown up enough to take care of themselves. There were no accidents at all, despite the fact that there weren't people in uniforms saying 'watch that step'. That added to the experience for the public, the fact that it was something that they were able to explore for themselves a bit like a walk in a forest, which has no roadmap either.

JM: You've talked about the importance of sound in H.G. *and various experiential events and referred to Bruce Gladwin's work with* Back To Back; *the intimacy and immediacy of the sound in headphones, whilst the action is played out at a distance within a vast arena of everyday activity. Could you clarify exactly what it is about that experience of sound that immerses us within the event?*

MM: *H.G.* came at a critical period in the technical potential of sound design; when sound could come from many different sources; when stereo became 5.1, literally surrounding, the term 'surround-sound' emerged at that time, which obviously has immersive qualities. The coming together of sound, image, action and participation seemed to go towards defining this experience that is now known as immersive. Sound is incredibly important, as is where that sound comes from. In the traditional theatre sound came from one source, over there, on stage. Now it's possible, even more so, to play with directionality and the architecture of sound. With Bruce Gladwin's work, I was very struck by *Food Court* at the Barbican, with live sound by The Necks, and also by *Small Metal Objects* at Stratford Station, experienced on headsets. Artangel has also worked in this area, beginning with Janet Cardiff's *The Missing Voice* in 1999, which took place throughout the streets of Whitechapel; the listener became a participant in a narrative which started at the Whitechapel Library and culminated on a platform at Liverpool Street Station. That sound-work was a piece of immersive theatre, yet the theatre was going on all around you, more or less left to chance. I remember the artist Chris Ofili had a studio in one of the streets that you walked down and the narrative referred to a green Cortina – which happened to be Chris's green Cortina – sometimes parked outside his studio and sometimes not. So there were times where you would think it was planted even though it was left to chance whether it was there or not, or references to banana skins that would sometimes be lying on the ground and sometimes not. So the work was as environmental as it was immersive. As indeed was Lavinia Greenlaw's more recent *Audio Obscura*, for Manchester Piccadilly Station and St Pancras International in 2011.

JM: *And there's also something in the intimacy of the sound as narrative, so close in your ear, really exercising the imagination and inviting you in further. You have often talked about Pina Bausch's influence, as well as your work with Robert Lepage. You referred to them breaking the fourth wall of the proscenium arch, yet still choosing to stick within the discipline of the stage space in order to explore the boundaries and possibilities, to test the edges of that space. For you, their work is an intensely theatrical and immersive experience, which it is, but I felt that in a wholly immersive piece, we would be backstage and rifling through the costume rail, touching that theatricality, feeling textures, sniffing it in. Would you expand a little further on this idea, how their practice illustrates a continuum in immersive experiences?*

MM: I do feel that what both Robert Lepage and Pina Bausch are doing is pushing at the walls of the proscenium. You couldn't deny their work is emotionally immersive for the audience, even though the audience is physically separate from it. Of course, in the recent Wim Wenders film [*Pina*], 3-D gives you a sense of being on the stage with the dancers. It's a very different thing, but that's something that Pina herself, at the end of her life, was interested to explore. I think somehow there's a way in which her performers are immersed in the particular worlds they inhabit, as a kind of bridge between the auditorium and the stage. She was aware of the work that we were doing at Artangel, but was puzzled as to how she could operate without the controls and technical parameters of the proscenium. The work that she made often appears to be improvised, but there's nothing improvised about it at all. Whereas, I think, there's always going to be an element of improvisation in a work where the audience is a participant because you don't know quite how they're going to behave or where they're going to go. In the past decade, we've seen a growing appetite for participation and interactivity. The days of passive audiences now feel numbered. There's a new audience that wants a much more visceral experience. I think that's going to be increasingly true as more and more people spend their time online. If you are going out, to something which is live, you're going to want to feel alive, and there's something very vital and very life-affirming about the experience of being immersed in a piece of art, rather than watching it from a distance.

JM: *Do you feel it's that that is the unique power of immersive practice? Or is it that* combined with *the social aspect and the sense of community that can evolve from this work?*

MM: I think it's both. It's the integration of form, content, experience and the fact that it has a transformative capacity and that you have to find your own pathway through it. In this work you need to make decisions in a way that you don't have to when you're sitting in an auditorium.

Felix Barrett of Punchdrunk

Immersive theatres – intimacy, immediacy, imagination

Josephine Machon: *What do you understand by the term 'immersive' when it's applied to theatre?*

Felix Barrett: It's the empowerment of the audience in the sense that they're put at the centre of the action; they're the pivot from which everything else spins. It's the creation of parallel theatrical universes within which audiences forget that they're an audience, and thus their status within the work shifts.

JM: *What are the vital theatrical elements needed to create those parallel universes for a Punchdrunk experience?*

FB: First, it's the fusion of all the disciplines and the belief that no one discipline is more important than another; the light is as important as the sound, which is as important as the action, which is as important as the space and so on. Also, what's crucially important is the detail in the work; the implication that you can always dig deeper and find something of merit. It's implied in the spatial detail, there are always secrets to find, but also in the work as a whole; to know there are other rooms, other scenes, more backstory to a certain character; a perfect angle to see a lighting transition from or to capture a little *son et lumière*. There's always the promise of more to discover.

Illustration 13 Punchdrunk's *The Crash of the Elysium* (2011). Performer: Danny Millar

[Photo credit: Tristam Kenton. Image courtesy of Manchester International Festival]

JM: *How does Punchdrunk inspire or help shape the intuitive and instinctive response that is required of the audience?*

FB: With different concepts and different performance structures it varies. The mask is a critical device – it can remove the audience from the picture, shifting their status and making them ghostlike. They're empowered because they have the ability to define and choose their evening without being judged for those decisions. They are also removed from the traditional role of the passive, hidden audience, as they become part of the scenography and sometimes actually create walls to frame the action, providing a more intimate environment. The impact of the mask differs for each audience member – for some, wearing the mask gives them a sense of character, enabling them to come out of their shell and adapt their behaviour accordingly. This is empowering because it means they have the freedom to act differently from who they are in day-to-day life. Since first using the mask in *Woyzeck* 12 years ago, this change was immediately apparent. People apologised afterwards because they felt they had acted out of their own control. The use of the mask divides opinion. It seems to affect people in very different ways depending on the individual's nature.

In other styles of our work, such as *The Crash of the Elysium* or one-on-one pieces, the audience are given a specific role to play, so there's no need for a mask as their status has already shifted – the key to audience immersion. That can be empowering because you're never consciously watching the action, you're part of it, you are the protagonist. If ever an audience becomes aware of themselves as *audience*, then we've probably slightly failed.

JM: Are you aware of the moments where that happens, or where frustrations are felt?

FB: Yes, of course. We can always make shows better; every time we try a new format it's not always 100 per cent effective. In *The Crash of the Elysium* the dilemma of how to have a performer talking to the audience on a video monitor, whilst ensuring the audience stayed present in the space rather than going to default, passive, 'I'm watching a screen' mode, was difficult. How can you keep the threat levels, the adrenalin levels up when you're shifting the performance language from being very live, very immediate, very tactile to suddenly being in something that counters and dilutes that? We failed initially and then we realised that you have to give them a job. If, as part of that job, they have ownership of that content, then they remain present. In terms of the bigger question, how we shape responses, we are manipulative, and we're always trying to keep the lid closed so no light from the real world enters in; figuratively and literally! Sometimes you can see the real world, but only if we've shifted the audience's perception to such a degree that they're viewing it through a filmic lens. In terms of where we're progressing to, we're trying to use the real world as a canvas. It's a different form; how can you heighten everything to such an extent that it's not the world that you know and you trudge through every day but a shiny, ethereal, unfamiliar, dangerous place? The basic way that we shape the response, whatever the work, is the choreography and manipulation of audience around a space. It relies on allowing them to think they're discovering things, whilst in reality we are gently flagging moments for them. If we *tell* the audience what to see, we break the spell. If they find it themselves and they think that they're the first person to come across it, that's where the power lies. Through sound, through light, through proximity to performers, through lack of performers, through levels of threat and tension around a building; it's a richly textured tapestry that's there, gently pointing them towards moments of interest. In the case of *Sleep No More* in New York, we have 14 synced soundtracks around the building. It's important that everything starts at the same time, but it also means we can control the sonic shape of the entire site to echo and support the narrative; when the dynamic's picking up on a certain floor we can lower or mute the acoustic environment either side of it. It's like a rocking ship – when one bow rears up and is prominent, everything else needs to dip into the water to accommodate it.

JM: For me, those moments are often located around the live, moving performer, that's where my focus is being drawn. Is a physical language vital to Punchdrunk's immersive form in that respect?

FB: Another living, moving human being is always going to pull focus because of his or her ability to engage with you, through the unspoken crackle of their presence or through direct eye contact or tactility. Touch is arguably the most pure and potent sense in these worlds. They can also physically lead you, whereas where your other senses guide you relies more on your intuition. Spectacle comes from a fusion of all disciplines and without performers, there's always further to travel to get there. They are often responsible for those peak moments, which are designed to attract the most audience. Conversely, you could go in the opposite direction to that scene and find the inverse of that sequence; a lone performer in a room that's been locked and only opens when 95 per cent of the audience are in the opposite side of the building. It depends what theatrical experience you're looking for. You get many who devote their evening trying to root out and discover all the one-on-ones, to locate all the secrets; it depends what game you're playing. Punchdrunk events are designed, idealistically, for one person but of course, for economic and sustainability reasons, we have to have more than one audience member. We need those big scenes to carry the narrative and provide a context to everything, but I would argue that the theatrical gems that people will live with forever, if they find them, are those moments at the opposite end of the building. A one-on-one, for me, is the purest form of Punchdrunk; it's distilled Punchdrunk. In relation to the physical language and the dance, it's the proximity of another person, not necessarily the 'language' that is used, that is most potent.

With *The Crash of the Elysium* there were moments that felt immersive, and certainly some of our target audience [6–12-year-olds] became completely lost in it, but that show had a very different physicality as a performance language. It was deliberately dissimilar because it was playing with a different form in which you become a character and are tasked with a mission to complete; the mask work creates a completely different audience status to that. Yet they're both Punchdrunk because the audience is at the heart of it. We always try and maintain a frisson of danger where you don't quite know what will happen next. In other company's work there can be the sense that the performers are the ethereal beings and the audience are solid, whereas with Punchdrunk it is often vice-versa.

JM: How have you honed your approach as a consequence of what you are continually learning and how is it inspiring you to experiment further? Is the use of technology in your explorations something that excites you or is it something that is proving to hinder the experience?

FB: In all of our experiments for new projects I have to experience it to know whether it works or not. The essence of Punchdrunk is that you have to *feel* it. Until I've actually felt it myself it's difficult to critique because it's about the senses. I think at the moment technology hinders that. The reasons why we're conducting these experiments is through a desire to innovate, to take risks, in the same way that we ask our audience to take risks, otherwise we'll stagnate. Technology can be flawed in that it tends to distance you from the work and make you more passive; the immediacy is gone because you're always going through the middleman, which is the technology. But I'm fascinated to think that there must be a way through this; it's exciting hacking through the digital jungle to try and find the clearing in the centre. The work that I'm really excited about, the future for us as a company, is the use of the real world as set and creating the same sort of immersive responses, sensibilities and reactions that we can in a completely controlled, designed space. Punchdrunk Travel was one of the most exciting theatrical things we've done for years, but unfortunately it's not currently economically viable. We really want to get under the skin of Punchdrunk Travel and all that it implies, where there aren't any maskings or designed spaces. It's just how you switch it on, how you change the audience's perceptions of the 'real world'. Within a masked show the one-on-one is the essence of that, the equivalent in a 'real world' show is Punchdrunk Travel, for two people only. Works start with the essence, mix it with a bit of water, slowly it will dilute into something that keeps the flavour but that more people can taste. I'm also fascinated by the idea of the point at which shows start – is it when you're trying to find the building, which we've deliberately made quite difficult to locate – and when does the show finish; is it as soon as you walk back into the bar, when you get back home, is it two weeks later? I'm fascinated by that murky hinterland that is the space between the show and real life and how we can theatricalise that. There's a lot more in there for the future.

JM: What experiences have you had of immersive practice as an audience member, perhaps that are influences in your own work, and through that, what does this reveal to you about the power and potential of the form?

FB: What was sublime about Robert Wilson's *H.G.* was that as an artwork it was densely atmospheric with huge, implied narrative, but you *never* came across performers who were telling that story. Performers felt present, but it was as though they had just left the space or they were just about to arrive. It was amazing to be in an environment that was so charged. The first time I experienced it was with very few audience members. It was the room to breathe, the amount of space your imagination had to fill in the gaps, which was totally seductive. Then, what was equally rewarding for me as a practitioner, but not as an audience member, was when I went back a week later with my family. Having said, 'you've got to see this, it's mind-blowing', every man and his dog had done the same and there was a queue around the block. When we finally got in it was packed with audience and the spell was broken because all I could see was other people and other people's readings and responses to it. Watching other people go 'wow' and enjoy the installation, as I had the week before, somehow dirtied the experience; I wanted it just to be me again. What I had felt was so pure, it was mine and mine alone, and to see someone else enjoying something so private and intimate undermined my memory of it. For me, it was clear that to have an immersive experience you need to remove the rest of the audience members *being the audience* from the picture. If they're comrades with you, on the same mission, or if they're part of the scenography then they're either excluded from, or a complementary addition to, your reading of the work. Deborah Warner's *St Pancras*

Project [1995] was hugely impressionable, although I didn't experience it; the *principle* of it was influential. I couldn't believe the ambition of it, that someone was doing that, that she was allowed to do it and that it could be perceived as a valid artwork, something that was so experiential was so empowering. Maybe at that point I was slightly closeted and thought that theatre had to be consumed *in theatres*. I know from hearsay that she put performers into other sites nearby so as you were walking through the building, exploring it and going on her journey, the potential for performer interaction was infinite; it could just be a look from someone across the street. Simply knowing that the fusion of performance and installation art, such as the work of Geraldine Pilgrim's company Corridor, was out there suddenly opened up the potential for me to explore and experiment with these ideas myself.

Conversations two

Bruce Gladwin of Back To Back Theatre

The intimate (im)mediacy of sound

Illustration 14   Back to Back Theatre's *Small Metal Objects*
[Photo credit: Jeff Busby. Image courtesy of Back to Back Theatre]

Bruce Gladwin: We're always aiming to make a work that's transformative so that people go to a new territory or are somehow changed. We've had a history of exploring the relationship between the actor and the architectural space in which the work is presented which stems from the fact that the actors we work with don't come from a traditional-training background. About ten years ago we thought it was unfair to put them on a large proscenium stage and expect them to play a very large auditorium so we started thinking about the physical space in which we presented the work. We made a show called *Soft* in 2002; we built our own venue, a large inflatable structure that was, basically, let's build something from the ground up that's going to support our actors. As a result of that, although our primary concern was about a framing for the actors, it also became a framing for the audience. That was a work that I would describe as immersive. It was in a large shed in the docklands in Melbourne, a clear, spanned space and the audience couldn't see the structure itself, it was hidden behind a large wall and you entered through an inflatable tube which snaked for probably about 150 metres through the space, like you were walking through an umbilical cord in a way. It also disorientated you; it had a number of curves in the space that then opened out into a single cell inflatable structure that encompassed a seating bank as well as defined the performing space (see Illustration 7). The walls, the floor and the ceiling were all connected as one and attached to the seating bank with a series of pneumatic pistons. There was a given point in the narrative where the inflatable was released from the seating bank and ripped the audience out of that immersive space.

Josephine Machon: Soft *was about a couple who choose to get rid of an unborn child that they know has Down's Syndrome. Was the design 'conceived' to be womblike, with the entering of a fallopian tube/umbilical cord to a soft space from which the audience will literally be ripped away?*

BG: That point where the inflatable ripped away from the audience was at the point where they decide to terminate the pregnancy. But it's not as though we had the narrative first and then we went, alright, what's a good design for it. Well before we had the narrative we started to play with building inflatable structures and finding a way of releasing them quickly; ideas merged as a part of dealing with presenting that work in that inflatable. It was like a symbiotic building in that it was housed in this bigger building which had a number of sound issues. We thought the best way to overcome the issue of delivering the sound to the audience was to put the speakers as close as possible to the ears of the audience, so we started working with headphones, with the actors radio-mic'ed and the audience sitting in a very traditional tribune.

Once we started doing that, being able to deliver this very high quality sound, we realised that, in that space at that time, this was creating an aural architecture. That set the grounds for the next work, which was *Small Metal Objects*, the idea being to test that theory, to take it to the busiest public space that we could. Even though the inflatable structure was a great development for the company, we were testing the theory of whether we actually needed a defined, physical space. In the end, the range of the radio-mics, their frequency strength, became our defining physical space. The actors could only ever get as far away from the audience or the sound operator as the radio signal would allow them.

JM: *For* Small Metal Objects *the audio experience was key to the 'immersiveness' of that immersive event. It was quite contradictory in that the headphones made it an incredibly individual, intimate experience and yet an oddly collective experience in that you're all laughing together at the jokes, sharing the intimacy. How are you developing that experience further with* Tour Guide?

BG: We've done a creative development on *Tour Guide* in Linz [Austria] but the show hasn't been made yet. We worked with a number of theatre companies to test this idea, to make a show where the audience wear headphones but in a wireless set-up. The idea was that the audience could walk around a central Linz district and be navigated by a narrator and a narrative so that they would be sent to a certain space and there a narrative would unfold that would lead them to another space. With *Small Metal Objects* and also *Soft* we used a single radio microphone mounted near the corner of the mouth on the jawline, which is fairly standard as a theatrical use of the mic. With *Tour Guide*, a number of performers had them mounted in their ears and it was a binaural rig so each performer had two mics, one in each ear, and those performers became like walking microphones in a way. The audience is always listening from their point of view, getting this stereo, binaural effect. If someone leant in to the right ear to talk to the character that had that mic set-up, you would get the very intimate sound of that person talking in your right ear. So you're always getting this soundtrack that is someone else's soundtrack. It's a beautiful effect but it's actually incredibly disorientating when you're asking 150 different people to be in a public space and to ignore their own sensory experience, have it replaced by someone else's sensory experience. In the end, the show took place in a central park in Linz, surrounded by cars and roads. It's quite disorientating in that the person with the microphone mounted in their ears might be facing in one direction and you're facing in the opposite direction, but all of a sudden your left and right becomes completely disorientated because you've got the perspective of someone else. It can almost become a little like seasickness. That was an interesting experience. The other issue that we had with *Tour Guide* is that if you have 150 people they get to choose their own point of view to the narrative or action that's taking place. Initially, they can be quite cautious and they stand back, but after about 15 minutes people want to get as close to the action as possible, to have the best view. As the makers, we were thinking people would hang back or sit on the grass, watch from 120 metres away, keep the bigger picture and listen to the soundtrack as it's happening. But the visuals dominate the experience. If you put a group of actors playing out a narrative in that space, then what happens is people crowd in the same way as with a fight in a schoolyard. For maybe about 40 of the audience, they get this really fantastic view of the action up close, but everyone else is watching the backs of the other audience members. That became quite problematic. It made me think about the type of story we tell in a public space and how we control the audience. Even though we say you choose your own point of view, in some way there has to be some sort of framing and there has to be some way of controlling 150 people in that space.

JM: *The way in which you're working with audio is giving the audience an amount of choice in perspective; there's a respect for them and how they engage with the work. I'm also aware with* Small Metal Objects *that there was the paying audience, who were seated with headphones, but also the passers-by who were still involved in that immersive experience in a different way. How far is the physical presence of the audience conceived as part of the event and how far does space, site or location become significant to the way in which the event is experienced? How much does that 'audience framing' shape the quality of sensory experience that you're exploring?*

BG: With *Small Metal Objects* we weren't quite sure what was going to happen, it felt like an experiment. There's two narratives; the story about the drug deal that goes wrong, but then there's also the narrative that is the power dynamic between the seated audience and the commuting public. The seated audience are both spectator and spectacle and that's the kind of phenomena that I love in theatre; that's so beautiful how that works in that show. Since then we've made another show, *Food Court*, which is back into a very traditional theatre environment and we've tried to take what we learnt from *Small Metal Objects* into that. So that even though it's in a traditional arrangement, there's the sense that the audience are being watched and that they are the spectacle just as much as the performance. But I don't think that when we set out to make *Small Metal Objects* that we knew all those dynamics and how they would work. It was really in the very first showing where there was someone who walked past and they had three poodles on leashes and all of a sudden 150 people all giggled at the same time. They're all asked to look at this same image, the same frame and you felt that the power sat with the audience, but then four or five drunk guys walked into the concourse, see the audience and front up to them and you could feel the audience shrinking in their seats. There was this constant power dynamic, which creates this tension for the audience. It is immersive, you're allowed to be a voyeur; I'm giving you a ticket to be a voyeur for an hour, but there's a bit of a trade-off in that you also are going to be watched as well.

JM: And those moments where the audience are recoiling makes them aware that you are physically present within the event. In that respect, how much is body language key to the vocabulary of each piece?

BG: When you give the actors a radio-mic and you say to them, 'you can start this performance 200 metres away', a lot of the conventions that you're dealing with in a traditional theatre environment, the weight and history of theatre, are liberated from the performer. They don't have to face the audience, arch their back and throw their voice to the back of the auditorium. They can stand there and have this very intimate conversation. We play with that sense of distance and depth of field. *Small Metal Objects* is not an 'easy read', you can't read facial expressions, gestures; it's purposefully blurred so you have to focus on the audio. The audio becomes very intimate in that moment; she leans down and whispers in his ear and says, 'You're lonely aren't you, I can organise someone to service you', and in the end she offers to do it herself. In pushing that image away it asks the audience to listen, to rely on listening to the words, the breath and the space. What I like about that show is the silence, the space in-between the words, which then allows the audience to see all this other space that's around them and all this other action. The script for that show is only about eight pages of text.

JM: *The intimacy as you say, seems to owe much more to film or web perform-ances than theatre. Back to Back have explored a variety of different forms and approaches in your history of productions and it's interesting that the audio experience seems to be shaping a lot of the work as you move forward. An element that your work always returns to is the interrogation of big moral, philosophical and political questions. In relation to the confrontational imagery, themes and ideas that you're exploring, how far have you discovered that the immersive form assists you in that? Is it a form that meets the view that you take of the world?*

BG: I think a lot of what we're dealing with in the work is about power, about the confluences of power that operate in society, within a group, within culture, the shared experience of whatever dynamic, size or group or country, or broader society. Our aim in the performance is to support and empower the actors, and the audio equipment is our principle tool in doing that. In *Small Metal Objects*, one of the other things that the audience isn't aware of is that I can direct the actors, they have in-ear foldback. We like to make sure the actors are fully empowered before we begin with whatever subject matter or content we're exploring; and maybe it's just coincidental that the subject matter is often about power. It's also aesthetic – composers and sound designers and people we work with, the engineers who operate the show – there's a shared desire, an aesthetic quality to sound, the delivery of sound and the production of sound. The quality of the sound has its own theatrical value. I think we've come to really appreciate that.

Lundahl & Seitl

Challenging the (im)mediate interface

Christer Lundahl: It's interesting to see why this work exists today and how it can exist within different traditions. To get to the source from where our practice grew I'm going to go back to my MA project, which was an exhibition that I wanted to make based on

Illustration 15 Lundahl & Seitl's *Symphony of a Missing Room*, National Museum Stockholm, 2010

[Photo credit: Tony Ahola. Image courtesy of Lundahl & Seitl]

human experience. It was important to me that artwork would not be objects on display but generated by human interaction; somehow providing instructions or rules for creating situations in the gallery to be experienced by the viewers; all the works were either instructions or choreographed encounters, not objects. I was also really interested in how those works created links in-between each other so that the experience between the works or meaning production, interpretation would be from one work to another and the connections you make, was equally as important as the works themselves. As a curator, I was working as a choreographer of time; it was most important that the experience was an overall concept not just the individual works. The reason that I wanted to do this exhibition was that I felt really dissatisfied with the exhibition format; working as an individual artist leaving objects for people to engage with without me being able to respond back. In the end, with this exhibition, I felt I had failed in what I wanted to do. A couple of years afterwards I asked myself the question, wouldn't it be easier to make the exhibition space inverted somehow? This question, alongside Martina's practice as a choreographer, led to the work that we started to do. Certainly with *Symphony of a Missing Room*, it has that quality of an exhibition space, but you're really using your imagination and your memory of what has happened previously in the work to create a sense of a virtual world, a virtual exhibition space. I think it's interesting to think about the exhibition space – it's a three-dimensional space in which you're wandering around, in comparison with the traditional proscenium theatre – theatre-makers are challenging that with immersive performance, making the visitor immersed, moving or navigating like in an exhibition space, while curators and visual artists are increasingly aware of the staging of an artwork or the dramaturgy of the visitor moving inside the exhibition space. It's interesting to think about the traditions that have given birth to this movement. Like Tino Sehgal, who has a background in dance and political economy, or our work, which exists not only in visual art but also in the theatre as well as in choreography and science; we're challenging that interface. Our practice is also a spiritual exploration, a journey of the universe and human consciousness. With art practice and the presentation of an art practice, it's always a relation between freedom and control. It is not always straightforward, sometimes contradictory. As in our work everything is pre-recorded, but still many people feel extremely liberated when they are experiencing our work.

Josephine Machon: *There's a sense of immediacy about your work and I think that has a lot to do with your participant audience member being incredibly* praesent *in the work, which is influenced by the instructions and the way in which you feel like someone is actually whispering in your ear, alongside the tactility of the hands that dance with you and lead you. The pre-recorded nature of it becomes immediate as a consequence.*

CL: With our new work, which we're preparing for The Royal National Theatre in Stockholm, we're wanting to introduce live voice which is three-dimensionally around you, which you can talk with but there is no *body* there. The most important question we're asking now, because the equipment is really expensive, is why do we want to have live voice, what can we do with live voice that we cannot do with pre-recorded? Because what we've always done with the pre-recorded voice is create the illusion of it being there in the present moment. For example, the voice says, 'I'm standing behind you, with my hand on your back', and then you feel that hand barely there, you're feeling the heat or energy of the hand; because of the instruction to put your attention there you *really feel* the hand there. That gives a sense that the voice is connecting to the action in real time. The only reason that we felt we could introduce the live voice is to have a conversation for that sense of realness, that feedback.

Martina Seitl: I think my identity is quite confused; I'm biologically from Czech Republic, I was born in Sweden but I never felt the need to identify myself with one or the other, it felt so abstract in a way. It's the same with our practice, the essence is beyond how we categorise it; is it theatre, dance or art? I recently decided that I'm not going to try and frame it, that it can be more fluid; it can be in that frame and then another frame. I'm not trying to fix it, to limit it down to one. I started painting very young, but then I wanted to go into something very time-based so I started to dance. I went to Laban in London and very quickly I got interested in choreography. After that I went to teach at the Duncan Centre in Prague, I did my MA in Performance and Choreography and I also did a year of Fine Art in Prague, painting. I discovered in my MA that I had very long rehearsal process and took the performers into a deep state of *being* – within the self – it was an *experience* to be in the rehearsal itself, a lot of guided imaginary, a lot of hypnosis and we would come up with material that would then inform my process. Whatever they would bring from their subconscious would drive the process forward; it felt organic. So I started the project with an intuitive sense of – it's indescribable I think – a feeling that I had a missing sense; if I could have *that sense* then I would understand how coincidences are connecting. So through that intuition we started just simply to explore blindfolded experiences within the rehearsal context. We went through a long journey and I was continuously sketching out what I experienced. There was one specific image, which kept coming back to me that was like a vessel or a passage, where I felt myself as a passage, quite emptied, just impulses. I started to question where does the sense of free will come from and through that question the instruction-based pieces that we do started to emerge. Also the removal of the vision, how does that change our experience of reality, what does that emphasise? Then, of course, working with Christer, with his background different to mine yet we connect, our essences feel very connected, so we are sharing the core somehow. In that way we can expand in many different directions because what connects us is still there.

JM: Is it that connection, in terms of an essential concept, which shapes how you might then realise your ideas in terms of a form or style? You talk about your work as asking fundamental questions about life, reality, existence, free will; how have those questions led you to explore your ideas in this form? How has the idea of immersion proven integral to your exploration and examination of those fundamental questions?

CL: That is the hardest question, how did our practice evolve and why did it evolve in this direction?

MS: And could it have been in another direction?

CL: It's a question you could ask of evolution as a whole, why do certain things go into certain habits. All disciplines go into a certain habit after a while and to break those habits but remain within the discipline is a fine line to balance. When we present the work in the visual art context it's inappropriate in a way because you don't *see* anything, but there's something else in the visual arts that I'm interested in; what kind of knowledge, what kind of *ways of seeing* has visual art created throughout it's evolution, the use of the gallery and the idea of exhibition space and experience we have there. By using performance as a vehicle, a participating viewer going through the same instructions as when one enters an exhibition, but instead of looking at an object or an artwork that is somehow going to mediate something for you, we're redirecting the visitor's gaze inwards at what's going on inside; using all the information the visitors have from their own experience of art, previous exhibitions, life experience, measured by the existing curatorial space that they're presently navigating. Rather than us adding another artwork in there, we're more like a curator looking at the existing exhibition and *re*writing it, *re*thinking it, guiding the visitors through it, guiding the visitor to find where *in themselves* they *experience* art. This is why we use the blindfold, taking away what's there but at the same time also highlighting what's there. It also allows the sound to be more prominent, stronger. Our medium is sensory illusion; taking apart sensory input from a visitor and putting it back again. I think there's a lot in what, in neurology, is called the multi-sensory binding problem; how is it that we have one unit, one coherent sensory experience of reality from all the sensory input that is fragmented, chaotic, a lot of things going on at the same time. Removing almost everything from your 'reality' and putting it back in an organised way as we do, we're creating a sense of meaning to things, or at least a meaning we want to give, creating a sense of synchronicity; this relates to that.

MS: You asked the question how did this immersiveness emerge. Previously, when I was talking about rehearsals and the performers were wearing the blindfold and we were exploring, what we found was disproportionate in that the process was very long and the way we were going to present it on stage was very limited, just a few days and it would be visual. We thought, how is this going to be *felt* by the audience if they're sitting down. We took the decision to let the audience do the rehearsal process, reversing it, the audience would put on the blindfold and we would explore similar but more refined exercises, with what we would call 'the visitor'; they're not audience anymore but visiting the experience. We could see the visitor but the visitor could not see us, so everything was reversed; it was the visitor that had the experience and the performer was the facilitator of that, similar to how the audience usually supports the performer. For the performer, it became like a practical, technical overview, like the way an audience can go into an objective way of looking at something, while the visitor had the freedom to immerse themselves in pure subjectivity, being removed from their analytical self, because that analytical self could remove them from the experience. They would often analyse more afterwards.

It became important to question how we teach the performer to communicate through physical contact, what principles this is built upon. This is where my dance practice became very useful. We discovered the visitor became overloaded very quickly because the performers are in a different world to the visitor. As a performer you often feel that you're not doing enough, but for the visitor there's more than enough, so we have to be very aware of this. Absences were felt much stronger than presences, so we started to call it 'choreographing absences'. It was important the way a touch started and how it disappeared, and how that would emphasise the absence. You have to be really aware that you're in different *moods* of being. If we wanted to give a timeless feeling or to give a feeling that the hands were disembodied, that they didn't belong to a physical body, we could communicate this in a limited way through Laban movement analysis, where everything is limited down to weight, space, time and flow – which is interesting because in a way it's limiting but in another way, how *can* we express these experiences? How we relate to weight, space, time and flow *is* a way to express it. So I could say we need an absence of weight or I need a 'Spell Drive', which is an absence of time, where there are no changes in time. In this way people have a limited sense of anticipation so everything seems more timeless. In the interaction with the human being it becomes more complex; if I interact with you it's about our chemistry, I have to respond to the dynamic between us two, I cannot keep to my own way. So first of all we would attune together to establish trust and then we would start to manipulate that. It's about a transformation; with the people that went into the room we noticed a transformation in their bodies, especially the people that were very tense in the beginning, you could feel there was a change. In the seminar that we've just done, 'Exhibiting Experience', we all talked a lot about transformative experiences where you end up somewhere different.[1]

JM: The relationship that you create with your audience relies a lot on the sensation of hapticity. In this respect, how far are your 'visitors' conceived or constructed as integral to the form of the work? I'm thinking of the significance of their imagination in the work; how far you move between manipulating that and accentuating it, nurturing their imagination, especially the gentleness of the voice that is guiding you in the space and leading you further into your imagination. Also, you're playing with dimension both externally with the space that you're present in, and internally, within imagination, within internal space; the haptic relationship between you and them is key to that.

CL: The work itself 'is in the eye of the beholder' and that's true of every artwork, all reality whether mediated or not, everything is due to your own perception.

JM: Perhaps that's the point, it's the nature of the 'beholding' that is of interest.

CL: Definitely so because the work is made so that the imagination is a trigger to be activated. With *Symphony*, if the museum would be 'destroyed' the work wouldn't exist, or it would have to be adapted to another museum. Or if the recording for that museum were destroyed it would obviously not work. If no-one knew how to participate in our work, in the leading; it wouldn't exist if no-one were there to teach you the refined technique, which can't really be notated as it's more like a tacit knowledge. The relation between the physical space and the virtual space; in neurology there is a concept called 'ideo-dynamic response' which is the process of where suggestion or instruction creates a physical response in the body. In *Symphony*, for example, you're crouching down and told that you're entering a narrow tunnel and many visitors have felt that they actually did that, smelt the dampness of the tunnel, left the museum for some parallel space away from the public space. I think that's interesting to think about in relation to that neurological notion because I think it's an ideo-dynamic response and back again. What it does is lead you to think about a narrow tunnel; with the sound you're already some way immersed in that, but with the physical leading, crouching down, you're confirming that image which has been implanted. These three components are creating a feedback loop, a full immersion of being in that low, narrow tunnel. The reason why these illusions work are that the suggestions trigger the visitor's archive of lived experience that is stored, images in their minds, but equally in their muscles, bones, nervous system and proprioceptive sense of the relations between their different body parts moving in space in certain positions, with a certain movement quality.

JM: *That both illustrates the manipulation of the imagination and how the visitors are the form; the experience of the work relies so heavily on their perception, which involves playing with their sense of dimension.*

MS: When we go into a museum we're not interested in what we look at necessarily but *how* we look at it. How we look at it will decide and manipulate our experience of it. This is our starting point, *how* do we look. John Berger talks about a sunset, how we know the earth is spinning around the sun, yet this doesn't quite fit that sight. In looking at the sunset I'm reminding myself that the horizon in front of me is rising and that behind me it's sinking, which makes me aware that the earth is spinning and so I'm on a moveable surface and then I realise this earth reveals new sky behind me and closes up the sky in front of me. Perceived only as a visual phenomenon it's not kinaesthetic, not felt within the body. But if I remind myself I'm on a moveable surface, suddenly I start experiencing the fact that the whole earth is moving, so it becomes a three-dimensional experience. It's that sense of *presence* that we want to activate within the visitor. We can't change the sunset but we can change the way we *feel* it in the body. We often think of ourselves in a museum as a two-dimensional surface, a two-dimensional being, because the eyes are placed on the front, but there are many different ways of relating; we're three-dimensional so what if we activate the body in a different way, how does that affect the experience, does it become a different artwork then?

CL: We use the internet more and more, which is such a visual medium; you're feeling that you're moving through a lot of things but in yourself you're static, which is a strange experience. When browsing the internet I feel the notion of semionauts; I feel like an astronaut diving through signs, from one thing to another, stepping from this to another hyperlink and so on.[2] What kind of information and knowledge is that creating? I already have an intellect like that, a lateral, wide band-width, which I need to narrow down to get a clearer sense of the world.

MS: You mean the difference between knowledge that's processed through the body and knowledge that's more like mental information?

CL: The difference in getting knowledge from a second-hand experience. Of course, that's an intellectual knowledge but there's something else, where if it's done through practice and you're binding your concepts into a physical experiment – testing it out and understanding what it means – through this kind of philosophy, I can understand it more.

MS: It's interesting that, artistically, the way we're going is connected to science. First, it was Newton and how the world is independent of the observer, but then moving on to Einstein and Heisenberg, Quantum Mechanics, and the observer is changing their reality, so we're getting more into that.

JM: You refer to your starting point as questioning how we look, whereas for me your work is about experiencing. To talk about focusing it on the visual almost limits it because it involves the multidimensional, the 'eyes in the back of my head', experiencing through my whole body. It's genuinely about engaging all our senses, becoming aware of individual presence. In terms of the way you're manipulating presence, it has a lot to do with the aural experience and the magical gentleness of the tactility, the playful hands, which influence the experience of space, the fusing of internal and external space. In attending to my own presence it made me very aware that I was part of that space.

MS: Yes not me *and* space, me *as part of* that space.

JM: *You're playing mind-games with space, whole-body games. I became aware of the edges of my body fusing into the space itself.*

MS: Yes, manipulating that; can we feel the edge of the body in a different way? Can we have the illusion of expanding our awareness into the room, the kinesphere. When we remove the vision we don't know what's happening behind us, so we reactivate some instincts in the body. When you walk home late in the evening, the sense of being followed is suddenly heightened. That's what happens first, that heightened awareness and through that we become much more aware of what's happening around our body. Then if the touch is very gentle, in fact sometimes we'll just blow a little air onto the skin, breathe on their hand so they just feel the heat, so it's on the borderline of knowing and not knowing, 'oh a hand is here'.

CL: And that's in relation to the aural description as well, it could be footsteps or the voice saying, 'I'm standing in front of you' and it feels like you're hearing the voice in front of you.

MS: Or the voice is recorded in mono so you can't determine location. I think Einstein refers to it as a 'ghost field'; in theory it's related to quantum mechanics, when you observe something it either collapses into a definite particle or into a wave particle, which is a more indefinite space, so before you take a decision it's spread out as a presence of possibilities. You're blindfolded, the voice is saying 'I'm still here', you know that soon there will be physical interaction because you're in the middle of an absence [of touch]. Therefore some people feel a heightened sense of presence, the kinesphere around the body; that the touch could come from any direction. Then, finally, when the touch is established on the left arm, the sense of presence around the body is more determined to this place. That's why the absence is important.

CL: Which links physical space and kinesphere with your mental image. In that moment of suspension, you're experiencing space around you, an interior architecture of that space, and then, all of sudden, when the touch is there, people talk of seeing a hand.

MS: Another technical thing is the way we bend the legs so that people cannot feel the footsteps, but instead more a floating around. It's also based on empathy. When I take the hand it's not [she takes and drops my hand, gesturing a heavy, staccato movement], it's almost imperceptible that I keep on moving the hand.

CL: Similar to when in space, how things move without gravity.

MS: We talk about this a lot, absence of gravity, absence of time.

JM: An element of that interaction via the hand is the sense that you're taking care of us. One of the things I felt very keenly after Rotating in A Room of Images, *because of the intimacy of that experience, was the memory of you taking care of me, of it being playful, sometimes slightly dangerous play, but all the while knowing that you were looking after me and wanting that connection through touch as much as I was waiting for the voice in my ear. You referred to an interior architecture, how far is architecture, space and location integral to your explorations?*

CL: Every museum is very different in the way it is built, dependent on when it was built. The first conception of *Symphony*, which was for the National Museum [Stockholm] in 2009, a very old museum, 1800s, and the space we used had eighteenth-century plaster sculptures.

CL: The last museum was in Salzburg [Museum of Modern Art, Mönchsberg] on a mountain and part of the museum is inside the mountain and in that museum we went into a real cave.

MS: Because that location is so important, half on the mountain and half in the mountain and also because Salzburg is so high up in the Alps, it's affected by weather so they have a lot of thunder, a lot of rain. In this aspect, astrology and how the weather affects them is quite mainstream, so this became part of the work; we recorded the weather, thunder, rain, we went into caves. In Birmingham you went down in the lift, in Salzburg the lift is in the mountain itself, so you have to go through the mountain and you think about it as Plato's Cave because, when you open your eyes, instead of looking into a painting, as you did in Birmingham, where you see your own reflection or a reflection of the room, here you see your own shadow on the white wall.[3] The sound of the cave slightly shifts over to the sound of a theatre because of the theatrical context of the Salzburg Festspiele that we were part of, so we did some recordings of the stage and applause. We realised that the sound of the rain was extremely similar to the sound of applause so we made it ambiguous in this way. The ending was totally different but you still saw the man on the carpet and you still lay down, but the series of spaces that you went through in your imagination were different.

JM: The final image in Rotating *where you were tempting me through the door and then not letting me through it, the image was like a reference to antiquated art, you were playing with the aesthetic of that.*

CL: We're playing with the memory we have of those images, from Vermeer or Caravaggio –

JM: – particularly in regards to the play with light and shade.

CL: This is something we're interested in, to re-enact or enact fragments of art history that people have in their memory. Not in detail, but the archetype of those images.

MS: It's a subconscious thing as well.

CL: Like a memory, its something that if you come too close to it, it moves away from you in proximity.

JM: More like dream than memory because it has that unheimlich *quality to it; it's familiar and yet strange, there's an inarticulable weirdness to it.*

MS: Some of the performers in *Rotating In A Room of Images* are moving barely perceptibly and as you move that would influence the way you look at it and the distance. If you come close and stand still you would look at it very differently than if you were far away and moving slowly towards it.

JM: You're playing with perception and perspective, those artistic ideals, which goes back to the manipulation of internal and external space. It means your work is a holistic experience rather than simply a visual experience.

CL: With *Infinite Conversation* we darkened one of the galleries, the visitors entered one at a time with one and a half minutes in between and when they came into the space they went into – similar to a photo-lab – two openings where the light cannot leak in or out. No headphones in this piece but instead they could hear voices in that space all around. The voices that they heard were other visitors so we had about five people that were there to facilitate the conversation, to guide them and keep it alive, but the voices and conversations and all the stories that came up in this room were from the visitors that came there. Some people stayed two hours in that space. When they wanted to leave they just put up their hand and we led them away as we had night-vision goggles.

MS: Unbelievable the stories that people shared and trusted us with. In this space, even if you were a performer you behaved as a visitor so it was more equal. There was no sense of –

CL: – they're doing this for us, or other people were responsible for the space. They felt that they should take care of each other.

MS: An interesting social rule that came out of this space was that they felt someone and they would interact and ask, 'how long have you been here?' They would very often answer, 'I don't know I've lost my concept of time.' So the discussions would become quite existential and the performers were there to support and direct that. I felt this was the internal driving force of the piece although we don't have ownership of what people are talking about. For example, one person talked of how her horse could always find its way home in total darkness. The imagination was very present in the space.

CL: In another work, *Observatory*, six visitors interacting in a room with an audio track of instructions, because they have individual instructions that are different to each other, they are acting on and reacting to each other's instructions, facilitated by us with night vision.

MS: Here also the habits happen, there were so many moments where I thought I had to check the recordings because on [audio channel] number 3 several different visitors who didn't know each other repeated the same odd behaviour at completely different timings of the day, but it was simply visitors forming habits.

CL: We've read Rupert Sheldrake's research about habit and 'morphic fields'; information doesn't necessarily stay in our head but in fields that we can tap into, and he has explored a lot of taboo research such as the sense of being stared at, he has a whole book on that.

MS: I don't find it supernatural, I find it instinctive. The same thing with intuition, I find it extremely animalistic. With the post-human state we're so technologically advanced, but what we are interested in is how the body has natural apparatus as well, like instinct, and we might not understand everything about it. What do we mean by understanding, does it necessarily mean that we uncover all the mystery. It's almost like a choreography to me. What are the consequences of when we start to manipulate the knowledge of our age?

JM: *That fear of science and how scientific knowledge might be abused; the questions that throws up in terms of our humanity and also in terms of our relationship with the environment. How crucial is technology, specifically the audio journeys and the virtual experience, to the concept and the experiential quality of your immersive practice?*

CL: Heidegger talks about how technology can be used in a way to change how we can use something, to make it more effective. In our practice, using the goggles, which is a very simple thing, it's not a blindfold because that would mean that I have to close my eyes, whereas here you can open your eyes and have some kind of space around you. It's designed by Jula Reindell. They give a sense of space around you so you're not feeling claustrophobic. Then there's the three-dimensional sound. A lot of components come together; the goggles as blindfold, the sensory deprivation, alongside the sensory stimulation of touch and movement synchronised with the acoustic sound that the visitor moves inside.

MS: We've selected to use three-dimensional recording, which takes up the architectural sounds of the room, but not head-tracking. Say, if I turn my head I hear some water dripping in my left ear, if I use head-tracking I move my head but the water stays the same, in our case it's coming with you. We have chosen not to use head-tracking because for us, it's you as a subject taking the room with you, it's an inner room, so therefore when you turn your head the dripping comes with you. We use white-out goggles, some people think there's a projector in them but there's not.

CL: What they see from the outside means they think that they're looking at something because they seem to be so vividly involved in it.

MS: It's a torch. It looks interesting from the outside, everyone is doing what's almost like the same choreography and the performers wear a necklace with a torch, and then you have the white goggles and you all have the same recording at the same time (see Illustrations 9 and 15).

There's a moment where there's the recorded sound of an old door which doesn't exist physically, but there's a light source from underneath, so you all see people leaning over and the shine is quite beautiful from the outside. That's also a technology but it's not very advanced. It's very interesting how people, with *Symphony* specifically, are very curious about the technology so they stay for the next group, the moment of the bench.

CL: If you're using virtual reality equipment, like goggles or other kinds of technologies, how far do you want to go towards creating a full reality and how much do you not want to involve some of the senses? How much do you respect the person experiencing this, the impressions that they have? How much is decoration and how much is stimulation if you're trying to create a realistic world, so that you can have someone go into a film or into an environment. I feel 3-D film almost pushes me back out of the film rather than immersing me in it. Why is that? Well, obviously, you're not moving, you're sitting in a chair and it just invites you to be motion-sick, all that movement without moving yourself, it's destabilising. There's many possibilities to get even more immersive. But more and more I've realised what makes our work successful or interesting is the building on sensory deprivation of vision and focusing on the hierarchically peripheral sense of hearing. The sound functions as suggestion and triggers the imagination; it all becomes dynamic and one coherent experience due to the fact that it includes movement.

JM: It's the fusion of technology with the sensual experience, the human experience. You were talking there about creating worlds, in relation to your own practice and other work that you've experienced, how would you describe and define immersive practice in general and immersive theatre specifically?

MS: To expand on the idea of the immersive; we've been in contact with a scientist called Henrik Ehrsson who's known for exploring out-of-body experience in the laboratory. He looks at the blind-spots of the brain, looks into the sense of self and how that can be dislocated. One of the tricks that he did was to place a head-mounted display so you see yourself from behind but his intention is that you not only see yourself, but kinaesthetically experience you behind yourself. He'll hold a pen behind your head, but also in front of the camera so that your brain can see that. This very simple trick makes the brain think, 'oh I'm actually located here', so you kinaesthetically feel you're behind yourself. What I want to highlight was the *preparation*. With immersiveness, for example *Symphony*, the ritual of how you are taken into the work – how does a person hold the energy when she greets you, how does she take you to the lift, how are you seated on the bench, what do the instructions say before you even get the goggles on? – is a process of preparing the body into that state. In science they don't want to do that because they don't want it to be dependent on how you feel.

JM: It's to do with that human connection and the nature of the interaction that you're invited and encouraging; taking us into another world, making that journey to that other world, equipping us with a way of being that's different to this reality, 'the everyday', to a world where we behave and comprehend in a different way.

MS: Yes, yes.

CL: It's the notion of the situated self; what kind of self am I in this situation and what kind of self am I if I go on a football match with my friends and what kind of self am I when I go to the theatre or when I'm on the street; all those situations where I'm confronted with creating a different type of self. When one works with immersive theatre or situation-based art, depending on where you want to place it, science inspired art forms, to look at the components, what makes up a situation, to try and understand it, it's almost like trying to paint a world in order to observe and understand it to bring someone into a new situation.

JM: It's something to do with the way in which this work forces you, or requires you, to be aware of the way in which you are attending to the work. It's forcing you to confront how you experience. On the flipside of that, it's also granting permission to experience in a holistic fashion in a way that a lot of other work doesn't.

MS: In the proscenium nature of work, I don't think I'm saying that the audience experience this any less, I think it can be quite similar. Could we say it's binocular, microscopic, whereas the way we direct the focus in our work is more directed to the visitor, so all the intangible processes that are going on could be going on in an audience in a 'normal' visual arts piece, it's just that we turn the way that we look at it, we're directing it internally.

JM: Exactly, in a lot of other work you're not invited to engage with it in that embodied way. You may engage with it experientially, but the nature of the set-up isn't automatically inviting you to do that.

MS: That's exactly it. Not saying that one is better than the other.

JM: Not at all, but that the ways in which we are required to engage are different.

Silvia Mercuriali

Immersive imaginations – the intimate and (im)mediate

Silvia Mercuriali: Despite the surrounding being fictional and narrative driven, immersive theatre is about making the performance *present* and absolutely real for people. It's not just you sitting down and watching a show, it's you becoming part of the show fully. All of the work I've done with Autoteatro and with my collaborator, Gemma Brockis, is about the audience becoming characters in the show, where everything around them makes sense within the fictional world that we create.

Josephine Machon: *In that respect, how do you define your audience?*

SM: We often call them participants or guest performers. As Rotozaza, with Antony Hampton, we started working on the idea of instruction-based theatre with different performers on stage every night. The performers weren't necessarily trained actors; we had truck drivers, journalists, musicians, all sorts. It was more about people who were confident about being watched, not putting up a mask. We were interested in 'real people', 'real' reaction. It wasn't about a character or a story but about the audience enjoying watching somebody having to make a decision. That moment, when you're not aware of what you're doing because your brain is working really fast to understand the instruction you've just been given and how you're going to perform it, that moment is what we got really interested in. That was our first step towards immersive theatre. We started off with one person on stage and a lot of pre-recorded instructions. Then we gave them headphones so what they were being instructed to do wasn't the same thing that we as audience members were seeing projected on screen; there was a discrepancy that only became apparent after a while. Slowly, slowly you see an attitude or a reaction that really cannot go with what you see. You begin to understand that 'the agent', as we called the person giving instruction, is lying to the audience and is *using* the guest performer to look at *how we look at* people; why do we go to the theatre; why do we sit down and watch; what is it that we're looking for?

Our audience said to us, the most interesting thing must be for you and Antony to see how different people react to the same instructions. So we thought, okay, let's do a show with two people on stage following exactly the same instructions. As always happens with Rotozaza, the structure dictates what the show will be about. From talking to the audience we found they had this strange desire to be instructed, 'it must be amazing not to have the responsibility, to just "do" without thinking' – maybe because we have so many responsibilities in life, so many decisions to take – relinquishing responsibility is liberating. That's how *Etiquette* came about, our first immersive theatre piece for two people in a café; talking to the audience and understanding that they want to see something that is 'real', but that they want to be part of it. It's genuine because somehow, it's not about the instruction, it's about how *you* do things. With *Etiquette* and *Wondermart*, even though the instructions are all the same all the time, no matter who is taking part in it, the way that *you* perform it is always different to how someone else will, it really is yours, your private experience, your private world, how *you* decide to take it on board. It becomes something that is only yours.

JM: You play a lot with clandestine relationships and the intimacy of instruction via the headphones. Would you expand on that to get to the heart of your particular style of immersive theatre?

SM: I think it's the sense of complicity between two people. *Wondermart*, for example, really asks of the audience a big investment, you have to believe in it and go for it completely in order to really enjoy it. What I want to create is this sense of being part of something special. It's like

Illustration 16 Rotozaza's *Etiquette*

[Photo credit: Ant Hampton. Image courtesy of Silvia Mercuriali]

a secret society, an underworld, something that if you then go to the supermarket and you see people with headphones, even if you don't interact with them you feel close to them because you know or you imagine what's happening there. Immersive theatre pushes that to the limit; you're not watching something special, you're doing it yourself. There isn't anyone watching, there isn't an audience, nobody's judging you and you're totally free within that yet you know there's a big group of people that have taken part in it. *Etiquette* has gone all around the world and you know you're now part of a really big group, a wider community. That little card that you find in your pocket to remind you of it, you can know that there are loads of other people who have done that; it's totally yours, not mass-produced, but it's also part of something bigger.

JM: *Is there a degree to which you have an unspoken contract in mind between you and your participants?*

SM: Absolutely. We would never ask people to do anything that's embarrassing or diminishing or something that people just wouldn't want to do; get naked, to touch other people in a sexual way, to stand up and sing in the middle of a room. It's really important because the guest-performers have to trust me, then I can trust them to do everything I tell them to do. I know for some people immersive theatre means one-to-one, means shocking and challenging. I'm not interested in challenging whatsoever, challenging slightly pisses me off because I feel abused a little. How I respond always has to be a decision that *I* make. For *Etiquette* and *Wondermart*, in order for the participants to say, 'okay, I will follow everything you ask me to do', I have to make them know, 'don't worry, you are well looked after'. That gentleness and looking after your audience is key for work of this kind. There's other stuff that will test you and then it's up to the taste of the audience as to whether you like it or not. Where one guest-performer is relying on another guest-performer to do what they're told in order to enjoy the show; 'if you don't do it, whatever I have to do doesn't make any sense'. Taking care of people is basic. The same for the outside world. For *Pinocchio*, made with Gemma Brockis, it's the same idea, you cannot go in a public space and somehow shock the people around you; not because I think that art shouldn't shock but because the people around you should be respected. The more you respect them, the more subtle your intervention in the space, the more you're making the most of the space. You're like a guest at somebody's house when you're performing in public spaces.

JM: *Is that the crux of it, if you create something that feels both safe and exciting then that might ignite the 'something special' that you referred to earlier?*

SM: Yes, I really believe that it's not about over-imposing something that's not by nature there that you create something special, but by pointing out the features of what already exists. Like working *with* the architecture of a public space in order to attract attention to the lines of a space. In *Pinocchio* when I'm running along the river, it's that horizontal line and the backdrop and the music, only for those three privileged audience members, that make the scene amazing. It's not big speakers in the street and everybody looking at Pinocchio running because otherwise suddenly the magic is gone. By respecting that surrounding around you, then you can create something that is extremely exciting, that feels dangerous. *Wondermart* is exactly that. *Wondermart* asks a lot of you because you are in a public space, nobody around you has any clue of what you're doing, nothing that you do actually attracts the attention of the people around you. You're totally anonymous, another shopper with headphones, you might be a very indecisive shopper but nobody would care about you. Yet when you're pushing your trolley and you're trying to find the person that you're following or you're looking at something and in your ear it's telling you what you would do if you were to steal it, suddenly you really are a bit apprehensive, looking around and thinking am I doing something weird, strange. So it's exciting, dangerous, without breaking the atmosphere for the people around you.

JM: How does this work relate back to the questions that you're asking about theatre?

SM: It depends on what kind of work I'm doing and who I'm working with. With Gemma, it's always about public spaces and telling people that it's not about how beautiful where you are is, but about in here [points to her chest], how you perceive it, which is a very simple idea. Your mood will make a place look beautiful or absolutely horrendous and the people around you will look special or absolutely banal depending on how you feel. What we try to do with our shows is to make everything special, to connect with emotions, to make it into an epic landscape or into a secret, tiny-little thing that nobody else is seeing. With Autoteatro it's instruction-based and creating something special for the audience, giving the audience 15 or 20 minutes of an exhilarating, crazy world as in *And the Birds Fell from the Sky* .... There you can go 100 per cent into something that, in real life, there's no way you'd want to be involved in, in a car with crazy people shooting stuff; creating that excitement that cinema can give but here live for you, so that you feel you're really experiencing it. The audience is always absolutely the focus, as theatre should be, otherwise you're self-indulgent.

JM: With And the Birds Fell from the Sky *...there's a strong sense of caricature and satirical expressionism, grotesque versions of human nature and the contrast between being sat in the car to the sudden image of the open landscape, the green hills and the vast sky; a fusion of an intense visual and theatrical aesthetic.*

SM: *And the Birds Fell From the Sky...* draws on all of the characters from [Frederico] Fellini's films, the big prostitutes, the boobs, the ugly make-up, to me it's charming, it's soft and it embraces you in its violence and ugliness, it kind of puts it's arms around you and holds you. Then, when you're suddenly at the hill, that's Pasolini coming back. It all came from a collaboration with Simon [Wilkinson] and it's not always rationally drawn from things. As an Italian, for me Fellini and Pasolini are amongst the biggest influences I have; I'm more influenced by film than theatre.

JM: *In relation to* Etiquette, Wondermart *and* And the Birds Fell From the Sky..., *would you expand a little more on the perceived intimacy resulting from the one-to-one experience that you're manipulating. In terms of the immersive experience, how far is intimacy a central feature of that, or perhaps a starting-point as opposed to the epic, immersive on a grand scale as with a Punchdrunk production? You referred earlier to how structure often defines the content; how far is intimacy key to the questions you're exploring?*

SM: Part of it is about the limits of technology, which really influences my work. Plus the idea that you're not watched. Punchdrunk, they're brilliant, how they transformed BAC for *Masque of the Red Death* was incredible, but I had a problem with it, I felt observed. I felt slightly silly because I was wearing a mask, which might have something to do with being a performer and dealing with masks in a very particular way, so suddenly I felt like I was being given a character but one that I didn't know how to move, one that was supposed to roam freely. I know loads of people who loved the fact that they had a mask on, so I know it was my own personal thing. They could hide behind the mask and become invisible, for me the mask made me more visible. And perhaps both experiences are part of Punchdrunk's thing because you as an audience member become even more present. But, for me, the idea of not being watched is absolutely key; not worrying about judgement, nobody's watching you and that really comes from the fact that I am a performer myself. I am the worst audience member for any interactive theatre because I get so self-conscious and so scared of fucking it up for them that I cannot enjoy it. That's why in *Etiquette*, in *Wondermart*, in *And the Birds fell from the Sky...* there isn't anyone watching, it's a small 'audience'; two people. For *And the Birds Fell from the Sky...*, really it's one person only, even though you're doing it with one other person, you can't see them. Their presence adds to the piece because you feel them, you know they're there and when you take your goggles off it's that idea of complicity, having shared something and you can go out talking about it together. I think you can only do *Etiquette* if you know that nobody else is [intentionally] watching you. That's why wherever we go in the world to set up *Etiquette* we say the ushers must stay away and make sure that nobody's standing there watching. In *And the Birds...*, even though you're watching a world that doesn't exist, even though you're next to someone who isn't really interacting with you, the knowledge that there's nobody watching allows people to do the weirdest things. I've seen all sorts of reactions to the piece; people being very vocal, screaming, laughing. That's why being an usher for *And the Birds...* is quite a fun thing to do because every single person is so different, especially the people who are hesitant, scared, and then they take the goggles off and they've had the most amazing experience because, by nature, they wouldn't 'go there'. If it's an intimate situation you can push them more.

When we started doing instruction-based performances with one person at a time onstage, we didn't want to drag somebody from the audience, we wanted to work with somebody that we knew was going to be okay being watched without having to wear a mask. The idea of you, yourself, being happy enough with what you are and being watched for what you are was key. It was a tricky strategy in a way because there aren't very many people who can let people watch them and be so confident not to be cocky, or funny, just to be themselves and let people see them for what they are with their weaknesses, their fears. With Punchdrunk, with Shunt, the audience is key but not because they are the focus; they become part of the show but they're not the focus, the focus is still the performance. That's why I think it has to be one-to-one, more intimate when you ask the audience to become the main character in the piece. Similarly, our site-specific work is really 'hands-off' the site. The work I do with Gemma is very filmic, it's all about framing; framing a public space to make it into a location, framing people; John Smith's, *The Girl Chewing Gum*, any of the work I have done with Gemma is heavily influenced by that little film. When we do workshops together it's the first thing we show people. It's an explanation of how you can make reality so interesting and gripping and exciting without having to do anything at all, just a commentary on top. You're not transforming reality, you're adding an element, over-imposing, heightening, without the reality being changed. I love it when that man is crossing the road and [Smith] is saying, 'the man might have a gun in his pocket and is about to go and rob the post-office'. I just love it because there's no truth in it but you can imagine it as truth. In *Pinocchio* you go in slowly. It comes first as a slap because you have to go to a secret place and wait for a car and it arrives and there's a body coming out of it and something pretty weird happens. Then when you're in the car and the performers are talking to you and what they're asking of you is not to look at them but to look at what's going on outside. Then slowly, slowly, as the outside becomes magical, fictional, slowly you find yourself becoming a donkey and suddenly you're within the story. In order for people to buy into what you want them to believe, you have to take it slowly. As with *Wondermart*, in supermarkets, in my imagination at least, when you enter those first doors, you're not in the supermarket yet, you need that clearing space, 'you are here, forget about your problems', before you can enter and be overwhelmed by all of the offers. In the same way, you've got to give people that space to slowly get into it, to then, bam, suddenly they're swinging from a trapeze. It's also exciting because of the expectation. In *Etiquette* it's a lot about expectation, the stage fright, the curtains opening, the lights going dark and then suddenly you're there in the middle. You need that in order to buy into it and to know that you're safe. That 'waiting room' experience tells you somebody's taking care of you.

JM: *It's a combination of knowing that you're safe because someone else is in control and they're not going to let anything bad happen and also putting yourself on edge, knowing that this will be dangerous play, you don't know what you're going to be doing next.*

SM: Definitely the waiting room in *And the Birds Fell from the Sky...* wants you to feel like that. For me, it's very much like when you're rehearsing or doing a show, you need a warm-up, don't you. Some people do it more, some less, but you still need to centre yourself in order to step in. A little moment of meditation, call it whatever you want, but it's what eases you into the action. I think it's great to create worlds that don't exist at all but are believed to the full by the audience, where the audience really is right in it. Of course you know that it's not true, but it's your brain that wants to believe almost, because it's got all this stimuli, smell, somebody touching you, the person sitting next to you, it makes it plausible.

JM: It's a dream, a nightmarish scenario, the what-if of a world where dangerous clowns abound and hold the key to something beyond your reach.

SM: The clowns are something that came from Simon [Wilkinson], and then the prostitutes came into it. I really enjoy that grotesque world. The Faruk are to him a model of life; where you have no boundaries between what you want to do and what is supposed to be right. The Faruk are a world, reminding people of all of the emotions that we can go through and imagining letting everything go, for one second you can go for everything you feel. It's like Italians having an argument, if there's a plate, it's gonna get smashed. You wouldn't do it as an English person but for 16 minutes it's, 'oh fuck it, smash it all', because you know it's not true, you can go for it.

JM: For me And the Birds Fell from the Sky...*felt like a starting-point, the start of something bigger, especially with the phone numbers you could call, it felt like you were tantalising us with a life in that world beyond that immediate experience.*

SM: It's interesting, a few people called that number in the waiting room but not many called it after the event, whereas Twitter or Facebook went crazy.

JM: How far has your performance aesthetic across all of your collaborations, been influenced by contemporary technologies?

SM: Technology is something that you can't deny is becoming more and more present in our lives, without realising it. The way in which Facebook was fundamental to aspects of The Arab Spring was inspiring because that's what is brilliant about the technology; the idea that you can use it to do something that's going to change the world, your environment. Technology is present, why deny it's there. However, I tried to put *Wondermart* online and it really didn't work; very few people went online and downloaded the track. I believe it's because when people 'go to the theatre', they still want to share something, and I'm very happy with that. It's not about the experience on your own. It's the investment in the evening, it's the meeting up, the being there, having the ticket, gripping it, going in. *And the Birds Fell from the*

Sky... uses high-tech equipment, such as the video goggles, but in a way it's pushing you to forget about all that, pushing you to go back to *real* experiences, *real* feeling; like in *Etiquette*, to inspire people to *talk* to people. It uses technology to tell you, you don't need to be the slave of technology, let go of it, enjoy the real 'stuff', enjoy 'real' communication; the message and the medium are playfully opposing. You can't not use the mediums that are becoming more and more elaborate and amazing; so why not use it to say that it's the personal relationship that is much more precious than anything. It allows you to create a world that doesn't exist, cannot exist unless you use the technology, enhancing your senses. Being able to say whatever you want to say through a fictional reality, that is best achieved through the use of technology where the audience can be *in it*. Technology is simply a medium, something that I use, I explore. The technology that's around, invented for something else, how might you make it more interesting for people? For *Wondermart*, how can you use headphones to make an environment like a supermarket – horrible places where you end up hating the people – to use that space in an artistic way, to make it more intimate and to open your eyes. *Wondermart* really is about opening your eyes and not seeing people as obstacles but as people.

JM: *Does the technology, then, allow you to create a more immersive theatre?*

SM: Absolutely. You can of course create intimate experiences without it, brilliant immersive theatre, as with the BAC one-to-ones where you go into different rooms and it's just you and the performer. But at the same time, you're always aware that the person you're there with is watching you live, they're the performer, they're in charge and you're following. Technology, in our work, allows you to abandon yourself because you feel you're not being watched. You're in charge of what you do even when you're following instructions.

JM: *The headphones take you into the world in that respect make you utterly focused, and heighten your senses in the same way that being blindfolded can.*

SM: Working with sound is amazing, the fact that you can create an atmosphere; we rely on our senses to believe in the things that are around us. Because it taps into, uses your senses to propose a new, a different reality, technology really helps with immersive theatre. You're tricked, the brain does amazing things, when tricked by technology, makes you believe things that aren't true, because it's programmed to make things plausible. That's why technology can bring something special, it can trick the brain in ways that you cannot do live.

JM: So you're using technology to make things plausible, to play with the in-between-ness of the plausible and implausible.

SM: To instil the doubt of what is and isn't real. That for me is what is dangerous; am I really somewhere where I have no control or do I still have control? Of course you always have control because at any moment you can always take your goggles off.

JM: You've used the word 'special' a lot to define what is significant to you about certain theatre experiences, what do you mean by that?

SM: Our lives are very set, boxed-in, you know what you're going to do, and many of us are so safe. We've pushed commodities to a level where real adventure is very hard to come by. Why cinema works so well is because it can create stories that are so extreme, so far from what your life is; our lives have been standardised so much we crave for that. And that is what I'd like to give back, something that you cannot have in real life.

Conversations three

Tassos Stevens of Coney

Playing with(in) the 'what is' and 'what if'

Tassos Stevens: Coney has a set of defining principles; although what makes something Coney is a more open question than it is with many companies. All our work has the audience experience at the heart of it, through active involvement.

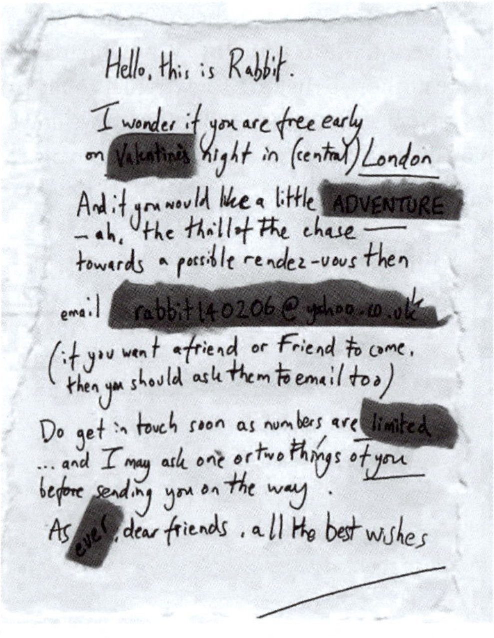

Hello, this is Rabbit.

I wonder if you are free early on Valentines Night in (central) London
And if you would like a little ADVENTURE
– ah, the thrill of the chase —
towards a possible rendez-vous then
email rabbit140206@yahoo.co.uk
(if you want a friend or Friend to come, then you should ask them to email too)

Do get in touch soon as numbers are limited
... and I may ask one or two things of you before sending you on the way.
As ever, dear friends, all the best wishes

Illustration 17   Rabbit: Valentine, 2006

[Image by Daniel Berzon and Tassos Stevens. Image courtesy of Coney]

Josephine Machon*: Is transmedia involvement always part of it?*

TS: Not always. Transmedia and cross-platform work – horrible vocabulary around it – *The Gold-bug* was the most transmedia thing that we did because it lasted for six months and there were lots of ways that you could engage with it. For us, the important thing about it is that it comes from a principle of gluing together a multi-layered audience experience. Coney doesn't follow a particular format, nor is there a particular set of people. There's a network of people who work on different projects; different teams are assembled across this network so that we can be agile. What makes it Coney is the type of practice that it is, the qualities and ethos that it has, which we semi-formalised in a set of principles that apply to all good interactive practice. The four key principles are; 'Curiosity' and rewarding curiosity; 'Reciprocity' – you get as much back as you put in – we don't demand engagement but invite it so people can choose the level of engagement they're most comfortable with. You can stay on the outside of something and get a different experience from someone who's at the heart of it; 'Adventure', making it as exciting as an adventure; and the principle of 'Loveliness', which is the most important and potent one. That's about making a gift of an experience that's surprising and delightful. I've been running a set of workshops in various places that are presented as a training programme for Playful Secret Agents, usually with a specific emphasis on the principle of Loveliness. Within the Playful Secret Agency, which of course doesn't exist, the alleged leader is something or someone called Rabbit. Rabbit pops up every so often and makes a few things happen. There are actions that are essentially a challenge about how to deliver a surprise present to a stranger, anonymously. There was an action that happened in Melbourne that Rabbit orchestrated where somebody who worked in a tea shop, on leaving the shop, got tapped on the shoulder by a stranger who presented him with a parcel, the contents of which later made that recipient dance; more than that I can't say on the record. Or a cup of tea that was delivered 4000 miles, still arriving hot. That was the first action, orchestrated by Rabbit, that made everybody else involved reflect on the power of this kind of operation. This coined the loveliness principle related to 'don't do "evil"' by deliberately trying to fuck people up or by negligence, not taking care of the action.

The other aspect that I've been exploring through these workshops is the *live* consideration of what's actually playing in a given situation, being alert to what's happening and not taking anything for granted. Although other precedents will be useful you cannot be guided by them alone. It's an active process of taking care. With the making-a-surprise-gift-to-a-stranger paradigm, there are various lines you need to be aware of; if the gift is personal it could be perfect, but too personal and it could be creepy; if there's a magic in the way it's delivered that's wonderful, but too much and it could become scary. There's no rule as to where those lines exist; you have to gauge where they are for you and empathise with the recipient enough to understand where those lines will be for them to ensure that you place it just the right side of the lines. That is a very active process. There are a lot of training assignments that would deal with that, if indeed that training programme existed, which of course it doesn't. *The Loveliness Principle*, as a piece, is a trail, a hunt, challenging you step by step to do a small, lovely thing for somebody, and there's a pleasurable twist that's at the end of it. Seeing how 'ordinary' people who have no experience of a playful-immersive-arts-thing were encountering it was such a joy. You might find a card lying on a table or mysteriously in your pocket, which may have a message written to you on it or stamped with a rabbit head and a line that says something like 'there's a message for you if you choose to call' with a number. That's a way in. But if someone finds that way in and they are uncertain about what will happen if they call that number – because they have no clue about who or what is behind it, what their intentions are, they can't read it as being in an art context because that's not where they are encountering it – then, in a way, they are taking themselves into an adventure if they choose to call. And it's beautiful to witness their delight when they do discover the intention. Erving Goffman's 'Frame Analysis' argues we're engaging in these encounters all the time. In this kind of experience, audiences are actively processing that information; what is the situation, how real is it, is that person an actor? In our pieces there will be various signifiers at the edge of the frame, like a card on a table rather than in a festival brochure, that will give you a clue. Signifiers that make you question how you attribute it but help you to know it's not sinister and not a marketing tool. The thing about play is that you should never forget what's real and what's play.

JM: *And that's a safety net for the player.*

TS: That's the place where reflection happens, that gap between 'what if' and 'what is'; and that's where the meaning lies, questioning how much those connect and reflect each other. It's useful to think about reflection and where that happens in the audience experience and to make sure there is space for it. I've done some research looking at Resilience Theory, specifically the framework that characterises resilience in terms of: agency – that your actions have meaning and influence; connectedness – social relationships and the networks that support you; adaptability – the things that you're good at and can develop; all of this powered by reflection. Resilience Theory is a framework for the bit of happiness that we have some control over.[1] The value of interactive art is how it engenders these other dimensions; the sense of agency, connectedness to the other people around you, how you suddenly discover you can do something you didn't realise that you could before. All these things will give you a fulfilment from the engagement, yet you need to build in reflection. That might be thinking about how you punctuate the action but it's also about what happens afterwards. With *A Small Town Anywhere* [2009] it was really important to us that when we took people back into The Historian's Salon, the liminal space through which they'd entered, it was worth us just giving everyone a glass of wine so no-one needed to go to the bar and thus keep the group together. In that space, with a drink, they would just talk to each other, which was necessary because over the course of those two hours there had been moral choices, actions being played out, where strangers made these intense, playful relationships. It was important to put people in a space that was no longer the show to give them that chance to playfully debrief, apologise, question. That's the best care-taking that we could do, allow space to tell stories about your own experience. Part of the resilience framework is that sense of telling stories to reflect on your own life, on what's happened to you, noting how those stories change over time.

JM: *Is that a crucial part of Coney's practice, story-making and its subsequent storytelling?*

TS: Making stories happen in the sense of a journey. I like the idea that we're making a world, or a lens for the real world. At the moment I'm thinking about play as a set of 'make-beliefs'; what make-beliefs make up this particular playful version of the world. You do this every time you walk into a theatre; you accept a number of make-beliefs and conventions that help you understand how it's going to work and sometimes you have to learn new conventions in terms of what's expected of you. It's lovely to make worlds that are ornate fictions, like *The Gold-bug* within *Masque of the Red Death*; the experience of immersion as something that is other, beautiful, scary. But I'm more interested in worlds that are quite like our own, the principle of minimum fiction; what's the least you need to do in order to transform something in people's imagination. Creating uncertainty about what's real and what's not because you've used what's 'really there' as part of the backdrop. It means that everything that's already there supports the fiction, everything becomes part of it, becomes charged. People pay attention in a different way, notice things that they wouldn't notice otherwise, make stories in their head about what's happening here. Paying attention more closely is a good objective for art. There's an intoxication within that first experience of immersion where you don't know what the conventions are, which wears off after a while because you learn, anticipate. That first thrill of immersion might start to wear thin if there's not something else added to the mix; small and unexpected things. I was involved on a panel following the Junction Arts Festival in Tasmania [2012], with somebody else who was involved in *The Loveliness Principle*, although I didn't know her real name until I asked her just before going on stage. She talked about how the simple fact of using a codename and the knowledge that there were other people out there on a similar mission to her, made everything feel exciting. Every moment in her everyday life had that bit of attention given to it because it might just turn out to be something magical.

JM: Does that potency of experience come from igniting the imagination or feeling like you have a role to play?

TS: Both of those and there being an uncertainty about what's going to happen. Because it's completely embedded in the real world, you don't know the limits of that, how far that extends, it's potentially limitless. The principle of loveliness is itself a safety net; there's an assurance that anyone else with a codename will be a like-minded person upholding that principle, so you feel okay about possible situations that may occur.

JM: *What do you understand by the term immersive in relation to theatre and how do you use it to define Coney's work?*

TS: Not everything we make is immersive. It's a tricky word. Interactive is trickier and both get misapplied. In immersive theatre the audience is immersed in the world, *present* in that world, and they *feel* their presence in that world whether or not their presence is acknowledged by the rest of that world. It's like imagining that playing space is a pool of water; the audience is in that pool rather than on the outside looking in. They also have agency, which is a more useful word than interaction. We refer to audience, players, 'playing audience', which I like because it plays on 'paying audience'.

JM: *Is 'players' adopted from gaming terminology?*

TS: There is a crossover with game worlds, but games tend to be a means rather than an end in our bigger projects. Game-design is a brilliant discipline because it gives you a set of tools to enable you to understand how and why audiences are interacting as they are. You can design the experience to facilitate particular types of action or play. I mean game-design not simply from the virtual world or games that are played on devices but any kind of game, back to charades, and what's at its heart; the formal system that's been designed. Live and pervasive gaming is really important as a sector and there are ways in which we're grouped as part of that because we're learning from it. *A Small Town Anywhere* is a marriage of game-design and dramaturgy. In terms of agency there are amazing immersive experiences, such as with Punchdrunk, where you have agency of exploration, but not over the outcome of the piece. Whereas with *A Small Town Anywhere*, there is an agency for the audience in terms of interaction *and* the outcome is made in response to, by and with them.

JM: *How important is technology to the Coney process?*

TS: The most important technologies are ones that enable us to be in touch with our audience in some way. The prevalence now of mobile phones or email makes it possible to be responsive in the type of play that's happening, it's essentially free, other than the time spent in the action. You can bring the audience to a place geographically, a location on the street, or imaginatively, before they start they know the world they're about to step into. Crucial to Coney is the idea that the experience of an event for any audience begins the moment they first hear about it and only finishes when they stop hearing or talking about it. It's potentially without end. I love work that leaves some kind of legacy for the audience. Some of our early work was premised on the ways in which the advance – the point before which the audience walks into the room – could be played with. You could seed ideas and expectations that they'd bring with them, that informs how they will then experience the work. A project *What About Tomorrow?*, on which we collaborated with BAC Young People's Theatre explored immersion in order to play with audience expectations.[2] That was useful, but ultimately we wouldn't do it again. It worked as an exercise in playfulness, but in fooling the audience in that way there was no real capacity for transformation. It was an amazing feat but it reflected back on the audience, on individual actions people had performed; although in some instances they did find themselves acting braver, more publicly than they normally would. We can understand the transformation in those terms. Equally, you can work with a company, especially in community work, where it's a transformative experience being part of that process. The player relationships we have with our audiences on some projects is similar to that. Creating actions that will have impact, be transformative, is a kind of optimism; that ordinary people can sometimes do extraordinary things and the everyday world can sometimes be magical. That 'sometimes', as a qualifier, is important; it's in the play between 'what is' and 'what if'.

Samantha Holdsworth of Nimble Fish

Immersivity and cultural production – 'permission to play'

Samantha Holdsworth: When I first started doing site-specific work ten years ago the term 'immersive theatre' didn't really exist. It was 'site-specific' and then it evolved into 'site-responsive'. It seems now that that's implied when you're [working] in a new space; everything is site-responsive and the 'fiction' of the space isn't as restricted as it was ten years ago; what are the 'ghosts' of the building, what are its stories. It's actually valid in and of itself to create a complete, fictional world in a new space. It's been interesting to see that progression. Nimble Fish began working immersively about five years ago on our first project, *Einstein's Dreams*, with Creative Partnerships. We couldn't get any traction with the school, they weren't accepting what we were doing, we weren't allowed to take the young people out of the school. We thought, even if we create something on the stage or discretely in the classroom, we're still in the locality of the school, so let's create a fictional place *within* the school. Because they were refurbishing we were able to pull down walls, put speakers into ceilings and create an alternative space, a universe within the school. That immersion suddenly ignited the imagination of the school; the kids, the headteacher, were suddenly, like, 'this is amazing, we're not in school anymore'. That allowed a dialogue around, 'let's get rid of the baggage of the space and in this fictional space school can be anything'.

From that impact it had on the entire school, Greg and I both felt there was something really meaningful and powerful in doing this. We recognised that the immersion was like a liberation from personal baggage, your own expectations, your own cultural baggage. It felt risky as well and that's why we liked it as practitioners. That's how Creative Partnerships' Head, Sue Lawther, said 'we've got this play *The Container*, do you want to do it?' Straightaway we knew the only way we want to do this is in an immersive way, otherwise this will just be another political play; we'll sit in the theatre, we'll all converse and then we'll leave. The writing was very traditional in a structured sense. We felt that the politics of being immersive at that point reflected the politics of that play; it felt like a subversive thing to get a 40-foot articulated lorry and put it in the street – that was how important and vital we felt the potential of this debate about migration was. If it were in a theatre, it would have just been another play around another social issue. Again, the fiction of the space *allows*. Everyone came in with bottles of water and sat on cartons and one of the critics afterwards said it was really hard not to feel like he should ration it because he didn't know how long he was going to be in there for – there's no fourth-wall, [the audience] are *it*. Also, there was only torchlight. Sometimes you would see audience members through this torchlight and they were absolutely complicit, performers, present within that play. It was the instinct that we need to escape from the boundaries of theatre; we don't feel, as practitioners, that we belong in the theatre.

Josephine Machon: With The Container, *was it the space itself that allowed, demanded direct connection with the politics? The space* actually *became politically active?*

SH: Absolutely. We were really conscious that if we were going to do it in the back of an artic lorry that it would be true to the language of that space; it does contain crates, there isn't light, it is hot. The politics of the space and the politics of the writing together created that massive impact. There was no escape from that issue, we were all in the journey together and after an hour you were let out into the air and into the light. Turkish and Kurdish migrants were in the performance; we got a letter from a Turkish guy who ran a café saying, 'thank you so much for raising this issue – I only knew about this play because I wondered what the big lorry was doing in the street.' So the immersive space itself contains its own relation to society; he would never have come to that play had it been in a theatre. It's a much more democratic approach. There aren't any rules, it's not white and middle class, it is what it is, a container in the street, and that ignites curiosity, which allowed him to access the space.

JM: Would you talk further about what you refer to as your 'pop-up' pieces, your community events which use this immersive form. What do you think it is that is 'persuasive' about that form, that enables you to be invited and funded to create those projects and what is it that encourages the audience to be excited or feel comfortable with that form in a way they may not with traditional theatre situations?

SH: The reason that we are always really keen to work in that way is that we feel it's a much more democratic process, it's more of, what we call an exchange; rather than participants, an exchange occurs, peer-to-peer development. We say to our 'audience' we're not telling you anything here, we need you to come and experience this so that we understand the space as well. I hope it doesn't happen that immersive theatre becomes another 'ism', simply another part of theatre where people go along because it might be an interesting evening out. We genuinely, with these exchanges, invite our participants to be co-creators. I hope for the audience that they have the freedom and that right to think they can leave the space because they've taken what they need from it or they're not getting anything from it, they feel they're not restricted to being there for an hour. There's no expectations around how they should behave, or need to behave, they just need to *be*. With the Sittingbourne pop-up space we had a couple of people just sitting on the bench, they didn't go into any of the experiences they just allowed themselves to witness it and be there but they were still participating by watching and witnessing. It's not behind a wall, it's not about us defining where the intellectual and creative space is, it's like this is your community, we are the visitors, if you don't join us and play with us this doesn't mean anything. That goes back to the democracy of always checking-in with that community; is this useful, is this valuable? Pop-up events, as we define them, are always in close connection with the community. We might go to a café like this and sit down for half a day and just chat with whoever comes in, try and connect with the world, the community, that we're in; that in itself is a form of immersion. It's about questioning how can we be accepted as part of this community rather than, here's a pop-up event for you, a show pony, and then we're off. As a result we ended up establishing something we called 'micro-commissions'. We got a budget for the Sittingbourne Festival and we didn't want to use that all on design or all on practitioners so we broke it up into micro-commissions and put a call out to the local community for artists with ideas and gave out small bursaries. One artist in particular said this was the first time she'd ever been paid to do something and she subsequently went on to create an installation in the Tower of London. That process directly resulted in her confidence as an artist.

JM: *Just to clarify, could you define exactly what you mean by 'pop-up events'; are you invited into a particular space or do you seek out a space?*

SH: [Sittingbourne] Council had heard of that phrase and how, especially in London, disused warehouses were used as galleries in order to draw people into the community, into the town centre rather than having lots of dead space; here's some money, here's some closed shops you could use. As it happened we decided not to use those spaces, the spaces we used were covered ways, the high street, we made friends with somebody who was renovating an A-listed building and, because it was part of the community and he realised that we were trying to create something with the community, we ended up using this phenomenal house. The only way we could have used it was by building that relationship with that man. He trusted us. It had vaults and a secret walkway underneath to the church. We ended up using the church space as well, which again was quite, 'do we want to use the church space, what does that mean?' But it was on the high street, it was relevant so it was included. We used a couple of dead spaces and we renovated them, put ceilings back in and the people in the community standing outside the shop were saying, 'what's happening, what are you doing here?' and came on to volunteer in the project. I don't know, is it theatre, is it community theatre? It was just a collaborative devising process for us. Even our proposal was written as if the person reading it was in the experience. There was none of that, okay this is the bit were we do the funding bid and so on, the whole experience followed the same motif including the people reading our tender, they're already playing the game, already part of that process from start to finish. The evaluation we did in the little, local cinema, invited people in and that was thematically linked. There's nothing that doesn't always serve the process and make sense in terms of the overriding arc of the piece. You know how you go to the theatre and you go, 'oh there it is I've seen it' and you leave and that's the end of the world, you leave that world, the fiction of that space? Well, a river flowed down the high street a long time ago so we created, with an artist and the community, a spray-paint river down the middle of the street, which is still there; that world still exists, the memory, the tangibility of that experience. Why would we ever want to do something that leaves; finishes and says, 'okay, thanks a lot, bye'?

JM: *Your work takes on its own life, its own history, the traces remain and become a story that continues for that community.*

SH: It has its own rhythm, its own structure. And even with the people who work on the process, whether that's the professionals or the community volunteers, there's no 'I am the designer', 'I am the performer', 'I am the project manager', you end up having a much richer vocabulary, because we're all designers, we're all interested in the community. We're really conscious of that, there are no 'experts' in this process.

JM: *It's a continuum of expertise and sharing and learning, discovering.*

SH: And that's why it's not that helpful to us when people say, 'great, can you do another pop-up project like that one', because in a way that's like going back to existing boundaries of theatre, of what's familiar; 'let's do a pop-up in a shop that we understand and know and it will have the same result'. That's not our process. We're concerned more with what's around that pop-up space and how we interact with that environment. We're tendering at the moment a concept that we're developing, a festival called *I Am an Artist*, the idea being that we do a call-out to everybody, anybody and you have a micro-budget each so this guy here could say, 'I've always wondered if I could paint this building red and I'd like to do this with it and that would represent this and would make me feel like this and to the best of our abilities we would try and translate that with him, try and make that happen. It goes back to Joseph Beuys's idea that 'everyone is an artist', you just need the vehicle and the space to support and encourage that. That's our long-term goal, to have a festival of 'non-experts'.

JM: *So you're artistic facilitators in a way.*

SH: Absolutely. And there would be no hierarchy about his idea having less value than that of somebody who went to Slade and studied sculpture for four years, they'd both be equally valuable, it would just acknowledge different artistic processes, that's all. A lot of the time there's a fear around 'Health & Safety' and legislation and that becomes an excuse or a reason not to do something; it's intimidating. We would hope to be the vessels for preventing that. Some of the community members in *re:bourne* would ask if they would be allowed to do something and our response was yes, we'll absorb some of that, you go ahead with the ideas and we'll figure that side of it out. And that's great because then you are really bouncing ideas around and there's no difference between who's the artist, who's the project manager and the producer.

JM: *And does that nourish you as artists?*

SH: All the time. It's very humbling. I spent a lot of money training; three undergraduate years, then an MA, then trained in clowning with Gaulier and I was like, initially, yeah, I'm a director in physical theatre and experimental theatre, but actually, now, ten years later, it's working with a community or with 'non-artists', non-experts, that offers more. It's an absolute appreciation of being able to create the environment in which *others* are free to create, to be non-experts, to be artists. That is deeply humbling. The ideas and the sensitivity and the understanding that people bring to a project is always mind-blowing and often those are the ideas that get honed, that grow. It doesn't make me feel less of a practitioner, it just makes me feel like it's a shame that art is so exclusive, that there isn't a robust dialogue around community art. Actually, for me, it's not even community it's just about the right to art, period.

JM: *Do you mean the right to engage in it perceiving yourself as an artist or the right to engage in it from any perspective, to experience it, to be an audience member, access to art via any means?*

SH: To be a member of it, to be a thinker around it, simply to witness it. One of the great things about working on *The Container* or on the high street in this way is that you have accidental witnesses; literally, people who are going to Iceland to buy their fish fingers and this little puppet came down to interact with a child through the window, and they weren't intending to be part of that but there they were (see Illustration 11). What an amazing place that is, where you have that potential, you have the vocabulary for that and it's valued, where that might be your Saturday afternoon –

JM: *– you go out for fish fingers and you get theatre. There's something in that idea, those moments where, by chance, people are engaging in art, serendipitously. The immersive experience surprises them, is all encompassing in that moment of engagement. Perhaps this refers back to how we define immersive practice; is there something in that initial lack of awareness of involvement, which sees to the individual becoming aware of that participation, that willingness to immerse themselves in an experience?*

SH: It's an interesting question. And how do you, if you're buying your fish fingers, reject the immersive experience if you don't want to witness, if you don't want to be part of it? Do you have to, by the very act of walking straight through the fantasy world, be part of it? Equally, if someone left *The Container*, for example, you appreciate how fragile the immersive world is, because the fiction of that world cannot support somebody leaving. If they do, boom, you're back into reality. There has to be massive complicity with the audience in accepting the invisible rules of the space. I was working with some teachers around how to use non-traditional learning spaces; I gave a teacher some masking-tape for an exercise in the playground and she made an imaginary plan of the local high street and the kids were working and going in and out of the houses and a boy had come out from the toilet through the playground and as he walked down the high street he suddenly did a jazzy little dance. As soon as he came to the end of the high street, he stopped, and walked off normally. When you create the fiction of a space, where you are *in it* and an *active participant* in it, then it gives you permission to play. He didn't feel he could do that on a blank part of the playground. That's so powerful.

JM: How important is site, space, to Nimble Fish's work and what have been your different experiences because of the different spaces with each of your projects?

SH: We feel like we've gone through different iterations around how we think about space. When we were doing *Einstein's Dream* in the school it genuinely was about what does the space offer, how do we respond to the space so that it can work with or enhance an idea and how might the idea come from the space itself. The core text we used was Alan Lightman's *Einstein's Dreams*, exploring Einstein's theories of relativity and time, how time is flexible. Because it was a dreamlike text, the freedom around the space *being* the narrative, rather than there being a traditional 'story', was liberating for us because we weren't thinking, 'what are we trying to say through this?', but more, 'how are we hoping people might *experience* this?' With *The Container* we chose that space deliberately because it was provocative, it was subversive, it was political, it's in-yer-face having a 40-foot artic lorry. It was a statement, it was our statement; *re:bourne*, with the pop-up spaces, the high street response, that was totally, we'll use the space we've got, it's there and we're simply practising in it. We didn't go, 'what are the stories in the buildings, in the walls?', instead, let's use the community to show us how they would like to use that space, the ideas for it they might have. Space and how we respond to it has always been at the centre of what we do but, as a company, we're still in dialogue as to how do we work around space, we still don't know. As a result of that, we've set up a programme of work called *Space to Learn* where we're working with teachers. Royal Opera House Creative Partnerships came to us saying, 'we hear you do interesting stuff with performers and with community work, could you do that with teachers?' – which was an interesting leap; suddenly we're finding ourselves in corridors going, 'well how could we have our lesson here?' and the end question that we're asking ourselves at the moment around that piece of work is 'what would a school look like if there was no building, if it had no particular space?' *Space to Learn* is allowing us really to reflect on why we think there's an important link between people, space and the creative process as opposed to people, narrative structure and process; the traditional text-based approach.

JM: *Bearing in mind that Greg is a writer, is there any link between the act of writing and explorations of space in your work?*

SH: It's an emerging language I think. It reminds me a little of 'Physical Theatre' of the eighties and early nineties when it was very physical, and then the likes of Frantic [Assembly] and DV8 started working with writers and it took Frantic in a completely different direction. I think for us it's something to do with understanding the language of what we're working with at the moment and articulating that; this is what it is *now* and we feel like we're pushing a boundary or expectations around that, so now that we're more comfortable with that let's see how far we can push it with text, or perhaps with non-performers or clowning. Something we really want to look at is how clowning and space works and that's purely from that position of, if space is the thing how do we celebrate it and how do we explode it? I'm a bit frightened of writing to be honest. I like the plurality of immersive work and writing feels like the interpretation of it; it's more restrictive. I know it's not, but in my head I feel it is. I made a list once of the different terms, because we were thinking, 'how are we going to describe what we're doing?' and there's hundreds; 'site-responsive', 'site-specific', 'immersive', 'pop-up', 'community responsive' and we're not sure where we fit in in all those words. There's something about opting into the experience. Again that's about getting rid of ideas around expertise, where does it become performance and where does it stop being the performer and me sharing an experience? I love the idea that we can all create a complete world without having to speak to the designer, who has to agree with the writer and the director and so on. I think that's partly why we've resisted the word artists; we very specifically chose the term 'cultural producing'.

JM: Would you clarify what that term means to you and what it offers you as practitioners; how does it enable you to collaborate with other immersive artists. How far is immersive practice central to the Nimble Fish approach to cultural producing?

SH: It's an ongoing definition. Currently it's about being able to set up a site, emotionally or geographically, where creative exchange can occur, which would always be between whoever is participating in it and the team working on the project; events where peer-to-peer sharing happens. It's a deliberately open term. At the moment we're doing a project with young people around 'cultural detecting' so we're analysing what 'culture' means. It's a wry term, we laugh about the fact that we're 'cultural producers' because we're not quite sure what we're doing –

JM: – you're defining it for yourselves –

SH: – as we're going along. What's really important for us is that we're always collaborators, that we're allowing that space to happen. In the same way that our process with a community is democratic, we aim for the same with other artists; let's not reinvent the wheel, let's try and use our knowledge to nurture this process. We hope that if we're as generous as we can be with the things that we've learnt, that we're creating a community whereby the practitioners have a shared value, a shared understanding that immersive theatre is about inclusion, literally in that you're included in our world but also come and join us, come and play, we don't want to be the auteurs we don't want to keep the knowledge to ourselves and let that create a mystique around us. We wouldn't be interested in producing a straight play, that doesn't represent what we're doing, so whilst we haven't necessarily said immersive is the only way, our instincts always lead us back to the same way of working which is around creating the *world* of a project, and that's linked to how we create the fiction of a space but also the values that go along with that. If we're inclusive and immersive, then our process, how we treat our practitioners, how we pay our artists is equally reflective of that accessible process. We never ever expect people to work for us for free because we feel that's inaccessible for some people. In order to have a democratic process, even if that means we have to do a smaller project, the value of everybody is important. That's the world of Nimble Fish, there's an aesthetic choice and for us there's also an ethical choice; an active rejection of the hierarchies of producer, director, designer, writer and then performers.

JM: In that respect, as an artistic form, is immersive practice ethically sound for you?

SH: Absolutely. When we're struggling with defining what we're doing we'll go back to, ethically, what are the values that are important to us? And that feeds into our immersive practice. It's an inclusive space. I guess that's where immersive theatre came from, the rejection of buildings and those values. The National Theatre of England, how may people does it actually represent?

JM: I hadn't thought before about the ethical choices for working with that form but it's interesting, placing the audience at the centre of the experience, that's hugely democratic, embracing and celebratory of the audience, something collaborative about that.

SH: And I think people instinctively feel that. They choose where they're able to go emotionally, if they want to go somewhere spiritually, intellectually, I'm not going to tell them how to do that, but I can provide them with the space where they choose to step in and play with me or not and that's fine either way. I'm really interested to see where this generation of people immersed in immersive theatre go with that next. That's so exciting.

Punchdrunk Enrichment

Immersion, enrichment and empowerment

Jen Thomas: Immersive theatre, in general, is about entering a full world, you're surrounded on all sides, it's three-dimensional, you're within a real space where there could be sound, smell and taste, all your senses are engaged. You're being *immersed*, you're stepping into an enclosed world that surrounds you and the characters are of that world.

Ralph Savoy: You're experiencing what's going on in the action and then you're immersed in it yourself, like reading a book, you become involved in it and you're also encountering the people in the book, again involved in what's happening.

Josephine Machon: In that respect, how is immersive theatre different to any other type of theatre?

RS: You're not a spectator, you're part of the scene, you become involved, doing things. I encouraged people to walk around with me in the soup kitchen, told them to look out for things so they might actually step back in time. I felt I'd like them to *feel* that experience.

Janet Evans: Just that sharing, you're taking people into the world that you're *in*; you're *in* this world aren't you and then you've got the audience, three participants in our case, and you can make them come in with you so that you're all sharing. If you're successful, then we all believe that we've been there. Some people came ready and willing to be there and others were more distant. It seemed easier for young people to think that this was an acceptable theatrical experience.

Pete Higgin: We didn't say anything to the audience; like, you will be expected to interact, we kept it unexpected so that it might be fresh for people; we didn't give them any instructions. Unless you draw the lines of engagement beforehand, some people don't know how to react. We worked to make the interaction as natural as possible.

JM: Thinking about an unspoken or prior contract, were you aware of, because of the nature of this project, having a different type of audience to the usual Punchdrunk fans.

PH: There was a mixture. We ensured that all of the participants' family and friends were able to see the piece and there was a big drive to get as many local Hackney residents as possible, who had no experience of Punchdrunk or The Arcola or this type of theatre, to come. The message to the press was that this was a project engaging Arcola 60+ in the creative process and if you want to come and review it as a standard Punchdrunk show then it's probably best not to come, but if you want to review it as a piece that's about creating work with a participatory community group and putting that work in a professional context, then that's interesting.

JM: *Why was an immersive form so crucial to the remit of this project, why did Arcola want to work with you on this project in this way?*

PH: Jen and I had talked about doing a project with a group from a community within Hackney for about a year beforehand and Jen had hooked into Dickens, so it needed to be something that was local and relevant to East London. There was a sense that we wanted to do an immersive group project which gave creative agency to a group of participants and that it needed to be in a found space, a surprising location, which was in the middle of Hackney. These guys had had experience devising, writing and creating and it would be a good next step, and an interesting development artistically and creatively, for 60+ Theatre Group. It was a nice marriage.

JM: *Ralph and Janet, what did working in this way reveal to you; what insight did it give you, how did it open up possibilities for you working as actors?*

RS: It helped us to loosen up ourselves a bit, instead of being restricted to the script, to be able actually to live the parts. In that way it was a wonderful experience.

JM: *You mentioned earlier that the space itself allowed you access to something unique in terms of your performances.*

RS: The atmosphere, the surroundings, unusual lighting which helped you with your character, you could grow your character in a sense, the furniture, you move about in that space in a certain way.

JE: What was brilliant about it was that you didn't have a 'script script' that you had to learn. Obviously you had things that you had to bring in, but you could vary it to some extent. If I liked a phrase, I'd keep using it. The fact that you actually were that person, meant you wouldn't go outside what would be authentic to that character.

JM: *How was the quality of experience working in this particular way different to the work that you'd done prior to this project?*

JE: You don't have to please a huge audience, you have to please three people; you could ask questions that were pertinent to the people that were there, that could draw them in.

JM: *Was there something powerful about the intimacy of that relationship?*

JE: Absolutely. My sister was supposed to have been burnt, so I would ask questions about whether any of them had a sister; you could play with the information that they'd give you.

RS: I could say to them, 'come with me', like I knew the people that I was talking to directly, 'follow me into the restaurant and I'll show you'. When they came back into the booth I would question them individually. You could give an impression of that on a stage but you couldn't do it individually. I would also get them either to choose whether they wanted to go along with me or they disagreed, so I had this little conflict situation going which was a challenge. Normally when you're on the stage nobody argues with you. I had to use diplomacy and tact, 'but think of the rewards sir', I became the character more.

JM: Does the immersive form then allow that creative agency to come to fruition much more powerfully than working with more traditional processes?

PH: When you look at a piece like this which could be, in a sense, compared to a distilled version of a bigger show; we had 16 characters

Illustration 18   Punchdrunk Enrichment's *The Uncommercial Traveller* (2011c). Performer Ralph Savoy

[Photo credit: Marco Berardi. Image courtesy of Punchdrunk Enrichment]

all devising 20 minutes of performance, all around the same structure and the same soundtrack, and in the same space but in different areas. There's no real way that a director, in this case three directors, can have oversight of all of those interactions. Even down to the fact that every interaction is different, what you inherently do, unconsciously and consciously, is hand over a certain amount of artistic control to the performers. Also, the space is big, it's an environment with a lot of detail to input, so I think it does lend itself to that. It would be a very different way of working if you were trying to control every single element and trying to have a model where the director was king or queen and everyone else was servicing the script or their vision. Because this piece was completely devised, it was about the characters that interested Ralph, Janet and all of the other performers, we didn't dictate that.

JE: When you feel that that's you're character, you're more prepared to do it for four weekends in a row because you're part of it.

RS: We did have a respect for each of our characters; we allowed for what the others were doing and meshed it in with what we were doing, didn't protrude on their space.

JM: You were clearly working in democratic ways because of the nature of the project but there's something about the form also speaking to that, a dialogue going on between form and experience and collaboration.

PH: Janet, when you said you first started, you varied your performance but as you got further into it you found yourself honing it down, that's a response to the environment itself and to the form and to you making decisions about what you thought worked. In a sense, because every interaction is different, it allows you to experiment but also forces you to make decisions in the moment, based on what you've done in the past.

JT: From what we had when we first did the sessions down on the site, there was a change in terms of the group dynamic and the experience, walking into the set for the first time and exploring that space, created by the designers for the cast, influenced by what they needed. The actual first experience for them of that shop unit was as complete as we could have made the self-supporting cooking depot. That had an effect on your characters and the investment because that space was speaking directly to all of your characters.

Illustration 19   Punchdrunk Enrichment's *The Uncommercial Traveller* (2011c). Performer Janet Evans

[Photo credit: Marco Berardi. Image courtesy of Punchdrunk Enrichment]

JE: When we went into that place it was like you'd given us a big gift, it was like Christmas. It was like we were doing our best here, going along with it not really knowing what you were on about and when we got it in there, we saw exactly what you were on about.

RS: We could really understand what we were meant to do with the audience, in a sense, bring them out of themselves.

JM: Owen, how do you define the immersive form and why was it that you particularly wanted to work with Punchdrunk in this way for this project?

Owen Calvert-Lyons: Immersive theatre creates a more democratic relationship between performer and audience. The moment an actor interacts with an audience member, for that moment that audience member is as much of a performer as the actor. In this instance, there are other audience members in there who are able to observe that moment and maybe a little while later that role will be reversed. That makes a fundamental shift in the relationship between actor and audience, which is hugely exciting for participatory theatre because you're already starting to play with those boundaries of who is the recipient of this piece of theatre and who is the giver of it. For Arcola 60+ that's really exciting to start exploring areas in which they are empowered and have more power than they might in a more traditional form of theatre, which is always what we're aiming at. We're always trying to devolve more of that power. Sometimes that's slightly inhibited by a more traditional style in which a director necessarily has to have more authority. In immersive theatre you *have* to devolve that, not just to the actors but the designers, the whole company. It *insists* on you being collaborative because, as Pete pointed out, there's no central focus. As a director a lot of your job is about framing what an audience are watching; once you've got multiple audiences watching multiple frames, you lose control of that which is great, it insists that you allow people to be in charge of that themselves, for them to decide where they want to look, interact at any given moment. That allows actors to be really playful because they choose when they are focused upon and when they're not. They can do something in a moment that attracts the attention of everybody and then they can give that up; they can constantly subvert that themselves.

RS: It's important to have a strong sense of story when you start, because you're leading them along so you don't want to go completely awry.

OCL: The amount of story that these guys created that the audience never saw, that's really exciting; there's much more behind a piece of theatre like this. The audience only see a tip of the iceberg yet they understand that the iceberg's there.

JM: Definitely, you feel that stuff, it doesn't need to be spoken, it's there in so many other ways.

OCL: Whereas you understand, as a traditional audience member, that if you chose to get up and cross that stage, you know you wouldn't find that world behind there. There's a sense with this style, and partly because of how much story there is, that you could follow that character, stay there into the night and those events would happen.

JE: I went to see *Betrayal* by [Harold] Pinter, expensive seats at the front and I just thought, they're over there and I'm over here; after doing this it made that division seem much greater. I also went up to Edinburgh [Festival] and it seems to me that this is the new way forward, everybody wants to immerse themselves, it's kind of happening, so much so that people were having one-on-one experiences. There seems to be a move to much more individual responses, being part of the drama, than there ever was before.

JM: It seemed space, specifically place, Hackney, the East End of London, was vital to your stories, your research, the piece as a whole. How did the form and the way in which you developed the project allow you a particular access to those histories, the politics of that place, to its community?

RS: I've been encouraged by this to read a book about the history of the period of Dickens and when I see how the people used to talk, the things they said, their attitude towards life in those days, accepting the hardships, it gelled with what we were doing. So a sense of another world had been really created by the set, a sense of the time.

JM: A direct connection with that history as it had been lived.

JT: Punchdrunk have been based in Hackney for a few years and we haven't directly connected with our local area or history or community particularly. The thing that struck me, all of us, about *The Uncommercial Traveller* was the way that Dickens experienced London was quite extraordinary. This book is a journal of his night-time and daytime wanderings, the things he discovered, the people he met. You get a window into the reality that existed and you can see the germination of his characters and the places that he creates in his fiction; many of them are based on the people that he seemed to encounter in this journal. We thought that that was a really interesting beginning; to open your eyes and wonder and allow yourself to go through a closed door in a quiet street, the people you find – the idea that these stories and characters are everyday and all around us. The knowledge of the East End, of the history of this area, came from the participants themselves. I didn't know there was an Ayahs' Hostel, I didn't know what an Ayah was; the whole story about the Indian immigrants, the British Raj and what happened when all the British people returned with their Indian nannies that was one story of many that was unearthed, discovered, by the community who lived there that we were working with; Dickens's idea that when you lift your head, open your eyes and look around yourself, push through the perceived 'privateness' of a community, these stories are all living. When we mirrored that in talking with this group and finding out what interested them, which characters and narratives they were drawn to, that was where those stories came from, where the research lay.

JM: And a power in that is, as a participant, you feel a very strong sense of an inhabiting *of history, the fusion of time, past to present, through these performances.*

OCL: Jen's got the right focus there, what we created was just a framework and an inspiration point in Dickens, in which we were then giving agency to the performers to go and find what those stories were. The thing that became interesting in those histories and geographies and the politics; they each came from an individual and their interests, their connections and their histories. We're talking about a very specific group who are already geographically based within Hackney and therefore already have that shared geography and all the things that come with that. Hackney is a very politicised borough and a borough that has a really strong sense of community in a way that, perhaps, if we'd put all these other parameters into another area it may not have elicited the same response.

RS: What I've learnt from doing this has encouraged me to research further. Doing these characters and creating this world, the potential is amazing as a learning experience. The sound effects from the period, the clocks, the carriages, evoked such an atmosphere, I don't think you would normally get that in a traditional dramatic production; that's something unique.

JM: In terms of that learning that was taking place, in many different ways for all those involved, I was very aware of the audience coming out and being politically engaged with the experience, historical injustices, political struggles for which this area is responsible.

PH: Dickens inherently gives the 'everyman' a voice. In a sense what this project did was give everybody a voice and, at points, a few people questioned when exactly this was. We were really clear that it isn't timeless exactly, but it isn't fixed on an actual date because that's restrictive to creativity. Dickens's canon of work goes over a long period so it could be anywhere within that. With the Dickensian working-class stories, it was all about giving voice, fighting oppression, getting the vote.

OCL: Some things didn't necessarily make it into the show in the end, but in terms of the rehearsal process a lot of time was spent on very political stories.

JT: We didn't aim for that at the outset, hadn't consciously considered that it would be part of it, but inevitably, the characters that were emerging had money problems, crime problems, problems with their families, their housing, their jobs. The characters were affected by the weight of what was happening at that time politically.

OCL: The minute you start talking to people about 'the self-supporting soup depot for the working classes', it's got a political edge to it; people have a political response to that, something that we hadn't anticipated or thought would be central.

JM: There's also something in the sensuality of the form and of the performers. The beauty of older performers, particularly in those intimate settings, is that you get a tangible, embodied sense of lived history through the skin, a performer's demeanour, In an intimate encounter you become aware of the bodies with which you're engaging.

OCL: When we first started to create roles, lots of the company would portray characters of a whole range of ages, which was really interesting but I think it was also a hangover of the fact that, as actors, the company were very used to playing characters of a completely different experience to themselves. I hope it was very freeing for us to say the company would be playing characters of around their own age. They could bring themselves to that part, become these wonderful characters who give a sense that they've lived in this place – whether that's Hackney or the self-supporting cooking depot – that they've inhabited this place for some time and they've got that sense of belonging and history.

PH: In terms of drawing the lines of engagement for the audience we were very aware that people would come in, begin an intimate conversation; very aware of making that change, from the real world into meeting this character then being taken even further into this character's story, as real as possible. As opposed to making anything historically specific, instead to draw parallels with what conversation could be now; family, the weather, worries of money. So there were fusions of time; from being there and in this moment, alongside the time that the performers brought in terms of their own experience and then drawing from now to this perceived 'then' without it feeling too much of a jolt. We thought a lot about what this form of engagement would be; that it would be conversational and that it was important that it was interactional and that we weren't asking the audience a question they couldn't respond to, or would need a prior knowledge of Dickensian London in order to respond. It had to be seamless. As with any Punchdrunk show, you don't go straight into it, you kind of get sucked into the experience slowly.

RS: Unlike, say, with the Hampton Court experience, where you can watch the performers in the costumes of the period sitting having a meal, but the people aren't sitting in with them enjoying the meal, they're watching as spectators. Here, they're in it and living it.

JS: Christine Taylor [a co-performer] said that she really thought it was the one show she could think of where it was an advantage to be old, to have more knowledge of certain things.

OCL: I think that's really important. For me it echoes the Youth Theatre movement. Young people were presented with the same plays that adults would be performing and being forced to play characters that they had no understanding of and were not relevant to them. That movement started 25 years ago, saying if young people are going to make theatre, then all those other parts of the industry should work with them so that they're performing plays that have young people central to them, where the characters are young people. We have the same problem with older actors; the writing isn't supportive of those age groups. Being able to create a production where those central characters, all of them, are older people and are played by people of that age is really important. There's not enough of that work around, which forces us to devise and create, which is exciting.

JM: *And it ends up communicating across ages. You've mentioned the effectiveness of the sound in the space. I'd like to talk about the significance of the headphone journey to the piece as a whole and in terms of place, geography. What were your intentions with it in terms of adding to the immersive quality of the piece?*

OCL: The vision for it was that it would have had the voices of our performers in it and that we would have elements and echoes of the stories that the audience were going to be presented with later on so there would have been a much greater sense of interaction between the live performance and the recorded piece. The format that it ended up in was still an exciting addition to the show, but it wasn't what we had set out to create.

PH: The walk itself, the journey of that walk was a journey that we'd all done as a group. The reason the walk is there is because of Dickens, the process of walking and observing, looking closer, getting the audience into the mind-frame of Dickens, trying to plant seeds of little things which might come back in the performance later on. Also to draw parallels between Hackney now and Hackney then; what would Dickens look at now, who are the characters now, what are the narratives you'd develop?

OCL: We had long conversations about how you would get the audience as close to the experience of 'the uncommercial traveller' as possible, not just the experience of reading it but Dickens's experience of walking around the streets. So in that respect the headphone journey is much closer to that experience than the live performance.

JT: We lifted a couple of passages from the journal itself and we all fed into other parts of the walk so that they could be modern-day; we were trying to make it fit both time periods. Ideally the vision of it was that you would be asked to engage and look at certain things, to ponder and then, just as Dickens happens upon the self-supporting cooking depot for the working classes, you would find a door and you choose to step through it. That was the point that we wanted to lead our audience to, the point of crossing the threshold. I think it achieved that goal, but we'd all agree that if we did it again we'd expand it further.

OCL: There was also something about only having a 25-minute show, being able to seed some ideas and create a thought-process in our audience before they walked through that door, over a journey in which they were encouraged to think and observe and *to be open*, they might then walk in the door and have a much richer experience.

PH: That sound world of the headphone journey, in a Punchdrunk way, relied very much on the random things that happen to structure meaning from it. There's something quite powerful about keying into someone's innate mechanisms for reading meaning into something that's happening around them. That's immersive, to be in that moment. You become both commentator and audience, you're listening and observing, watching other people. It lifts you away from who you are almost, because you're listening but also taking on the role of thinking, almost taking on the role of a character. The way you walk listening to that is different to the way you walk if you were just in your own world.

JM: *How does this project fit in with Punchdrunk's broader mission and aesthetic and what insights have you gained? How might it move the ways in which you work forward, finding new formulae for how you work?*

PH: Work that travels across environment and expands out of the four walls of a building is incredibly important and it's something as a company that we'll continue to explore. The audio experience, how you can make the reach of your performance further than when you enter the door of the space, how you can begin to pervade people's lives beyond that – the people who saw the stream of participants every hour – how does that impact? So there's something about reach, something about what we define as space and how you use an uncontrollable environment – the world itself and the fabric of an urban landscape, rural landscape or cityscape – to begin to define your work. That's part of a wider thing that we'll explore as a company. For the Enrichment Department, collaboration is key. Because we're nomadic and not building-based that's exciting, and it's also a wider movement in terms of the arts world and the climate we're in. What we can bring is our experience of working the way we do and what other organisations bring is their specific interests and their groups and artistic direction.

JM: *How has working with Punchdrunk added to the mission of Arcola and the ways in which you might choose to work in the future?*

OCL: I think for Arcola Creative Learning, we're now keen to embark on a series of co-productions which mirror the professional model and that's in big part due to how successful and exciting this project has been. In terms of the specifics of Arcola 60+, this as a style really suited that group in a way that it may not for all of our community companies. There were so many facets to it that solved problems that we hadn't solved over the last couple of productions with that company. The sense that I get from this group is that people would like to have another go at immersive theatre in a different format.

PH: The process and the product are exciting but what's more exciting is the ongoing impact and the legacy of that involvement, that we don't always see but which inspires. That's at the core of what Punchdrunk Enrichment will continue to facilitate, to try and create responses that go on beyond that initial impact and experience of a piece of theatre or the process of creating theatre, which is at the heart of what Punchdrunk does anyway.

JT: What was extraordinary about this, being there at weekends and meeting the audiences as they came out was, firstly, the audience didn't realise that the actors weren't professional, which says a huge amount about what was created by the company and the power of that. Secondly, something that we always strive for as a company, audiences came out and they were in a group that they hadn't previously known, they'd lost the person that they'd come with, and they would stand outside the door chatting nineteen-to-the-dozen about the experience they'd just had, waiting for the next group to come out so they could find out what their experience had been. All this dialogue going on to the extent that sometimes our stage manager was moving people on because the next cast had to come out or the next audience was due in; people were still buzzing about it. Something that we haven't explored before is the fact that the entire company of actors were community members, non-professionals, they weren't supported by professional performers from the company in the cast and for that reason there was a freedom there and a space there and a real empowerment.

JE: Speaking as a former teacher, you're always aiming to try to interest your audience. You did feel that you were able to get hold of people and draw them in to what you were trying to say. That in itself is a unique experience, because you don't get that in life.

RS: I did a little bit of acting through the years, but this was a completely new way of looking at acting; to be able to relate to a small number of people, feel that they're with you, it was just something new and fresh; the small significant things that we could do to be effective, keeping things to a minimum.

PH: The audience bring that final response and that energy to the work. And that was incredibly poignant and inherent to this piece.

OCL: Something really fascinating about the process was, if we were doing this on an unlimited budget we could have built the set from the outset and rehearsed in that environment for all of that time. Instead, all that work on how you create space, imagine space was what we spent most of the process on. To take a group and develop them to the point of going on an imaginative journey which was so important because it could have ended up in any of these worlds that was invented on the way. It also meant that our actors had these powers of imagination and a trust in their own skills, they could have taken those people on a journey into a space in a blank room and that meant that they already had reached a certain level. The environment added a layer on top of that but as actors they were never reliant on that space; they were reliant on their own skills and the space augmented that.

PH: How do you make something that is Punchdrunk in its nature satisfying in only a 20-minute journey; that takes the arc from the subtle beginnings of the one-on-one to crescendo? It's about shifting the audience expectations, shifting what an audience member thinks this will be. That is inherently Punchdrunk. With our one-on-ones there's always a need for that character to reveal something, to share a secret, they *have* to communicate with that audience member; I need you to help me with my mission, I have this guilt that I have to get off my chest; that need for communication to be natural, real and then that *shift* to the revelation, that's what's Punchdrunk about it.

Conversations four

Louise Ann Wilson

Immersed in the environment – 'off the beaten track'

Louise Ann Wilson: I'm interested in how the act of walking might engage an 'attendant' audience in the manner of a pilgrimage, where duration, immersion and the challenge of the physical journey are fundamental to the process of exploration and reflection. I don't construct my work with specific terminology in my head and prefer not to be too conscious of words that define what I do, because they can guide, direct and impose too much. I'm also wary of assuming that I know what the audience experience is going to be, rather I try to create a space where people can engage and bring themselves fully to the experience. wilson+wilson asked audiences to be deeply involved, experiencing many layers of material with all of their senses; where the piece itself revealed clues and gradually built a non-linear thematic narrative. We wanted audiences to notice details and link these, detective-like, to something that happened later in the piece. This engaged them imaginatively and intellectually and required them to be fully switched on. Sometimes the auditorium lights going down means an audience can be present and not-present at the same time. In all of my site-specific work, I've taken audiences on a physical journey where they've travelled on foot or by bus, tram, off-road buggy, pedalo or elevator. Asking people to walk, to make a journey, physically engages them; they have to climb and struggle up narrow stairways or steep mountainsides, squeeze themselves into a tiny room or a cave along with other participants and performers. *House* encouraged audience members to look inside drawers and behind closed doors, and they found themselves in the same room as the performers; an old man, asleep in a chair in front of the fire, surrounded by the artefacts of his life, providing clues to the rest of

Illustration 20 wilson+wilson's *House* (1998). Performer: Leader Hawkins

[Photo credit: Fiver. Image courtesy of wilson+wilson]

the piece. Some just froze, as if they were actually in someone's private space, whereas others were bolder; one person even prodded him to see if he was real.

I think audiences are now more used to being close to performers and to performers coming close to them. With wilson+wilson, and it remains the case with my current work, we treated our audience with respect and didn't shock them or make them feel embarrassed or self-conscious. Many of them were non-theatregoers. A lot were from an older generation who knew they were going to be intellectually, artistically and physically challenged and engaged, yet in a safe space. We may have lost them, or other potential audiences, if we'd made the pieces too confrontational, interactive or exposing.

JM: How are you able to embrace a non-theatre going audience? Is it due to the spaces that you use?

LAW: Firstly, because the spaces are 'real', 'everyday' places that people have lived, spent leisure-time, or worked in they feel invited in –

JM: *there's no sense of exclusivity, instead 'I'm allowed here because I have a connection with this space'* –

LAW: – I'm allowed here, I'm a citizen of this place or of this land. Secondly, people who have an intimate and specific understanding of a place or landscape are involved in the creative process and they, and their community, become interested in seeing the final production. Sometimes, as with *Fissure*, these 'experts' actually appear in the final performance. This means that the place and the people of that place are embedded within the very bones and fabric of each piece, which grows from the site; it's indigenous. *Jack Scout*, a walking performance specific to Jack Scout, an intimate location on Morecambe Bay, arose from four 'Dialogues' that the creative team had with the place and people with different knowledges of that place; an 'Underworld Dialogue' with National Trust wardens and plant ecologists about the site's unique flora and fauna; an 'Overworld Dialogue' with the Royal Society for the Protection of Birds about the behaviour of indigenous species of birds, butterflies and bats on the heath and migratory birds on the beach; an 'Innerworld Dialogue' with pupils at a nearby school for urban children with special needs; and a 'Waterworld Dialogue' with cross-bay guides and fishermen concerning fishing traditions and the Bay's tides, shipwrecks and drownings. We used cartography, writing, improvisation, drawing and photography to register and distil our own experience of the place and to evolve material that was transformed into the final performance.

JM: *There's a beautiful creativity about that, it has its own narrative. It's clear that space, place and audience are central to your work and it seems a lot of environmental questions underpin each concept.*

LAW: My recent work has focused on the rural landscape as a place for performance in which the relationship between the personal and the environment can be re-imagined. It seeks to explore ways in which the earth and biological sciences, ecology, art and performance can dramatise, articulate and reflect upon significant life-events, creating multi-sensory experiences that transform how people perceive and relate to their surroundings. The form, shape and content of the pieces I make respond to the physical nature of a place; its geology, biology, geography, history and ecology. In planning the route for *Fissure* I looked for fissured, symbolic and diverse locations; limestone pavements, shake-holes, cairns, scars, subterranean rivers, caves and mountain tops. These location choices were underpinned with neuro-scientific knowledge of the brain's structure and its function and dysfunction. Through conversations with neurologists, I discovered striking analogies between geography and neurology; neuro-scientists describe brain ventricles as 'caverns filled with fluid', and explore the white-matter pathways of the brain as 'finding a path in a field'. The shape and dramaturgy of the whole piece was divided into six phases based on my memories of and notes from Professor Michael Brada, the neuro-oncologist who treated my sister, about key moments in her illness, death and the time since. In *Fissure* I wanted the audience to hear directly from the various 'experts' that had informed the piece so I placed them in particular phases and locations to deliver their words; Michael Brada described how brain tumours grow; Dr Chris Clark, a neuro-imager, described how he uses water to map the pathways of the brain; and Dr Mike Kelly, a geologist, described how caves are formed by water seeping and flowing through the bedding planes and vertical joints of the rock. I also worked on the ground with local specialists, such as an ecologist from Natural England who later spoke to the audience about the ecology of the flower meadow they met him in, and a caver who took the creative team on underground trips, which informed the content and form of the piece and who later worked with the dancers who performed in the cave passages.

JM: *It becomes part of an evolving methodology; whatever the final form and shape of the piece, all along there's a respect for the creative exchange between location, the people of that location and the ideas that exist in your work. Perhaps that's where the environmental ideas emerge, because you're working so closely within an immediate landscape and its community, where the local ideas around environment merge with wider arguments of ecology.*

LAW: The locals and experts I collaborate with have a huge investment in, understanding of, and passion for, the places in which they work and live and it's vital when making this work that I listen to, and respect, what they're saying. As part of the research and development for *Fissure*, I went to the Yorkshire Dales with Michael Brada and asked him if it was possible to draw parallels between neurological systems, a brain tumour and the landscape around us. The neurological parallels were many, but he said, 'there is nothing here that is as devastating to the land as a

Illustration 21 Louise Ann Wilson's *Fissure* (2011). Commissioned by artevents. 'Day Two – Ingleborough Cave'

[Photo credit: Bethany Clarke. Image courtesy of artevents]

tumour to the brain, and the patient.' The landscape around us had been formed and gouged out by repeated ice ages, tsunamis and tectonic plate movement, but over time it repairs itself; the body, affected by a tumour, can't repair itself in this way – there is no recovery, it's terminal. Later, at Ribblehead Quarry, a disused limestone quarry, I could see where the stone had been gouged out leaving a massive crater, but that the land inside was beginning to recover and repair itself. This became one of the locations for *Fissure*; in the performance the audience walked to the top edge of the quarry, where harsh sounds of brain surgery combined with sounds of quarrying, recorded from a nearby working quarry, could be heard rising up from below. They then walked down inside the quarry to pools, dams, waterfalls and isolated figures; here, juxtaposed with the sounds, Elizabeth Burns's poetry is sung, 'the body of the land begins to heal, water flows over it, things start to grow' – speedwell, tormentil, primrose, eyebright, forget-me-not – 'but this is not the body of the land, able to renew itself over and over again, this is the body of a woman'. *Fissure* was about facing up to and recovering from the terrible loss caused by the death of someone you love. The quarry experience on the first evening became a microcosm that reflected the three-day journey of the whole piece.

JM: *This is work that can't be made in a studio, it has to be experienced in the space itself, it can't be transposed.*

LAW: It has to be experienced in the place in which and for which it has been created, otherwise it becomes something else. It needs its whole context; the performance, the landscape, the natural sound-scapes, the walking and the weather. We'd been rehearsing all week in terrible rain but on the Friday, as we left to collect the audience from Settle train station, the sky cleared. The piece began on the train with musicians playing and singing about the landscape we were passing through and a song of two sisters which established the overarching dramaturgy; this was then followed by the scene in the quarry, at the end of which the setting sun created the most awe-inspiring backdrop. On Sunday morning, having descended into the subterranean world of Ingleborough Cave the night before, we resurged and began to ascend Ingleborough, but a strong wind blew up and it became too dangerous to proceed; we re-routed off the mountain and down into the village of Clapham. As we approached, church bells were ringing, children were arriving with their pet lambs tucked under their arms ready for a naming ceremony. Looking back I'm struck by the fact that the piece had to respond to external forces that were beyond our control and which, quite literally, blew us off course. This, in terms of the piece, is very symbolic; when making this sort of work you have to be constantly open to and embrace the forces of nature, particularly the weather, which bring their own challenges, and rewards. With *Jack Scout*, the performance led to discovery, or rediscovery of the place. The immersive experience made audience members more aware of the place and the 'natural' environment, even those familiar with it experienced it afresh, through different eyes, walked through it differently –

JM: – because you've allowed it to 'speak' for itself?

LAW: Yes, people could *be* in the world and observe and *feel it* more fully.

JM: It can make you aware of your responsibility in that 'environment'. I think this practice in general makes you aware of the ways in which you're complicit in the situation. There's a connection with humanity in some way, being aware of your presence, of how you impact on the situation; it's specific to a particular piece, its setting and the duration of time over which it occurs.

LAW: At the end of *Fissure* I said to the audience, 'you were meant to be the people who took this walk and made this journey'; not only were they walking with me but alone, with absent friends, each other, and the landscape. A number of them had chosen to come along because the subject matter was particularly meaningful to them. I know that some emotional shifts and 'big' conversations took place along the way. These, combined with the enjoyment of being in the landscape, meant people experienced everything in a full and sensory way. With any piece each audience group develops its own dynamic, each individual within the group feels and responds to the work in a way that is unique to them. It was important that the audience remained together throughout *Fissure*; walking, eating and staying together, they became a community of individuals. They didn't socialise with the performers at all until the Sunday morning when the dancers and singers emerged from the caves – into which they had disappeared the night before – and joined the audience as they walked. The shape and form of the piece was inspired, in part, by the Easter Triduum and in particular a Maundy Thursday service I attended at Ripon Cathedral where, during the hours of 'darkness', a carving of Christ on a crucifix was wrapped up and taken down into the crypt where it remained until Sunday morning. I visited the crypt every day and sat with the Christ figure, keeping 'it', 'him' company, in that stone-carved tomb. I realise now that this powerful experience was part of my grieving process; that I was sitting, in the quiet and darkness, with my absent sister; it informed *Fissure* very directly.

JM: By exploring that metaphor that is so felt by you, it has the potential to open up that experience to others. There's an essential experience there that articulates ideas around grief and loss, the individuality of it. Confronting the darkness.

LAW: Yes, I felt the need to create a space, where the anxiety and fear caused by the diagnosis of a terminal illness and its implications could be expressed, talked about, explored openly. My aim was to make a piece that transformed the silence, isolation and emotional pain of this very personal 'life-changing' experience into a work of art that resonated with others. Throughout her illness and diagnosis I tried to face the reality of what was happening, as far as I could, with her – a sort of mirroring. This became a theme of the piece where the brain – which is divided in two halves by a longitudinal fissure – was a symbol of two sisters fissured by the death of one of them. I wanted to try and understand what had happened to my sister physically and metaphys-ically. That's why I worked with neurologists, including Michael Brada who told us that my sister's condition was terminal and so delivered the worst news imaginable – in *Fissure*, death arrived suddenly, on a train, dressed in a suit singing 'One Day You'll Fall' – and neuro-surgeon Andy McEvoy, who I observed and recorded performing brain surgery. Seeing this, and the material of the brain and a tumour, answered my need to understand some of what had happened to her and took away the fear.

JM: It also goes beyond an emotional connection; understanding that we're simply flesh and bone at a material level, something of the natural world.

LAW: The idea of making *Fissure* a walking performance came about because I wanted to create a space where my family could talk about the loss of my sister – which we were struggling to know how to do. From that first impulse, the piece gradually evolved. Initially it was going to involve two separate audiences walking from different sides of the country, following a river-route that traced the sea back to its source, where they would join and become one whole group. This idea gradually focused down to an area of hills, streams and rivers in the Yorkshire Dales, a landscape my family knows well, and I began collaborating with the choreographer Nigel Stewart, writer Elizabeth Burns and composer Jocelyn Pook to evolve an interdisciplinary piece that attempted to find a language, where few exist, for death and grief.

JM: It's a cultural problem. Many western rituals for death are about hiding it; the fleshly connection with death is lost, unlike those communities and cultures where the body is present with the family, part of life. We're lacking in the 'everydayness' of dealing with death; another example of removing our connection with all things natural, understanding how we're part of natural cycles.

LAW: Yes, we've become afraid of death and our own mortality and materiality; we walked through landscape where the limestone beneath our feet, which is made from the shells of millions of sea creatures, and the skulls of dead sheep that I gathered and placed amongst the stones of a cairn began to speak of our transience; we are here for just a brief moment in time.

JM: How far is collaboration, particularly in relation to the written, spoken and aural element in your work, central to your concept and key to the wider experience of the work?

LAW: wilson+wilson predominantly worked with poets because they're less bound by the established structures of playwriting. With some site-specific or visual work, the spoken word can be a weak aspect and it was important to us that all the creative elements were equally strong. In *House* we collaborated with Simon Armitage; his poetry interwove with the other art-forms in such a way that a non-linear, multidisciplinary language and narrative developed that worked fragmentally. I asked Elizabeth Burns to write for *Fissure* because, in her existing poetry, she'd imagined the death of her sister and how terrible that would be, and how interconnected they are, which she refers to as telepathy. She uses language like it's colour, making her writing beautifully evocative, like you're stepping into a painting. *Fissure* had two sisters at its core and I wanted them to be performed abstractly through dance, but rather than having two dancers, who might be seen as representational, I worked with six who became interchangeable. I made the decision that all of the poetry would be sung and Jocelyn set Elizabeth's words to music. Interwoven through the piece were the words spoken about neurology and geology. *Jack Scout* was performed by two dancers, two musicians, and a guide whose words were honed down to the essentials in order that the spoken word didn't dominate; instead, dance, live-art installations, sound, music and the environment were all equally layered. I'm now interested in making work with little or no speech or text; I've just created *Ghost Bird*, a silent walk and Live Art installation in the Trough of Bowland which developed the scenographic and visual language of my work.

JM: *The fusion of all of the elements in your work is getting to something essential about those experiences that you've researched. Perhaps that's why you're moving towards the body. Would you expand on how the human body is significant to your work, including the perceiving body?*

LAW: Following *Fissure*, I'm interested in exploring ways to investigate and metaphorically emplace the 'interior landscape' of the human body within the physical 'exterior landscapes'. I work with materials and phenomena of what a place or landscape affords – the indigenous, in relation to the performer and the audience: a singer's voice echoing in a cave passage; the sound of rain on a tin roof of a barn and the glow of a peat fire on a pregnant dancer's body heard and seen inside; a trace of heather placed in the cracks of a dry-stone wall shooting butt, inside which a naked person is curled up; a dancer emerging from a cave passage, causing the water inside to gloop; and skylarks underscoring the gentle chatter of resting walkers lying in a meadow of flowers. The work fully immerses the audience in many different ways – the sensory, spatial, artistic, scientific, emotional and physical – audience members can navigate through these different aspects in a way that suits them. To an extent, they construct their experience. I like to take people into places and environments that they might not normally visit, into the unexpected yet still everyday. I've been learning to bell-ring and I'm creating a piece in the extraordinary/ordinary world of the church bell-tower; another on a sheep farm where, in the same shed, lambs are born and dead lambs are skinned – everyday activities on a farm that we rarely see.

JM: *Worlds that have their own particular aesthetic, choreography, environment, which we don't know unless we're involved with them.*

LAW: By taking audiences into these worlds and placing the 'real' and the 'everyday' next to the scientific, the artistic, and the poetic, it creates a place for revelation and transformation.

JM: *In choosing to work with poets and dancers it feels like you're wanting to get to something essential, to the core of the subject; to relay a strong impression of it* and *interrogate the experience of it, in its simplest or most distilled form.*

LAW: I think so. It's the juxtaposition and joining-up of each distilled element that makes them powerful and revealing; hearing a neuro-physicist lecture on how he creates cartographic maps by mapping the water in the brain, followed by a geologist describing how the water-filled cave passages you're looking into have been created by water, then seeing two dancers emerge, physically struggle up, from that same passage. It's how I layer the neurological, geological, sung word, dance, visual image – each a poetic fragment of the whole – into one sculpture, that makes the work what it is.

JM: *How is* Fissure *exemplary of your particular style of immersive practice, and an illustration of all your work to date; especially in that you've just referred to it as 'sculpture'?*

LAW: Immersion through walking, distance, and duration are particular features of my work. The audience, or participants, are asked to arrive in a particular place – often they will have travelled and planned just to get there and, from that moment, they'll be taken on a journey requiring them to focus on where they are and leave their busy, often urban, lives and worries behind. They become immersed, step-by-step into the world of the piece. In *Fissure* the collective experience was important to ensure participants didn't experience that physically and emotionally challenging piece alone. At the end, after three days, they were safely deposited back in the 'real' world and their journeys home allowed time to fully emerge from the piece. Responses showed deeply felt memories and impressions stayed with them long after the event. The interdisciplinary forms, the landscape, the walking and the overarching dramaturgy – all of which were informed by rites of passage and religious rituals – came together in a way that felt absolutely right for *Fissure*. It became a pilgrimage.

JM: *Walking is now an artistic language. There are Walking Artists groups creating art, philosophising around art, located around walking or through walking locations. I wonder if that's about making us reconnect with the wider world, with each other, with ourselves, with our 'presentness'.*

LAW: Yes I think so and perhaps that's why people undertake pilgrimages; walking can be a solitary or communal activity, a place to be quiet or talk, but you have to be present. Increasingly I'm making work that is off the beaten-track and that takes participants to places that are challenging and difficult to get to, physically and metaphorically; where the difficult journey embodies journeys through difficult life-events. I remember and can feel *Fissure* in my body and the route under my feet, as we talk about it now. I know how and where to place my feet in a certain terrain; I know which bits are hard, where the wind blows in a particular way. But, as you say, it is much more than a physical journey alone – it's deeply engaged.

JM: *That bodily memory we have of walking, not only does the physical impact of the work remain with you in a very different way to work that you might receive 'intellectually', it also plays beautifully as a metaphor for ideas traversed; you navigate the ideas and hold onto them as a bodily memory.*

LAW: The physical journey the audience will take is one of the first things I develop but during the actual event I don't step into their experience, I step back to hold the space, so that they can enter in and become immersed.

Bill Mitchell and Sue Hill of WildWorks

Immersive communitas – space, place and people

Bill Mitchell: Immersive is an interesting term, it's not one we used, it's come up recently. Way back, we started working with community theatres and TIE companies, talking to people, working up stories with people from scratch. We didn't do extant scripts; everything came from us. Because of the nature of the work we were working very closely with our audiences – being interactive was part-and-parcel of everything. Skipping forward to the Kneehigh years, Sue started this process of taking small groups of audiences through the woods –

Sue Hill: – called 'Wild Walks', where the audience is moving rather than settled –

BM: – and 'immersive' would have been a really good title had we thought of it. We called it 'Landscape Theatre'. It was an idea to work on the beach or work in a quarry, find out what that gave us. As a designer I'm used to working in that way, whether it's from a text or from a space, you can gradually work out the narrative. We called this Landscape Theatre, because the world was given us. We used to describe it as filming without cameras.

SH: The audience becomes the camera because you're taking the audience's attention and finding ways in which you focus it on certain things or certain actions, which then help you tell the story. You end up talking about the work in film terminology; long-shot or close-up. In a black-box theatre you've got lights to tell the audience where to look, what's important. If you work in the open landscape you've got this incredible panorama, but how does the audience know where the story is, where the close-ups are? You can put somebody half a mile away on a hilltop, with a flaming torch but *they've* got to find it. The idea of the audience being a camera became a significant thing.

BM: The very first time it happened to me, on a show, outside, landscapey. There was a really interesting cliff that dropped down, there was this long road and an old dynamite works. I remember I couldn't move the audience that much, but I could bring the audience up to the edge of the cliff and they could look down. There happened to be a lump of corrugated iron so I said, 'put some rope on it, put some rocks on it and drag it from as far away as you can'. With the real sound of dragging corrugated iron, you suddenly feel that everything is then yours; the sea, the horizon-line, the cliffs, all this becomes part of the world; you could hold an audience's attention far longer outside.

SH: There were some key moments where things changed for us. When we first started working with Kneehigh we were making work indoors, in village halls. That step of making work outside and discovering a whole load of new toys – we could play with fire, we could play with distance, we could play with sunset, with water. There was one particular Wild Walk piece on a beach on the North Coast of Cornwall [*Ghost Nets*] and, as part of the show, the company would run into the sea, pull out the nets and harvest a catch. One night, where the tide was a lot further out, we ended up running for a long way and we found the audience was running with us. We reached the sea and some of them actually came into the sea. We hadn't done that hideous, 'now it's your turn to do this', they had volunteered themselves into our world. It was such an intensely interesting thing, that somehow we'd created a world that was strong enough that they felt they could inhabit it without breaking any rules or without behaving in a way where they had to 'perform', they were still an audience. That has become part of the journey for us; how do you create a world that's strong enough, in which the audience knows how to behave, they know what's expected of them so that they can be more interactive than they would be if they were in a conventional theatre situation?

BM: From my background as a designer, having real things to play with is rather wonderful but it's what it does to an audience; it does *change* them. If you know what the ritual of theatre is; you go into the dark and you sit there and of course you're transported but physically there's a degree of comfort, you know what the focus is, it's a set-up that doesn't have to be explained to you. As soon as you put an audience in a situation where they're waiting on a cliff-edge or they're waiting on one side of a wall to go into a deserted department store, there's an element of anticipation and –

SH: – anxiety –

BM: – because people don't know what the rules are, they're already in the moment, waiting for everything. One of the things we've found, it's one of our tenets now, we don't overdo, don't have to put everything there, we choose the clues that we want to give for that world, all they need is the smallest hint and encouragement and they work it out for themselves. That receptivity, the space that we can create with this type of work, I find the most fascinating thing; it's a really interesting place for audiences to *imagine*, to have to work out what's real and not real. It's probably the thing I enjoy most, certainly most consistently. When we were doing *The Passion*, all of us in some odd way had lost contact with quite what was real and what wasn't real. For us and for the audience; they were engaged in a way I've not seen before, it was like being part of a sports event, being part of something where you don't know the end of it, what's going to happen next.

SH: There was one long scene on Good Friday; the story was that the town was being occupied by this force that was run by the corporation, ICU, the scene where the Chief Executive is addressing the town and telling them his plans for Port Talbot and there's a group of community members who've been enrolled as insurgents, who are starting the chant and then you hear the rest of the audience joining in with the chant. Later on a member of this insurgent crew is shot, very close up to members of the audience, and caught by Michael [Sheen], cradled by him. The palpable shock of being that close to that violence, people were really angry and upset. We'd been working with a women's refuge and they didn't want to be part of the performance activity but they wanted to contribute to the event, so they made a shrine that was placed at the site of the shooting. People had said, 'that will've gone by the morning, people will've taken the teddy bears', but the next morning, there were more things there not less, the community had added to it. People feel they can, that they own it enough to be able to contribute to it.

BM: The thing that makes our work distinctive and why I think it's such an interesting form is the way we include the people of the place. There was a sort of a click with Malta [*A Very Old Man With Enormous Wings: 3 Island Project* (2003)] where we were in an urban situation for the first time, given a site that was a town. We were immersed in the people of that landscape, surrounded by people who were wondering who we were and what our role was. Our instinct was, we want to work with you, we want you to tell us your story.

SH: What happens in these moments is a thread will arrive that then finds its place in later projects. So this thread, which started in Malta, was how do you really listen to a community? How do you find ways in which they can tell you their deepest feelings?

BM: We're not parachuting in, bringing a show.

SH: We had to really, genuinely attend to them. Mercedes [Kemp] came up with this wonderful idea of, bring me your photographs, bring me your ephemera, bring me the programmes for the boat races – we're strangers here, aliens – bring us the things that are important, the memories. That thread of memory has been a really strong theme and we've found other ways of harvesting it. In *Souterrain* we worked with a local artist, Sue Craig, and she'd been using tea parties as a way of encouraging people to come and play. So tea and cake have become a very powerful form of generosity from us to a community – we haven't very much to give you other than our ears and cake.

BM: There's a real value in being a foolish artist. Being somewhere that you don't know, it's a lovely relationship, because we need help, it's a way into a community. We did it with the foothills of *BABEL*; the company were introduced to all sorts of quirky individuals. The chat started with, we're from Cornwall, how does the city work? And people tell you; they'll tell you about certain areas that they're slightly fearful of but they'll also tell you the wonder. People are very generous. As with Malta, when people bring photographs in, they're bringing their families to meet you, though they might be long dead, and they're also bringing their values. That relationship informed a lot of that work. A lot of our work is honouring the past and looking ahead –

SH: – imagining a future.

BM: So immersion is interesting. The form is so young, a number of words can describe it.

JM: Yet elements of the form are ancient, the ideas around participatory practice have existed as religious festivals and ceremonial pageants for years and years. Of course current practice is defined by intention, by a crafting of that form.

SH: In terms of the craft of it there are some skills that we've developed related to how you take an audience on that journey without puncturing the world. It's very easy to behave in a way that turns them back into passive receivers rather than active participants. We tend not to have stewards, or if we have stewards their role is a safety-net way back from the action. The people who are actually guiding, acting as stewards, are there in role as angels and they're finding ways in which to help the audience to follow the story, to get to the places they need to get to, without any 'walk this way madam'. We create opportunities for the audience to intuit where they should be next; you might hear a distant saxophone, that's where your attention is drawn, there's a pathway and you know to go there or there might be a string of bunting so you follow that. Finding ways that the audience can be as self-navigated as possible. Community members will often become these angels, we find ways in which we enrol them so that they understand how they can support the audience's experience. It's quite a delicate skill.

BM: It takes time because you aren't just trying to build up the trust of the company to make a piece of work, you're having to develop the idea of what that company is. So you've got ripples going out and everybody has to trust everybody else; it's to do with ownership. We will lead the process, we're very clear about that but it's like a catalyst; we don't fully understand what happens –

SH: – and we don't know what the destination is, what it's going to look like when it's finished.

BM: What happens is a lot of the time the process has pulled something up, caused something to happen which wasn't of our making. Our intention is to work honestly with people, to build up trust and mutual generosity, make the best piece of work we can. What's amazing to me is the things that come out of it and the new connections and friendships that happen, new ideas that arise when we've gone. That's not necessarily everybody's goal with this sort of work, but it is one of ours. We've done it for long enough to realise that, you go into an area, into a community and work with them for as long as we do, there is a fair bit of responsibility at the end of that, it can't just be, oh well, we're not there anymore. Somehow all of that has to be looked after.

JM: Other contributors that I've spoken with have talked about the creative exchange that occurs and how immersive practice is democratic in form; learning occurs for the practitioners; community members come to see themselves as artists; and there's something in the ownership of material and the respect for space and place. Could you expand on the relationship that you build with audiences? You've talked of the codes of conduct, the clear boundaries you set and the shaping of a safe space in which the participants might immerse themselves. How do those unspoken contracts influence the form of the work as much as they provide a methodology for practice for you? Secondly the way in which you interact with the audience is like choreography so how does that also shape the form? Both strategies serve to ignite the audience imagination.

BM: Having a contract with the audience is really important for them to get the best out of it and to have some sort of rigour or discipline as the performance goes round. A lot of the time it can be quite hard to see and hear so you have to get just a simple contract across, which is, 'this will move around so be active, move into the right place. Curiosity will be rewarded.' What we try and do now is build that as much as we can into the start of the piece because the audience need to feel safe in the space they're in. In terms of their imagination, there's interest and there's danger and there's an adventure. We use their curiosity. Once you've found the site, you have to find a route and it has to be the right route; once you know the site and the route they tell you so much.

SH: Physical spaces change audiences in very powerful ways. You compress an audience by putting them in an enclosed space and you allow them to breathe by putting them into an open space. The opening and closing of space, at its most basic level, or the lightening and darkening of space, changes an audience so powerfully. The site tells us what the story is and the physical change of spaces influences the way in which an audience can *be* with itself; if you end up taking them down a long narrow path, they're going to get spread out, they're going to have a more solitary experience. It also means that the end of that, the first cohort of the audience will be waiting for the rest to catch up, so another element of the story needs to happen there that can busk until everybody arrives. So there are technical things about the way an audience physically behaves alongside the emotional state space puts it in. We're very interested in concealment. When you're looking at a site, it's lovely to have the big view but you also want to have the element of surprise, you want to be able to turn a corner, so enclosure or compression or screening becomes really important in order to articulate a story that isn't all immediately visible. We're passionate about narrative and for narrative to work you need to have a curiosity about what happens next.

BM: We're describing the physical journey but there's also the emotional journey we want to take the audience on. Quite early on – and this is something to do with a methodology – we realised that audiences always start off as voyeurs, coming in to watch something. Everything that we've described so far helps an audience walk along, wonder what's going to happen next, start to get involved in characters. With *A Very Old Man*, where people needed to be part of a village, they started off looking at the village, wondering who's in there, what are the relationships. After a while, they feel like they're so much part of the village they can be addressed as the village, they can be involved in it. We've stumbled upon things because we thought they were interesting things to do in order to tell the story, but then we realise the power of them in themselves. In *Souterrain* you reach a point where Eurydice has been lost into the underworld, the audience have chosen to go into the underworld, and to them at this stage, it's a game. But then we introduce the idea of Lethe, the River of Forgetting in the underworld, which becomes a dramatic point because if Eurydice reaches Lethe, she will lose her memory and that means Orpheus may never get her again. We always found our Lethe, sometimes it literally was a stream, sometimes something else but we would find the point of water and washing, where all your memories would disappear, the pool of oblivion. And of course the audience is on their way to Lethe too. Because memory is so much part of what we do, we thought wouldn't it be wonderful if people wrote down their most important memory to leave here. It was an innocent story point when it started – 35,000 or so of these things later, some in English, some in French, we have this archive, which Mercedes now calls 'The Archive of the Human Heart', because people are so honest. There were categories to help frame the memory –

SH: – we had luggage labels with one question on each, and there were six different questions; what does your heart want to remember?; what do your eyes want to remember?; what do your hands want to remember?; what does your heart want to forget?; what do your eyes want to forget?; what do your hands want to forget?

BM: Some of the answers were funny, some of them were direct, some of them were really powerful. In itself, it was a powerful thing, in the context of that show it was fundamental, because after that people were engaged to a level I've never felt before. Similarly with *The Passion*, they fully got behind it with a couple of triggers that go so deep that you're no longer watching it from the outside –

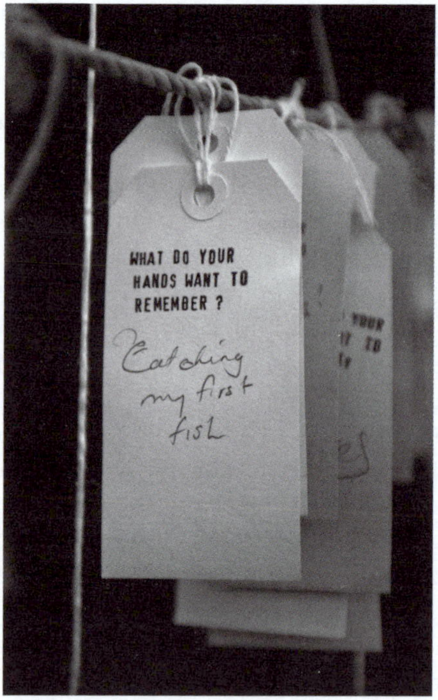

Illustration 22 WildWorks' *Souterrain* (2007). 'Memories: The Archive of the Human Heart'

[Photo credit: Steve Tanner. Image courtesy of WildWorks and Steve Tanner]

JM*: – you're in it and not just in the narrative of the event but immersed in the concept, the themes –*

BM: – absolutely immersed in the emotional world. You've effectively become a character in there because you've contributed something of yourself. This is pretty profound stuff. We don't always get that right but we are always looking for that moment. I've seen it in a number of our shows where we've achieved an emotional arc where people go, *now* I feel it, this is happening to *me*.

SH: So people are physically immersed; in the space, enabled to be part of the physical world and then there's the emotional immersion, which often happens as a result of one particular question, activity or moment where people are offered the opportunity to dive into it, place themselves in it.

JM: Could we talk in more depth about 'landscape theatre' and your very strong focus on place as much as space; place and its inherent politics. Expanding on what you were just saying, I'm interested in the idea of immersing yourself in the political as much as the historical and emotional, which are fused in the landscape. Specifically in terms of the histories and authenticity of voices in a place. It's what you've described, Bill, as the 'warp and weft' that's worked into the fabric of each piece combined with the idea of space, site, becoming 'both script and stage'.

BM: I think it's a really interesting and complex area. I'm a designer so I think of 'worlds' when imagining spaces. When we started working outside you've got riches; the whole sky to play with, a whole beach to play with, light – a very old thing, Shakespeare wrote his plays around the fading of the light – so did we.

SH: Stories that went into darkness.

JM: Practical and also elemental.

BM: For me, as a designer, place and object are really important things and it's good to make a bridge between that and people, human emotions. Early on, we were looking for the right places and listening to those places. For instance, we were asked to do it [*A Very Old Man With Enormous Wings*] in Cyprus and there was a whole debate about where we could do it; people showed us potential sites, beautiful places. To understand the island we were also shown the Green Line, through Nicosia, so you start to understand Cyprus as two 'Cypruses' that are at war with each other and that there's a wall and it's about territory. In being asked to create something about Cyprus I felt absolutely compelled to do it there, rather than on the beautiful beach we were being offered as a site. This simple story suddenly starts to *mean* more; it becomes more than theatre. It felt like the right place to do it, it felt like we should have people in it from both sides of that divide – as well as Maltese, as well as Cornish players – and to bring in audiences from both sides. We set our partners in the project the massive task of trying to nail this project in this site and to waive a whole load of border issues so that people could come together. That piece of work, although it was the same story we did in Cornwall and in Malta, it had a different meaning there, it resonated the themes of that conflict. So the site tells a story, it gives you the emotional narrative and sometimes, choosing the right place, not deliberately putting it in a 'place of politics' but putting it in an area that has tensions, makes the meaning more profound.

SH: It's not judgemental, in no sense is it making a recommendation about what people's actions should be, it's not saying this is right and that's wrong. When we go to a place we are very accepting of what is, rather than trying to force an issue, it's never political in that campaign sense, it's more about trying to tease out the meanings and what the relationships are.

JM: And how do you feel the form allows that?

SH: It's less focused on text. As soon as you commit stuff to text, it makes things very explicit. We use a lot of words but it's not in the form of dialogue; there's a lot of poetic text that becomes part of the work, but it's much more rooted in imagery and sound and music than in narrative text.

BM: Practically it's much more difficult to rely on text to tell a story because if it's windy you can't hear it.

SH: But it's not just about audibility; as part of *The Passion*, we'd written this whole scene that took place in the slipway that was written like a traditional piece of theatre and at part of it you could feel the audience not wanting to be bothered with it; it was beautiful text but the way in which an audience receives words outdoors is *just different*. We haven't abandoned words but we've tried to work with them as they behave; they're a different kind of animal so you use them for lyric quality or emotional content rather than trying to tell a story or to elucidate a character. Work that's based more on visual imagery and music crosses boundaries of culture and language. People from different cultural backgrounds can be witnessing it and they'll bring their own experience to bear. Anyone going on the journey of a show with us will be making their own show, telling their own story, because of the things that are being put to them. They're active in that sense as well, which means that they're not in receipt of a manifesto, they're forming the experience.

BM: Trusting that people will pick up narrative in a number of different ways. Music is massively important because it will change mood. Leaving space is important, for people just to *be* somewhere and reflect and read what's around them, because the site is so important. If you work against the site then you have so much more work to do and also you're fairly foolish. If you're working *with* the site, then you can rely on the audience to pick up the atmosphere of that space. With Cyprus, you're in a place that's got a border control right next to you, barbed wire all around you, yet we don't refer to it in the piece. We rarely tell the actual story of the place that we're in; it's more of a *feeling* of the place. You heighten the reality because you've got so much 'reality' there, you can use it as a springboard to tell another story; so a man will fly or a man will be nailed to a cross and *that* becomes as real as everything else. It's like some chemical equation, some alchemy happens.

JM: Something that's clear in your work is the fusion of the epic and the intimate, as with The Enchanted Palace, *it's the idea of encountering lived histories, personal histories within a larger social history. You allow very intimate stories to connect with grand narratives; a person might be having a personal, playful experience in a room full of toy soldiers, but in the same moment that makes wider connections with ideas around war, power, class and children playing at war, adults playing at soldiers whilst real wars are waged across oceans.*

SH: We're looking for that in the sites. The place will allow you to make both intimate and epic encounters. We use proxies; in *The Beautiful Journey* there's a point in the event where a ton of ice is landed, a huge lump of real ice is craned out of the dock and into the space where the audience is. Six hundred members of the audience can't touch the ice but ten children can, and there's a lovely thing which happens where you have this extraordinary image, a crane lifting this huge piece of ice out of the sea, dripping with water and it's beautifully lit and you can see the audience thinking it's a fibreglass prop until the first child puts its hand on it and gasps; something so personal, intimate happens yet the whole audience has the experience of it (see Illustration 23). These are ways in which you can give people a sense of their connection to it. It's the hardest thing we do; how do you enable 600 people or a 1000 people or 12,000 people to feel they've had a personal experience?

JM: And there's something in that related to the sensory experience.

BM: A lot of the early work was intimate, certainly in the woods; you're working very close to people, it's interactive, you get people involved. Our work started out valuing the role of interactivity and intimacy. As

Illustration 23 WildWorks' *The Beautiful Journey* **(2009) Newcastle upon Tyne. 'The ice arrives'. Performer: Mae Voogd**

[Photo credit: Steve Tanner. Image courtesy of WildWorks and Steve Tanner]

we developed and the work demanded bigger audiences, we ended up doing more epic things. If you have a landscape or docks to play in you need a number of people to convince an audience that this place is populated, has a cross-section of the world in it. Then, with the beautiful and poetic images, you need to fill that space in different ways; you hang something from a crane and so on. At the same time, one of the things we held onto was not wanting to lose the intimate, so we found ways, as Sue described, of making sure that becomes true.

SH: It's worth qualifying that epic doesn't just mean spectacle. With Kneehigh we would tour to theatre festivals and we would see endless amounts of extraordinary spectacle that was simply like firework displays, beautiful but no content. The thing about 'epic' work is it's spectacular but it also has powerful meaning.

JM: In relation to landscape, I'm always very aware that if I attend to my experience of space, in one and the same moment I'm aware of the vastness, the power of the environment, the distance my eye can extend – which can happen as much in the city as it does in open countryside – yet attention is

also drawn to my intimate relationship with it, what I can smell, touch, the
surroundings with which I'm immediately in contact.

SH: Yes, and this relates back to what I was saying earlier, there's also something about your connection with time. We're working with people's consciousness about their relationship with the place in terms of time. Bill grew up in the city and has an urban experience of place which is fast-changing and ephemeral, and I grew up in Cornwall, a mining area which, essentially, is a manmade landscape but set in wildness and incredible sea and cliffs; with a sense of deep connection, back through generations, a sense that people have inhabited this place before me and had touched it in the same ways I'm touching it. Earlier when you talked of the way in which we're working in a framework that has historical precedence, there's a form we've used several times now where we create a ring of performance space. With *A Very Old Man with Enormous Wings* it was the village; the houses were raised performance spaces and the audience was in the middle, completely surrounded by performance. In *The Beautiful Journey*, the shanty was all round the audience. We didn't really clock until later that this is the ancient Cornish form of theatre; the 'plen an gwarries', the playing area is a 'bund', a big bank, and the audience is in the middle, heaven is on one side and hell is on the other and the performance happens all the way round the outside of the audience. In this sense, we're treading on territory that has already been explored which fascinates me.

JM: It suggests that it's innate; that there's something elemental in it. It's interesting that you bring us to time because I'd like to discuss duration, which is a key part of your practice in two ways; in terms of the actual experience of the event, however long that performance might be; and in terms of you creating an event that journeys across its own distinct time and across lands; this involves an additional idea of duration in terms of the life that continues after the event. There's a fusion of past, present and future in your work, which is very powerful.

SH: In terms of what happens after we've gone, we're very interested in the stories that communities tell about themselves. We're taking stories that have happened before we've arrived, so the memories, the stories of a place become part of the event, then the stories that people tell about themselves after we've gone become different stories.

Hayle in Cornwall, where we did *A Very Old Man With Enormous Wings*, which is a funny little Cinderella town to its more glamorous sister St Ives; a post-industrial town, constantly waiting for this promise of regeneration and redevelopment that never happens. The fact that for one summer, an angel flew above their town is now part of the narrative that they tell about the place. Those threads feed back and become part of the warp and weft of that community's thought (see Illustration 4).

BM: We make a heightened world, it's not what you see every day, particularly as it goes through into night and we use lighting to heighten the beauty of the place. With *Souterrain*, people were maybe completely blasé or negative about where they lived, but then became incredibly proud of where they lived, this show was pulling people in who had never seen this place looking like this before. *Souterrain* typifies what you're talking about. The big story is; whether it's Cornwall or elsewhere, we've met tin miners, all sorts of people, who identified, described themselves through the work they did, yet typically, in Western Europe, that's gone. So when we're offered a site, it's usually in one of those places –

SH: – a place that has lost its original meaning –

BM: – usually the people are aware that some sort of construction company is going to come in and build a marina or a casino, everyone has heard these rumours, or that nothing is going to happen and nobody knows what the future holds. The thing about *Souterrain* that makes it exemplary is the personal stories that ran through the middle of it, about death and grieving for something that has gone, looking at the stages of grief that people have to go through in order to come out the other end. *Souterrain* was a ritual, hung on the Eurydice story. We took a character through every one of those stages of grief and therefore every audience member went through that too; some of them funny, some of them achingly beautiful some of them incredibly sad. Yet it was also referring to Sue's loss, she'd lost both her parents within a month as we were preparing for that show. So we understood the emotional heart of it but you could also expand it to each larger context; this particular tin mine has gone, this area of Cornwall is going through a similar process, or the whole of Cornwall is going through it, because each is trying to understand how it handles it. Therefore, from the very specific you go right the way through to the universal.

SH: It also relates to the work I've been involved in at the Eden Project. When a regeneration company moves into a failing, economically challenged area, the first thing it often does is build things, a new college or a road or factories. We started to explore the idea that the engine of regeneration is the stories that people tell about themselves. It's true of health as well. Stroke-victims who tell stories about themselves that accept the stroke – the story is about meeting the challenge and becoming a new person – will do better than the person who tells the story of themselves being a victim. The narrative becomes the important engine of change. At Eden, Dr Tony Kendle was using *Souterrain* specifically as an example of the way in which a community can start to tell a different story about itself. You can tell a story that honours the past without being helpless about it. This loops back to our past practice and the fact that we're both socialists and, without being evangelical or missionary about it, we want to have an effect, to have agency. The sense of agency that we have expresses itself through how we find ways in which people can tell new stories about themselves that are supporting and healthier.

JM: That's also a great way of thinking about the epic and the intimate; understanding that the personal is political. Equally, the way that you were just thinking about grief expands on the epic within the intimate; it's an archetypal emotion that enables you to understand the idea of the heroic within the everyday, in struggling through the overwhelming impact of grief, knowing you will come out the other side and will be stronger for it –

SH: – recognising that it will be one of the most important experiences of your life. It's a primary life experience that has moments of absolute wonder and beauty, where you feel yourself changing into a different creature and that's part of your life's journey –

JM: – it's mythical –

SH: – mythical and an important thing to do; you have to live it and not deny it. Apply that to a community undergoing change and the meta-text for it is: this is something that's powerful for you if you look it in the eye and live it. Honour what is gone, make space to value it, then look to the future, see what's coming over the horizon and shape yourself for it. The hero of the everyday, that's a lovely way of expressing it.

255

JM: What you give people with your work is a sense of seeing the everyday as the magical, the mythical and the imaginative, so the space they're in becomes something special, becomes part of a bigger history.

BM: With *The Enchanted Palace* we found the princesses stories particularly moving. Think of them as human beings going through something extraordinary; that's worth sharing. The emotional journey should be, whether it's conscious or not, that you feel like you don't belong to this place, you're not quite sure where you are, whether this is yours or not. The emotional arc is that you begin looking at it like a stranger but by the end you've played in there, you've sat on a knitted throne with knitted crown jewels; you can have a knitted coronation.

SH: We worked with fashion designers and, rather than giving them a worthy brief, we gave them a kind of jackdaw pack, so they had a list of possible dress titles; 'a dress for dancing all night in the woods without permission'; 'a dress to hide beauty', provocations so that they had as much of an imaginative springboard as possible rather than us cramping their style. We also wrote a list for ourselves of all the things you're not supposed to do in a palace and then we tried to do all of them.

BM: *The Passion* was one of the most ephemeral works, each scene was only played once, it was really powerful for people, a big thing in the life of that town. After three days it was gone and people were left reeling from it, it was such an intense experience. This Easter they want to get back together again to mark it, so the people of the town are coming together with the National Theatre of Wales to build a memory palace of *The Passion* and people can come in, can talk about what it meant to them, their memories of the day, what's happened to them since; a lot of organisations and groups have sprung up as a consequence, people attending to their place in a different way.

JM: Which goes beyond a simple exercise of giving people activities to engage in, it's the sense of being so marked by something that it continues to live and people are compelled to illustrate that in concrete ways. Would you summarise, then, what you consider to be the key elements in your work that define the particular 'immersivity' of WildWorks.

BM: For me it would be involving people – audience, participants and us – in a world that evolves and where we share a moment that's uniquely special. We were trying to define legacy for *BABEL* and when we asked about the city, almost every borough did this, in Newham alone there's 120 different languages, cultures from all over the world and we, in our innocence, asked where they 'talked', where did those groups come together? We started to make maps, maps of love, of grief, of celebration. One of the areas where people came together was around disaster, where people who would not normally talk are impelled to have conversation. I would love the work to be about something that's so particular, it's more than theatre, something we share has happened that you can't help talking about, even if it's difficult because you don't share a language, so you just make eye contact, you feel like you need to keep talking about it. Something about the work is then amplified; the truths, the memories, the values are heightened, which means that you don't quite know whether it's real or not.

SH: If I had to track the essence of the process, it's not having too much prediction about what you'll find; to be open-eyed, open-eared and open-hearted about what is really there. Most artistic processes try to close the doors quite quickly, close down the options, but Bill leaves all the doors banging open until quite near the end, which is quite frightening for people used to working in a more closely constructed way. It's a very porous process, things can come into it very easily, it's very open; you might be working with students and one of them brings something in which has a particular resonance and it can become part of the piece because you haven't closed your mind or the doors to things. That's a very important thing that the process is very accepting of what is given. We artists that work on it become the truffle hunters, rooting around, finding treasure that becomes part of the work. It then has authenticity; finding ways in which you can really attend to the place and really attend to the people of the place, then condensing all that into a powerful elixir which becomes enlarged into the event, going with the grain rather than trying to make something happen.

BM: If you're a control freak you really shouldn't work with this form. You need to work with what *is*, rather than what you want it to be. Bad weather for an audience *and* the story is magnificent because you have that sense of communion, you're in this together, you know you're in the same world.

SH: Like with *A Very Old Man With Enormous Wings* [Hayle, 2005], at the point where the money is pouring into the village and everything is fabulous and the sun is going down and sparkling on the sea and it's wonderful, then, as the second half progresses and things get darker and darker literally and emotionally and the village is shattering, halfway through this second act the biggest rainstorm happens, the sky is literally weeping and you know that that audience has had the most intense experience that we could possibly make for them, with the help of the climate. You have to treat that as a gift; it's not going to happen every night but the ones that have that experience know they're receiving something special.

BM: One of the things I learnt from Kneehigh, which is to do with the French training [of Jacques Lecoq], anything that happens is a gift and you go with it. That's a fundamental thing that goes all the way through our work. Now we're working with communities, somebody reminded me that community means gift –

SH: – 'together in gift'[1] –

BM: – we give and people give back and mutually the work is made.

JM: Why all the wings, the presence of flight in all of your works? Even in The Enchanted Palace, *the hundreds of paper birds that make up Victoria's dress and the sweeping flight of Vivienne Westwood's dress, all of these are suggestive of flights of freedom, flights of the imagination.*

BM: It *is* about freedom and flight – flights of fancy, flights of the imagination – and it's something in the ritual of it. A lot of the time it's in the stories that we choose – any of the Greek myths – we end up with the Hermes character in so many shows. It's a mutual interest [within the creative team] in magical realism.

SH: It flows through naturalism, through the domestic.

BM: That's why I love where you get a gritty mining site, with barbed wire and a boarded-up gate, and it's difficult to work your way through, and then you see something fly and you question whether it's real or not. I think that's a really interesting, creative place to be, a place that artists are in a lot of the time but it's wonderful that you can bring an audience into it. That's been there since the earliest days, from walking through the woods where we had altered and added certain things.

After a while, if it's an attentive audience, everything they see they think it's significant –

SH: – a log in a lake becomes a crocodile because of a previous installation –

BM: – it's an interesting world where you can imagine and create when you're in that state.[2]

Conversations five

Adrian Howells

The epic in the intimate

Adrian Howells: Touch is something that is much more acquainted with and has become associated with the work that I do; through the three years of my Creative Fellowship at Glasgow University and since. Over the next two years, during my artist's residency with The Arches at TouchBase, I'm going to be exploring it even more. I'm really interested in touch-based and non-verbal communication. I'm going to be creating two projects over a two-year period that will definitely be interactive and experiential as opposed to spectatorial. I don't like spectatorial performance because I think that it encourages judgement. I've done a workshop this week with post-grads at the Royal Scottish Academy of Music and Drama and there was a stunning realisation from everybody in the room between two exercises; one when we were all sat in a circle and [the participants] introduced themselves and completed statements, 'intimacy is...' and then, 'a significant moment of intimacy in my life has been...'. After that we went into a semi-circle and I placed a chair in the centre. Randomly, when they wanted to, they could come and sit in the chair and complete a statement which started, 'I am...', which could be anything about themselves, something autobiographical, revelatory, they were in control of the degree of how exposing that might be. What was very interesting after this exercise was the number of voices saying how the tone had completely changed; how a lot of people had started to become dramatic in what they were saying to impress other people. What had started to happen was people were making judgements about what people did or said when they sat in this chair. That didn't happen when we were all sat in the circle together because we were all participants, there wasn't an audience and somebody performing.

That spectatorial arrangement encourages judgement. That for me was a crystal clear re-emphasis of something that I had already known; I do not want to put individuals from TouchBase in that setting – and not from the idea of 'velvet oppression'; a great expression of over-caring to the point at which you are denying individuals their human rights to experience things. I often use the expression 'audience-participants'; there's equality in the dynamic between performers and audience.

JM: Would you summarise the approach you take when creating work?

AH: Often I get an image of the end-piece even before I'm aware of what I'm wanting to explore or my 'research question'. It's like working backwards; I arrive at the end point and then I have to work backwards to fill in the gaps. Quite often within that are ideas of ritual and symbolism taken from different world religions. I'm imbued with the connection between the different rituals and symbols in world religions and their potential to help us explore our humanity and community. I'm struck by Mary Douglas, an anthropologist, who said you can have a society without language but you cannot have a society without ritual; it's fundamental. Tony Fisher at Central School of Speech and Drama said that he understood why I was attracted to ritual; because it has an in-built dramaturgical element. I think that's very true. I'm looking for these opportunities all the time for people to have community with one another; for people to have opportunities to nurture themselves and each other. I'm talking about that very specifically within the one-to-one dynamic, experiences that I set up to do with foot washing or bathing the whole body, I'm wanting individuals to be deeply nurtured and deeply nourished but in return I'm nurtured by being allowed to nurture other people. What I want to move towards much more is an actual community and I think that that's where I'm going with this idea with TouchBase and the audience-participants who might be involved with that. I've done one-to-one work for the last ten years now and, not to negate how passionate I am about it and how important I think it is, but I have started to get a bit concerned by how my one-to-ones might in some way be encouraging individualism. I've always argued, if ever I've come up against that criticism, that what I offer in one-to-ones is an opportunity for people to take time to invest in themselves; to have qualitative time and recharge, to then go back into society and be an effective member of their community. But because of the very particular times that we're living in since the economic downturn, the phone-hacking scandal; the way that people have been seriously abused by those in authority and power, all of this has been preying on my mind that it's coming from an individualist society where people are out for themselves. So I feel I need to return to the idea of community. I was asked to revive *An Audience with Adrienne* for the Brighton Festival and I did it in a real living room space for 12 people, as opposed to 25, because we could only seat that many; the quality of people sharing and opening up was incredible. These people that didn't know each other at the beginning of the evening, after an hour and a half were friends and wanted to carry on their friendship. En masse they would go downstairs to the pub to carry on talking and having drinks together. For me that's an example of community happening from performance; how might that then have greater ramifications? With *May I Have the Pleasure...?* at the Edinburgh Fringe I intend to take the one-to-one element – me dancing with individuals – and put it within the communal experience to see if that has an impact. I got very interested in that when I was asked to do a workshop experiment at Leeds last year, performing *Foot Washing For The Sole* for a group of post-grad students and a panel of experts, from the Psychology and Ethics departments, who were allowed to contribute their thoughts and ideas on my work in terms of the ethics of the work. I'm normally fiercely protective of the one-to-ones for the individual because it's not about it being a spectatorial experience, but one thing I'd never thought about was that it could be enriching, nurturing and nourishing for somebody to spectate this. When I'd finished this experiment, with a willing volunteer, people from the panel were crying, they were so moved by this. So all these things have started to dovetail.

JM: There is something about the charged quality to the space of a one-to-one. It's about engaging in a shared sense of ritual and additionally it's to do with the charged intensity of that shared moment; it's a quality contained within that where observing itself becomes experiential.

AH: Yes, it was an intimate experience for those people spectating. So when you ask me why I'm interested in intimacy, partly I need and want to answer that by saying I so crave it myself; I have my own questions about it which is why I create work around it. It's pertinent and salient to say that I'm very sure and comfortable about being intimate with someone in a performative frame and I'm really not very good at negotiating intimacy outside of that frame. I think we're living in very brutalised and unloving times and we need to learn to 'tenderise' ourselves through intimacy. Our society is not very good at being intimate, at touching and really engaging in that qualitative, loving-kindness type of touch. I think what we do is perfunctory; we do 'hugging' that's the equivalent to a pat on the back –

JM: *– that's about keeping a distance rather than letting someone in –*

AH: – yes, when actually hugging, cuddling, cradling, stroking, what all those things can do for our mental well-being as much as our physical well-being, is enormous. That's why I'm interested in intimacy.

JM: *How significant is the audience in terms of form? Talk a little more about the presence of the audience within your work.*

AH: I always refer to the 'audience-participant' in my one-on-one work, equally in *An Audience with Adrienne* and in *May I Have The Pleasure...?* because they're not a passive spectator; they co-create, co-author the piece with me. Yes, *Foot Washing for the Sole* is highly structured and the content is quite fixed, but I would never want it to be so inflexible that it didn't allow for people to really bring their own contribution verbally and bodily. One of the significant things about *The Pleasure of Being* is that people are co-authoring with their bodies. Often very little is actually exchanged verbally but a hell of a lot is contributed and exchanged bodily. I would love to be able to say that there's an equality of experience but it's very much that I'm in control and I'm guiding it –

JM: *– yes, that's what makes it 'safe'.*

AH: I was asked yesterday, in the plenary of the conference, how would I define what I'm doing with the audience and I said that I think it's 'a loving manipulation'; the way that a parent who so loves their child might manipulate them because they want them to have a particular experience that's going to be safe, 'boundaried'. I think that's quite a good definition, 'loving-manipulation', because there's always a tendency to think that manipulation is a negative thing because it takes away agency and ownership from individuals. Something I'm very aware of is empowering individuals to have agency. With *The Pleasure of*

Being it's very deliberate that you sit in a cubicle, fully dressed, and you engage with these guidelines; it's not me speaking to you in the space because you wouldn't hear me.

JM: *It's also part of the ritual, part of the structure and discipline and the preparation that you enter into before you go through the final experience. For you, then, why is it theatre and not therapy?*

AH: When you come to a piece of my work I think you're asking a whole different set of questions. Everything is signalling something different to what you might have if you were going to a professional therapist. With *Foot Washing for the Sole*, the moment you come into the space you're already asking questions about why I've set things up the way that I have and it's candlelit, as with *The Pleasure of Being*, so the space is theatricalised. With the *Pleasure of Being* at Battersea [BAC] it's very deliberately white, pristine, clinical. I very much wanted the gold feet of the bath to be there and the red rose petals; the aesthetic is deliberate. So people are automatically being alerted to the layout, the colour scheme and I think you're asking a whole different set of questions. And of course I'm eliciting a different set of responses than you would expect from a professional therapist. But I would not want to diminish the fact that I think the experiences are often therapeutic. I am aiming for a transformational, cathartic experience; I'm not uncomfortable with embracing the idea of it being therapeutic for people.

JM: *You're beginning to touch upon it so could you expand on how significant space and site is to the work, to the aesthetic, the form of the work.*

AH: It's very interesting with space because I feel like I have to feel that I own it in some way, that I'm 'at home' in it in order to be very relaxed about performing in it. It's quite a challenge, for example, when you're part of a conference and they've given you a room where they might not have given it that much thought, irrespective of the fact that I might have stressed specifications. I have to be able to rearrange things in order to feel that I have some ownership over the space. If I'm creating a piece I'm existing in that space for two weeks, making it mine. Homeliness is quite important; by doing that I hope that it will also be homely for the person entering into it. It's important that it's a space where people don't feel intimidated, don't feel threatened, don't feel uncomfortable or anxious. Adrienne's living room should create a feeling that people can put their feet up. So my work is site-responsive.

JM: *In terms of the way in which space informs form is it high up on that list of priorities or is it something that happens by choice or design 'along the way'?*

AH: It's not the main priority. One of the things that I discovered when I was doing my Creative Fellowship at Glasgow University was that the most important thing is my engagement with the individual and their engagement with me.

JM: *So the space becomes important only in as much as it allows that engagement to occur?*

AH: Exactly. With the *Garden of Adrian* a journey was facilitated by me that I wanted people to go on; a series of tactile and 'tacular' interactions with me within a larger frame of each locale within the garden, each focused around a different sense. I can't emphasise how significant and important the environment was for facilitating that experience for people. That was the first project during the course of my Creative Fellowship, where there was a focus on the environment as well as issues of intimacy and risk in the course of a one-to-one performance context. I worked with Minty Donald, a visual artist and designer, and what she created extraordinarily supported what I was trying to do as a performer. In a way I became part of the environment, to facilitate this experience, so I don't want to negate the importance of space. With *Foot Washing for the Sole*, which is a much more flexible piece, environment isn't so important; other than in terms of how I feel about it. I'd be more particular about the bathroom [for *The Pleasure of Being...*].

JM: *At BAC it was so special because there was something otherworldly about the bathroom; the white wasn't simply clinical, it had a sense of luxury, faded glory, the feel that it was of a different time. It was perfect in terms of the ambient sounds of that bathroom space, it felt womblike with the echoey sounds of the plumbing. In terms of form, are there particular artistic or performance influences in your work?*

AH: One of the biggest influences on my work in the last ten years has been an artist called Helen Herbertson who is based in Australia. She's a dance-maker, probably in her mid-fifties, and she came to the National Review of Live Art in 2003 at The Arches with a piece, about 20 minutes long, called *Morphia Series*. There were only 12 of us as an audience and we were taken one at a time, by an usher wearing a headlamp strapped to the forehead, who led us very gently and carefully into a space that was completely pitch dark. We were given what looked like a dessert with exotic fruit on the top but when you ate it, it was a combination of sweet and savoury, really exquisite in it's presentation – the detail of it – and exquisite to taste. Then you were given a tiny, dainty glass of dessert wine, which was also exquisite, all in the dark, you could just see from the light of being shown what you were picking up and putting into your mouth. Then we were individually led to a seat and when all 12 people were sat, way down in the distance, after a period of time of just looking, questioning if something was there, the light started to grow, so far away and then you felt that it was getting nearer, and were wondering how it was travelling. Then you realised that we were getting nearer to it. As we got nearer, it was actually light on Helen Herbertson's moving back. So at first it looked like an amoeba and then you realised it was a human back and then the light grew more on her and it was her completely naked body and she was in a box. We were being pushed forward on tracks and our seating area could fit inside the box in which Helen was performing. We came to the very edge and Helen was so close you could touch her, hear her breathing. Sometimes there was a sound-scape around us ambiently but you couldn't necessarily discern specific words. The whole thing was exquisite in its simplicity, it was stripped down, the naked body in a space, gorgeous to see an older woman's naked body. I then did a three-day winter school with Helen and what she talked about was how it takes her such a long time to get to that simplicity, to get to that minimalism. It's all about paring it down to the essentials, you only put in front of an audience what you really, really need to. That made a huge impact on me; the beauty of the simplicity, of the bare essentials. It's how I feel about bathing, the pleasure of being – washing, feeding, holding, they're the basics. A journalist in Edinburgh asked me recently, *'The Pleasure of Being, May I have the Pleasure...?*, what's the interest in "pleasure"?, is it about the fact that we live in an age of instant gratification where pleasure comes from spending money on iPads or whatever', and that's exactly what it's about. These are very simple things which give enormous pleasure; dancing one-on-one with somebody, having their body close, hearing them breathe, feeling their breath, smelling them and bathing somebody; these are simple, basic things, pared down to the bare essentials, but they're powerful and beautiful, important.

JM: In an artistic way, it gets back to that primal, instinctive, initial pleasure that is fleshly, that is about human contact, the parent and the child, skin-on-skin contact. There's a sense of formal distance and yet it still gets to the heart of what that experience is because it reconnects us to our own bodies, to the power of human connection, human capacity for connection, which has been lost in this technological world. To finish, how would you define immersive theatre in relation to your own practice?

AH: My understanding of immersive practice is that its absolutely about being really, really *present*, being in the moment, sitting with stillness and silence or whatever has been set up, it's about really entering into that; being fully immersed in what the condition is. It's about *really* slowing down, *really* paying attention. I stressed this to the students in the workshop that I just took; we're going to do a Five Senses Meditation and it's about *really* looking, *really* touching and so on. For me immersion is about really entering into that condition that's been set up, that action that's happening, that exchange, that connection and *really being* with it, being fully alive in it. *The Pleasure of Being* is about being fully alive with your being, with another's being. And an amazing kind of dance happens when you're really alive to somebody else's being. For your being to be with someone else's being, to be alive and alert, there's a need to let go of the analytical, the self-analytical, the self-reflexive, and to really engage with somebody else. It is predominantly about a bodily experience, a bodily exchange and connection. I live in my head a lot and I'm constantly anxious about how I'm coming across, how I'm being understood. I think it's a relinquishing, a surrendering of all that; and I use the term 'dance' because it puts you in your body.

JM: The type of dance where you give in to the music.

AH: And dance is beyond verbalised language. A full body massage puts me back into my body, but I also experience that when I dance, when I let go and surrender to a piece of music.

Illustration 24 Howells's *May I Have The Pleasure...?* The Penthouse Suite, The Point Hotel, Edinburgh, August 2011

[Photo credit: Niall Walker]

Tristan Sharps of dreamthinkspeak

The intimate in the epic

Tristan Sharps: I find it hard to define what immersive, site-specific, site-responsive, site-sympathetic means. I understand they're really handy hooks for people to hang things on; a shorthand means of discussing these things. I don't mind at all what people like to call our work – I wouldn't presume to define it so specifically. It's less important how people choose to label our work, and more that they appreciate it. I just follow my nose and do it. For me, the act of creating is also the act of discovering. I don't have a blueprint or a manifesto. When I finish creating, then I'll be able to understand what my manifesto was. When I started working in this kind of way in the mid-nineties it felt a little bit lonely; now it's a more crowded landscape and there are many more labels attached to this kind of work. I'm really happy that the labels are there, I think if they help other people than that's wonderful.

Josephine Machon: _Do you think of your work as theatre or do you think of it more as art?_

TS: Again, they're categories. Should theatre be a big enough house that it can have all these different rooms in it that might involve the sort of work that we do or do we need to stop using the word theatre and create other labels? I'd much rather leave that as a conundrum for other people to work out. My first love was visual art and then I got heavily into architecture, then film and then into theatre, so the work is a mix of all those different experiences, all coming together at a point where I felt, I'm not seeing any of this stuff out there as an audience member so I better start creating it myself. _The Rest is Silence_, the audience are completely locked within a world, immersed, and I use that as a verb, within a world that we are creating around them. _Before I Sleep_ in 2010, we placed them in a world but we were using the architecture of the building, there were moments where the building itself burst through the scenic elements; there'd be a gaping hole in a room where you'd see the wall of the Co-operative Building which you could contrast and compare with the wall that we had built around it. So I don't know if that means that we were completely immersing the audience in a world or if we were partly responding to the world that housed the world that we were in; it's a dialogue between the two things, a dialogue within the space. _Before I Sleep_ was inspired by _The Cherry Orchard_; it had its roots in the soil of that play. We were formed in Brighton in 1999 but there was a period between 2005 and 2010 where we were doing a lot of work outside of Brighton, in other countries or other places in the UK, so we were looking for something to do in Brighton and I noticed the Co-operative Building in 2009; I always describe these ideas that are floating around in my head as planes that are waiting to land and for some reason the runway is never quite prepared and then a runway is suddenly there and you're being told that that one can come in.

Often the space, the site and the context of the site becomes the catalyst that really makes that idea extremely concrete. It was a big, disused building, it was a hub of the local community in London Road, a relatively run-down area in Brighton that was due for a big burst of regeneration, which had stalled. So this limbo moment allowed me to come in. I thought a lot about the ending of *The Cherry Orchard*, the sense of an old world fading and this new world arriving; the first Russian Revolution is just around the corner. But Chekhov is less interested in that, his interest is in a new kind of world that he sees, in Lopakhin chopping down the orchard and wanting to build these holiday homes, dachas for the townsfolk. So you gradually get a sense of this world becoming very urbanised and you wonder what will happen to it, what will happen when Lopakhin builds the dachas. If you were to fast-forward that to where Brighton was in 2009 in the London Road area, lots of apartments had gone up all around the station and yet no one was buying them; they'd been built and there was suddenly a big downturn. I began to link into that and into the Co-operative being a much-loved building that was about to be knocked down. Yet it's also a department store, an image of a globalised world where you can get lots of different things under one roof; a representation of the world and where we are now. On the other hand the Co-operative is democratically run, Lopakhin, even Trofimov, would have been impressed with its values. So it sat between these worlds; it was Brighton's 'cherry orchard' yet it also represented the new world. It was a perfect space for presenting this piece. All the shows begin with me on my own in the building, spending time with the thoughts that I've had and soaking up the detail, thinking a lot about the social and geographical context of the space. It's a little bit like a ripple in the middle of a lake. It begins with a little ripple, which radiates out; as I move further forward through the process more and more collaborators come on board until there's a large gang of us and the project belongs to a vast range of people and finally the ripples meet the shore and the show is open. I spent a lot of time on the different floors; in the basement, lots of partitions had been taken out to create a bigger area; upper floors became more expansive, the first floor was vast, endless. I get a sense of the shape and the feel of the space and then I get a feel for the way the audience will move through this space. The basement is the world of *The Cherry Orchard* house. So I wanted to design that house; I looked to Russian architecture and also to Georgian and Victorian architecture of which there's a fusion around this area of Brighton. I redesigned my notion of what I thought the house was and then deconstructed it over the basement level. So you found yourself going through the various rooms of the house but already a couple of years after it had been deserted, the drawing room, the dining room, the ballroom, the nursery, the kitchen with the little recipe for cherry jam that Firs mentions. As we built up these spaces, we tried to follow the line of the previous partitions, as if the reconstructing of *The Cherry Orchard* house was in parallel to the reconstruction of the former Co-op. Through the window of the drawing room you see Ranevskaya and Gayev, her brother, having coffee on a patio and you're not sure if it's real or a hallucination, a hologram. You began with what that world once was, a world of ghosts, but not scary ghost-train type ghosts where audiences experience them like this [he motions pulling back, fearful] but here you're like this –

JM: *– curious, peering through to see more –*

TS: – sensitised to it. You're aware of the ghosts, it's discomforting, unsettling but at the same time you want to explore, your curiosity's aroused. When you found yourself on the ground floor, coming up from the basement, you open the door and suddenly you're in a department store peopled by characters who speak a whole range of different languages. English is spoken at the Customer Services desk where they can explain what's going on. There's all the different departments where you can buy anything you want, literally bid for the sofa; we sold all those pieces of furniture. Each department matched up, in a modern context, with all the interiors that you'd been in in the basement; you slip from one world to another, it mirrors it but also contrasts with it with visual motifs from what you'd seen downstairs. It was hard to find a corresponding department for the ballroom so we decided on the fashion department. Each area had references that developed ideas established in the basement. Model-making was key in that respect. One of the first things you saw was a model of the house, surrounded by trees and snow landscape with footprints, then a huge dining table with a tiny model of Ranevskaya and Gayev in a candle forest and a little Firs with a cup of coffee trying to find them (see Illustration 25). There's also a doll's house in the nursery in the basement, which is itself another version of the house; if you open it up you see all the interiors that you've just walked through (see Illustration 10). Then, when you go into the department store there's a Wendy House version of it in the nursery, and in that Wendy House when you open it up there's another doll's house which has got very modern interiors, which are those that you see later on when you go onto the upper floors. We play a lot with

Illustration 25 dreamthinkspeak's *Before I Sleep* (2010). Ranevskaya and Gayev in the candle forest

[Photo credit: Jim Stephenson. Image courtesy of dreamthinkspeak]

the sense that you're going through the past, the 'Cherry Orchard World' and then you go through a series of mirrors almost and you end up on the topmost floor in a future version of how these rooms would be in a very modern context, yet these are already dilapidated because you've zoomed forward in time; the faster the pace of regeneration, the faster the pace of degeneration. When new buildings are built they're not built to last, they're built to be homogenous and easy to knock down and I can see that cycle about to continue in London Road.

JM: *Those images themselves are like lateral thinking games, or children's rhymes about the house within a house within a house, a hall of mirrors eternally repeating itself or an Escher drawing.*

TS: Although Escher is very empty. A lot of work that's form-led, design-led, is very empty, whereas this is completely connected, nothing is there for show, everything is there for a reason. Not because I've thought it all through cerebrally; the act of creating it is also the act of me understanding what I'm doing. I work very strongly on intuition. Often the kind of work that I do gets lumped in with other practitioners. When I started in 1995, I didn't see other work that was like this and now there's a lot of this work and that's great, but to lump them all in together is like saying, *The Birthday Party* by Harold Pinter and *The Cocktail Party* by T. S. Eliot are the same play because they're both plays about parties written for the stage. The differences between companies are as rich as the similarities. The landscape of this work gets talked about as something that is quite superficial, visual, doesn't have any meat on the bones and that really annoys me. There's a lot of design within this work but there are reasons why things are happening; there's a dialogue within the space and also a dialogue between the geographical and social context. London Road has become economically run down but there are lots of wonderful things there including the Co-operative Building, which will be swept away with this new regeneration drive. What do we want with our spaces and our places and our lives? It's the end of *The Cherry Orchard*; there's nothing else on the table apart from Lopakhin's offer, the only way of moving forward. Similarly we don't have anything else on the table but this blind idea that if we regenerate and let the big corporations come along and build then everyone will be happy. Look at the people in *The Cherry Orchard*; it doesn't make them happy that the orchard is chopped down yet they're also absolutists.

You can't stick to ideals, there's a need to change and adapt, to explore new ideals. It's the death of ideology, which has been playing in politics since the Blair years. That infused every single strand, every layer of media that we used to create this work.

JM: Is place – the socio-political, historical and geographical location – always important to your work?

TS: It depends. *Don't Look Back* has been adapted to many different places and spaces around the world. *One Step Forward and One Step Back* I thought would be adaptable to many different places, but once we'd finished I knew there was no way you could take it out of Liverpool, outside of that cathedral. Even though it was about the world and there was a timelessness to it, it was specific to that building, to that city and that particular time. *Before I Sleep* I thought was also tied, yet the Holland Festival were interested in the show. They didn't have a defunct department store, instead some office blocks that had large ground floor windows which were set up for retail space, in a brand new business district in the centre of Amsterdam, like Canary Wharf before it was inhabited. I spent a lot of time walking around there and it was like London Road in 15 years time once all the regeneration has happened; it's all been built but no one's inhabiting it – an empty, soulless place where everything's 'To Let'. It's the world of Lopakhin. We had two buildings directly opposite, the audience inhabited the 'old rooms' or 'the Cherry Orchard House' in one building, but they could see through to the new To Let apartment blocks opposite. It suddenly became this extraordinarily rich series of visual relations that resonated through our piece. So the space is extremely relevant; a piece can be transposed and yet can never happen anywhere else.

JM: It becomes responsive to, resonates with, the politics and the history of the particular place and space.

TS: I work very much with improvisation in the space; all the live performance work is created through workshops. For the Holland Festival the space became a wonderful playground which the performers could be let loose on. We created a number of silent scenes that the audience could see in the building opposite, a whole range of things, which were going on on different floors. We do a lot of playing between buildings. With *Underground* at the Theatre Royal, there was a bank of buildings that morphed into the dressing rooms. You could be in one dressing room, look over the courtyard and see the murder happening constantly on a loop; see him going along the skyline then entering the room. Without that live performance element the piece wouldn't work.

JM: Is that the point at which the work becomes 'alive' for you?

TS: Yes – without the live performance element, the work would not live.

JM: You've adapted Orpheus, The Cherry Orchard, Crime and Punishment, Hamlet, *beautiful, detailed, literary forms which you've translated into a three-dimensional experience involving a kaleidoscopic play with narrative, time, theme and form. That allows access to the ideas in the original works in a sensual way, opened further by themes generated by the space and place.*

TS: *Don't Look Back* was inspired by the myth of Orpheus. I was really interested in the Ovid version because there's something about that Greek culture where certain things are understood, in the blood, that now we have to examine cerebrally. The story of a living person going to the Underworld; he loses Eurydice on their wedding day and he can't accept that she's died so he has to go down to the Underworld and the gods are flabbergasted that he's come. For the audience, it's like we are the living so there should be a sense that we shouldn't really be there, aware that you're trespassing. In Somerset House [London] there were a lot of moments where you would be gazed at by the performers, a series of hauntings –

JM: – thrilling moments where you feel observed rather than being the observer.

TS: Yet it also works quite subtly on you, gets under your skin, becomes incredibly potent because you start to feel you really are part of this world, even if you're trespassing; you feel that it's connecting with what's going on in Ovid's work but in a live, living way, that isn't easy to talk about cerebrally.

JM: With Don't Look Back *in particular there was also feeling that you were submerged in a different medium, it felt like everything was slowed down. The models added to that, the honing in on detail, and then the final, breath-taking image.*

TS: All of that emerged from the workshops with the performers. We worked a lot on rhythm and pace and we realised in the underworld you have all the time in the world; work continues because there's a lot of processing of new people but you've got time to take. Which means that, when doing all this work, when you stop, it's a momentous thing. In later versions of the piece we extended that; we had parallel worlds of 'The Documents'. In Romania where we worked with a troupe of 40 performers, the audience could go down a stairwell and find 15 undertakers walking up and down with boxes full of Birth, Death and Marriage Certificates. Every now and then the rest bell would sound, they'd put the documents down and slowly curl up on the stairs and go to sleep; you could be walking up the stairs with sleeping clerks all around you. Timelessness, that calmness, if it stops, can be unsettling for an audience.

JM: Alongside the moments where you found your name amongst the piles of information being processed.

TS: At Somerset House, we were able to take everyone's names because they had booked in advance. So there was a moment where you walked past and saw your name being sliced by one of the clerks. In Moscow we performed in a vast, partially disused, old paper factory. They had huge rollers, one of which was still operating, so we made these huge sheets of paper printing in big Cyrillic the names of the people who came to see the show, which they saw rolling out very slowly as they walked past in the engine room of the underworld, processing all the names. That sense of you and your surname being present became a powerful part of it; it's about *your* journey. The lift moment where you see her through a two-way mirror and that's the last time you see her before the end means that it becomes very much about *your* journey to the underworld rather than you following her (see Illustration 3).

JM: You play a lot with reflection and illusion, upturning perception. Related to that and the multimedia explorations in your work, as well as referring back to the significance of site, I'm intrigued to know how you have responded to the translation of The Rest is Silence *from a warehouse that is in-between towns, on geographical thresholds, to a black-box studio in West London.*

TS: I'm intrigued to find out myself. This really is focusing in; like the drawing room in *Before I Sleep*, or the hotel room in *Absent* where there's a mirror, then you see through to another mirror and there's film playing. *The Rest is Silence* is taking that out and magnifying that. It's responding to architecture but not in the same way that *Don't Look Back* responded to Somerset House and then to the paper factory; it's responding more to a world of lots of warehouse conversions that are going on, loft-style conversions, shiny minimalist interiors. It's relating to the wider context of the space it's in but it is its own architecture that can be taken out and put in another place. Riverside Studios has had a lot of its own renovation, slick, lovely interior which this will fit snugly within. In the act of doing it I will find out.

Conclusion: Immersive Theatres

The book has examined what it is that makes up those immersive theatres that are physical, locational and participatory. Immersive theatres always exploit the imaginative possibilities that exist in the sensual realm of live performance. Historical and artistic affiliations with past innovators of interdisciplinary forms are clear in this work; specifically those that prioritised embodied audience involvement, rethought the impact of space and overturned any hierarchies of performance.

The scale of immersivity proposes central features that are identifiable in immersive theatres, which help to gauge to what extent an event is/was immersive. In brief, the event must establish a unique **'in-its-own-world'**-ness, which is created through a dexterous use of **space**, **scenography**, **sound**, **duration** within **interdisciplinary** (or hybridised) **practice**. **Bodies** are prioritised in this world; performing and perceiving bodies; the latter belonging to the individuals who make up the **audience** – a pivotal feature of this practice – whose direct insertion in and interaction with the world shapes the outcomes of the event. With this audience a **'contract for participation'** is either explicitly or implicitly shared in order to allow full immersion in the world. The level of immersion experienced is ultimately influenced by the artist's **intention** and **expertise** in the execution of the work.

This is not to say that the onus is solely on the artist to enable total immersion to be achieved. A willingness to negotiate and give in to the demands of the work (where care and attention has been assigned by the artist in realising these) is the responsibility of the audience-participant. Immersive work has to *enable* the audience to be willing participants, to invite curiosity and complicity. Artists can encourage this desire to engage through pre-performance techniques. These may include the journey to the event; practical instruction and guidance in the idiolect of the world; or antechambers which steep us in the aesthetic and mood of the work, where the act of waiting is charged with 'immanence'. Such techniques gently immerse each individual in the world, which ensures that the imagination and proprioceptive senses are engaged enabling them to intuit their way through the event.

Where an event is wholly immersive, the audience-participant is *always* fundamentally complicit within the concept, content and form of the work. Audience-participants are integral to the sensual heart of the work and a living part of the form and aesthetic. This enables artist and audience together to move to new territories within the live performance exchange in a mobile, intuitive and *praesent* manner. Consequently, immersive theatres create a space for reinvigorating human interaction, however 'fictionalised' the encounter might be. At the very least, it causes an audience member to attend to the exchange occurring in the moment. Furthermore, immersive theatres that inhabit geographical landscapes are able to locate the audience-inhabitant organically within, and as a continuum of, this wider environment; haptically and politically. The very nature and activity of this work evolves the idea and the *practice* of audience or spectator beyond the conventional attitude and action of 'listener' and 'viewer' into a decision-making collaborator in the work. Immersive theatres explore innovative approaches to creative agency for artist and audience alike, establishing relationships that traverse a range of responsibilities including creative comrades, collaborators and co-authors. What is always the case is that the audience-participant is sensorially and sentiently engaged with the immersive world.

The live(d) experience of *praesence*, the participant's whole body responding within an imaginative, sensual environment, is a tangible fact and a pivotal element of theatrical immersion. In immersive theatres, the full human sensorium is called into play. Haptic perception is crucial within the experience and to an individual's immediate or subsequent interpretation of that experience. Audience-immersants are encouraged *to attend to* the situations, narratives and ideas within the world, and by extension, to relate these to the equivalent in the wider, 'real' world. It is this reawakening of the holistic sentience of the human body in immersive theatres that allows for an immediate and intimate connection with the ideas as much as with the artists and other participants in that immersive world.

The embodied experience of the work is paramount and has an influential bearing on any intellectual decisions taken during each *praesent* moment of the performance and in any subsequent process of recall and interpretation. By giving credence to embodied knowledge immersive theatres force us to rethink the ways in which humans 'think'. The prioritisation of all the human senses in immersive theatres opens up – indeed, requires – a new taxonomy for holistic appreciation. As the proceeding chapters have shown, analysis of immersive practice provides a bridge that links sensual, relational, spatial and environmental aesthetics.

Although diverse in form and outcome what is clear is that all immersive theatres produce *shared qualities of experience* that involve some degree of immediacy; that can engender the epic in the intimate and uncover the intimate in the epic. The critical reflections throughout this book have sought to demonstrate the unique and all-encompassing way in which immersive theatres impact on an individual; encouraging a reconnection with the self as well as with others. The active decision-making and sensual involvement that is required in this work can be transformative on a number of levels; from the playful way in which a participant influences the shape of the event or physiologically, via the engagement of sensory awareness, to the radically transformative; transforming an individual psychologically or ideologically. The 'lasting' nature of this work functions on a variety of levels. It can be as personal and private as an individual's corporeal memory of the piece that cites the shared experience. It can be a more widely felt collective memory that lingers within a community and its environs. It can be the physical remains of the art in the space that evidences civic engagement with a place and its inhabitants, honouring *communitas* in every sense of the word. These are precious outcomes and a privilege to encounter; outcomes that are proof of the power and potential of immersive theatre.

Notes

Introduction

1. *You Me Bum Bum Train* is the invention of Kate Bond and Morgan Lloyd, both of whom come from a background in fine art and illustration (notably, scenographic design is key to the total immersion in the event). It has been running in various guises since 2004, evolved from interactive club nights run by Bond and Lloyd. In 2010 the experience was sited in a disused office block in East London, produced with the support of The Barbican and was reinvented as part of the Cultural Olympiad 2012. The experience begins with a clear contract for participation; you entrust your belongings to your guide who summarises what will be expected of you. Significantly, you are made aware that should you become uncomfortable in any way and wish to be removed from the experience, returned to 'normality', you must fold your arms or shout 'escape'. You are then placed in a wheelchair and taken to the start of your personal adventure where you are placed in assorted roles: delivering a sermon, burgling a house, teaching secondary school pupils, coaching a soccer team, heading up MI5, before your final exit, which involves a rubbish chute and karaoke.

2. BAC has historically supported much of that practice which is identified as immersive theatre today. It has programmed a range of work across recent years that explore sensory and participatory practice, such as the former Artist Director, Tom Morris's 'Playing in the Dark' season in 1998, of which Sound & Fury were key contributors (see Martin Welton's *Feeling Theatre*, 2011).

3. The BAC One-on-One Festivals (2012, 2011) proved to engage a diverse audience. Jubb clarifies how people with a concern for the civic function of the space were particularly drawn to the work:

   > The audience for the one-on-one festival, both times, is the most diverse audience we've ever had in the building; culturally, ethnically, age-wise, loads of over-60s came to the one-one-one festival... Adrian Howells had a woman who came to see the piece in 2010, she'd heard about it on the radio and she had just started having to bathe her mother and she wanted to know what it felt like... My theatre-going friends are used to audience participation meaning people being ritually humiliated, pulled up on stage, the hierarchy of artist and audience being exacerbated in that moment by saying 'look at the gimp on stage, let's all laugh at them' and one-on-one practice is about subverting that (Jubb and Machon, 2012: n. pag.).

4. Many conversations in Part Two compare the 'traditional theatre' set-up with immersive practice. Morris, Gladwin and Lundahl and Seitl in their conversations in Part Two use 'proscenium arch' as a shorthand to denote this type of theatrical experience as much as to identify the architectural feature.

5. In Part Two Wilson refers to pilgrimages in relation to her work and Hill's describes how WildWorks practice naturally and unintentionally alighted on the ancient form of 'plen an gwarries'. See *The Theatre of Cornwall* by Alan M. Kent (2010) for a detailed critical consideration of ancient and modern Cornish theatre practices.

6. To illustrate Kaprow references: a meandering end of day conversation with friends versus the speedy, disturbing and infiltrating time of the siren outside the window during this conversation alongside the 'endlessness of artwork that transcends palpable time, such as 'the slow decomposition of a mountain of sandstone' to reinforce the *felt* nature of time in such events where duration becomes key to the affective experience of the work (1995: 238).

7. Kaprow clarifies, 'composition is understood as an operation dependent upon the materials (including people and nature) and phenomenally indistinct from them. Such materials and their associations and meanings…generate the relationships and movements of the Happening, instead of the reverse. The adage that "form follows function" is still useful advice' (1995: 242).

8. See Machon, 2011 (in particular, pp. 35–7) for an explanation of Friedrich Nietzsche's 'Dionysian' (immediate and intoxicating) and 'Apollinian' (measured and restrained) in (syn)aesthetic practice. In immersive theatre, these two approaches marry themselves to lesser and greater degrees according to the type of immersive event in which one might be participating; a feeling of randomness or spontaneity balanced by a careful structure. For Kaprow, an Apollinian, 'formal art', such as Bach's fugues or Shakespeare's sonnets, 'is primarily manipulative. As in a chess game, the manipulation is intellectual, whereby elements of the work are moved according to strict, sometimes self-imposed, regulations…at once stable and general in meanings' (Kaprow, 1995: 243).

9. 'Ritualised' here defines that performance work which, to borrow from Schechner's outline, strives to 'seek roots, explore and maybe even plunder religious experiences, expressions, practices, and liturgies' (1995: 19–20). This occurs in theme and form where the style exploits customs of cultural rituals, 'ordinary behaviour transformed by means of condensation, exaggeration, repetition, and rhythm' (Schechner, 1995: 228), stressing the role of heightened and meaningful experiences involving degrees of risk and investment from performer and spectator alike.

10. It is notable that Lundahl comes from a visual and installation arts background with a history of curating exhibitions, a factor that he sees as part of the aesthetic of Lundahl & Seitl. Mitchell and Wilson both trained as designers.

Sharps is influenced by design and architecture as much as theatre. The formal aesthetic of film permeates Mercuriali's work and Stevens highlights game-design as a working aesthetic in Coney's practice. Holdsworth cites Pilgrim's Corridor as an influence as does Barrett who, from a young age, was also inspired by the scenographic innovation of Edward Gordon Craig, and later Wilson and Kuhn's *H.G.* alongside other performance-installation work.

11. Haptic technology involves a tactile feedback system that applies vibration, force or other forms of motion to a user through equipment held or worn on any part of the human body. Other immersive technologies referenced include audio technologies that are experienced usually via headphones and video technologies, which are usually displayed through goggles that block out any other visuals other than those digitally generated. These are discussed in more depth in Part One, Chapters 1 and 2.

12. *Communitas*, a Latin noun, defines both the very spirit of community and/ or a community in which there is equality amongst all members. It describes a powerful community spirit, involving a feeling of great solidarity and togetherness.

13. I would recommend viewing *Passion in Port Talbot* (Edwards, 2011a, 2011b) or *The Gospel of Us* (McKean, 2012), which provides documentary evidence of the transformative power that this work can have on individuals and a community.

14. Here 'haptic', 'haptically', 'hapticity' (from the Greek, *haptikos* and *haptesthai*, to grasp, sense, perceive, 'lay hold of'), is used in relation to the performing/ perceiving, sensual body, alongside 'tactile' as the latter tends to connote only the external quality of touch by hand. 'Haptic' emphasises the tactile perceptual experience of the body as a whole (rather than merely the fingers) and also highlights the perceptive faculty of bodily kinaesthetics (the body's locomotion in space), which involves proprioception (stimulation produced and perceived *within* the body relating to position and movement *of* the body). Haptic perception encompasses the sensate experience of an individual's moving body, and that individual's perceptual experience of the moving bodies of others. Hence the use of the term in 'haptic technologies'.

Part One   Defining Immersive Theatres

Chapter I   Definitions and details

1. Following Marvin Minksy, Calleja demonstrates how a sense of 'presence' (derived from telepresence in relation to technology) is established via a combination of operator/player action and the subsequent video, audio and haptic 'feedback' with the technology, creating a sense of inhabiting the

game space, fusing the 'physically proximal' with the 'physically remote' (see Calleja, 2011: 18–19). In general, then, 'telepresence' refers to the use of technologies to allow a person to feel present, to give the appearance of being present, or to be affective via these technological means in a remote space, a place other than their actual location.

2. I use 'noetic' (from the Greek derived, *noēsis, noētikos, nous*, meaning inner wisdom, subjective intellect or understanding) to denote knowledge that is experienced directly and can incorporate sensations of transcendence. Noetic understanding traverses the ineffable (that which cannot be put into words) in that it can make physically manifest complex emotional or social experiences that defy explanation yet are *felt* and consequently the thing shown *feels understood*.

3. As Sandy Craig summarises, Welfare State redefined 'the nature of the theatrical environment...the central element of their work has been the disparity between the theatrically-created image and the surrounding social reality' (1980: 25).

4. See Steve Dixon's *Digital Performance* (2007) and Salter's *Entangled* (2010) for more detailed analysis of this practice.

5. See Steve Benford et al., 1999. There is a rich selection of archive materials available via Blast Theory's website, including an extensive back catalogue of articles and reports written since 1999, which foreground Blast Theory's experimentation with digital technologies.

6. Diana Lorentz provides analysis of such practice (see Lorentz, 2006), a recent example of which is the interactive event, *Journey Through the Afterlife: Ancient Egyptian Book of the Dead* (2011), held at the British Museum to enrapture an audience within the world of the museum and this specific exhibition. The intention with this was to create a grand spectacle involving a series of performances from a range of contributors (including spoken word performances, music, dance, film and workshops) in various locations across the Museum's Great Court and ground-floor galleries, curated by the site-responsive and outdoor, participatory theatre company, Periplum.

Chapter 2   Features and finer details: A scale of immersivity

1. In addition to Bennett's analysis of theatre audiences, Oddey and White et al. provide a clear-cut outline of 'modes of spectating' in current interdisciplinary artistic and cultural practice, unpacking the complexities of the practice of spectating within a range of performance/performative encounters. In doing so they ask necessary questions about the nature of current audience spectating in theatre (see Oddey and White, 2009).

2. Referring back to the immersive inheritance, Bishop highlights how the emphasis on critical and sensuous involvement in performance practice, with a focus on the relationship of the audience with/to the event via a close

and involved proximity in the performing space, arose out of a Modernist sensibility. In particular she cites Artaud and Bertolt Brecht as innovators of such practice (see Bishop, 2006: 11).

3. Charlotte Davies refers to the 'immersant' in her haptically enhanced (for instance, via a sensor-filled vest) virtual art. Her work, influenced by her own passion for diving, exploits technological immersion drawing on this 'physically intimate synthesis of the technical and organic' which fuses the visual and physical (Grau, 2003: 198). Here 'immersant' is an active and appropriate term for the respondents to these works of art who interact without a cohabiting performing partner present within the immersive experience.

4. Neurological researchers argue that from birth the human capacity for cerebral meaning-making resides in *experience*, due to the 'limbic system', the area of the brain and the neurological impulses associated with sensual, emotional and cognitive memory, which develops early in humans. As Richard E. Cytowic asserts, 'all sensory inputs, external and visceral, must pass through the emotional limbic brain before being distributed to the cortex for analysis' (see 2002: 253, 271–93). Interpretation triggered by smell, taste or touch in particular is therefore affective and experiential, semantic sense (cerebral meaning-making) cannot be disassociated from somatic *sense* (embodied *feeling*). I develop this idea in Chapter 3 in my reference to (syn)aesthetics (see also Machon, 2011: 20, 200 n.5).

5. Oshodi refers to the 'glossing over of detail' and draws an interesting point regarding sighted people who watch audio-described films with her; 'often I'll ask if they mind it being on and they'll say, 'no, no, it's really good, it's really making me look at that blue door because I wouldn't have noticed that otherwise'. In relation to Extant's experiments with haptic technologies, Oshodi shared how 'working tactilely in the dark' fuses immersive techniques with sensory deprivation which forces the participant to focus on other senses, which 'brings a particular level of awareness' (Oshodi and Machon, 2011: n. pag.).

6. The Recommended Reading & Research section provides a delightful video illustration of this.

7. Oddey provides an interesting analysis of the intimate and immediate connection inspired by soundscapes in/from space, corresponding to ambulation in/through that space and how this encourages the 'spectator/ performer/protagonist' to 'tune-in' to space in an intricate and imaginative manner (see Oddey, 2009). She highlights how such sensual practice encourages a reciprocal, sensual relationship between the self and space (immediate surroundings and the wider landscape) and other people within that space; the focus on our aural rather than visual capacity, thereby stimulating all the senses in the experience of the work. This resonates further in my more detailed consideration of space in this chapter and in Chapter 3.

8. Scott Palmer clarifies: in contemporary performance practice the term 'scenography' is replacing theatre or set design as it best represents, 'the complex interrelationships between space, object, material, light and sound that define the space and place of performance...the term advocates a more active intervention and holistic approach to design for performance...a space created for performing bodies to interact with rather than against' (2011b: 52).

9. Higgin continues, '[I]t's not just about arriving at the door, going through and then you're somewhere else. It's about the journey, in this project, from a week before that: [the pupils'] first interaction...with a workshop facilitator, in role as a character, then from the letter they receive and then the journey on from that.... It's about making sure that [Weevil's Bric-a-Brac] shop feels like a real environment, a real shop as opposed to a very staged theatre set. It's very much an environment where you can open drawers, you can touch things, you can sit on things' (Higgin and Machon: 2011: n. pag.).

10. Lotos Collective's *Trial of The Mariner*, inspired by Samuel Taylor Coleridge's *The Rime of the Ancient Mariner*, is set in 2111, where a group of sailors on the Ship of Fools are lost at sea and become drunk on rum and mad with cabin fever. They arrive at the Plastic Continent of the Pacific Ocean Gyre, where the non-degradable detritus of the world has come to life. Saul Eisenberg's Junk Orchestra is created from recycled rubbish. The soundscapes he performs for productions establish strange atmospheres as a consequence of these found objects and invented instruments. The presence and interaction of The Junk Orchestra in *The Trial of the Mariner* added to the environmental themes at the heart of the work.

Chapter 3   Immersive perspectives

1. In appropriating certain features of the neurological condition of synaesthesia I accept that this is an actual, proven, sensory experience. The terms of (syn)aesthetic analysis *adopt and adapt* terminology and frames of reference from the scientific study of synaesthesia in order to establish a discourse for the experiential qualities of the arts in general, and certain performance works in particular. It does so to help describe the stylistic approach in performance and a *quality of experience* felt in appreciation, including any subsequent affective interpretation. See Machon (2011: 13–24) for a more detailed explication.

2. Somatic, meaning 'affecting the body' or 'absorbed through the body', and the semantic as in the 'mental reading' of signs. This fusing of sense (semantic 'meaning-making') with sense (somatic *feeling*, both sensation and emotion) establishes a double-edged rendering of making-sense/*sense*-making and foregrounds a fused somatic/semantic nature at the heart of (syn)aesthetic forms in intention and practice. The play with the duality of the word 'sense'

is fundamental to (syn)aesthetics. The term 'making-sense/*sense*-making' plays on the fact that human perception translates received information through the sense organs and simultaneously combines this with perception as cerebral insight, involving memory, cognition and expectation, to establish a holistic sense arrived at through sensory information. Thus, perception as sensation, that is, corporeally mediated,, and perception as cognition, intellectually mediated (accepting that the latter also involves cultural and social mediation).

3. Steven Feld's analysis of the sensual experience of and attitude to making sense/*sense* of place according to the practices of the Laluli people of Bosavi, Papua New Guinea extends this approach (Feld, 2006). Additionally, Constance Classen, Dorinne Kondo, Marina Roseman and Lisa Law provide further discussion of the ways in which non-Western cultures naturally accept embodied ways of 'knowing' and have a sensual, linguistic and physical taxonomy for corresponding according to this attitude (in Howes, 2006: 143–241). There is a range of discussion around how non-Western cultural attitudes to embodied knowing exists within, arises out of and leads to holistic appreciation and analysis in performance processes in the following; Schechner (1994, 2007); Diedre Sklar (2007); Louise Steinman (1995); and Phillip B. Zarilli (2007, 2009).

4. Geurts goes on to explain that currently in elementary schools, students learn that 'hearing touch, taste, smell and sight are senses, but they do not learn to categorize balance as a sensation or sense. Yet balance is clearly treated as a sense in contemporary textbooks from ... biology, psychology, and medicine' (2003: 3–4). Geurts also highlights how the 'sixth-sense' ranges across an assortment of possibilities, all of which are understood as extrasensory perception, rather than located within the body.

5. *Seselelame* refers to a specific sense 'or physical sensation that we might call tingling in the skin', like that associated with impending illness; it can also refer to sexual arousal, heartache, passion and pain alongside inspiration, such as 'to dance or speak' and can also describe intuition or situations where uncertainty arises as to the source of the feeling. Lastly, *seselelame* also encompasses a generalised, similar to synaesthetic, feeling within or through the body (Geurts, 2006: 167, see also Geurts, 2003: 52–85 for a more detailed explication of the synaesthetic and kinaesthetic features of *seselelame*).

6. 'Every performance *explains* the composition but does not *exhaust* it. Every performance makes the work an actuality, but is itself only complementary to all possible other performances of the work. ... [E]very performance offers us a complete and satisfying version of the work, but at the same time makes it incomplete for us, because it cannot simultaneously give all the other artistic solutions which the work may admit' (Eco, 2006: 33).

7. Here the politics of a work of art are not to be understood solely as a didactic sharing of party-political thought, with the intention of invoking direct political action, but instead understanding that political thought and intervention can work more subtly via a resonant engagement with what it is

to be human. Through this, what we as humans are capable of questioning and how we might shift attitudes and sensibilities during and subsequent to a performance event, in and of itself marks its own political action. Rancière remarks:

> There is no reason why the sensory oddity produced by the clash of heterogeneous elements should bring about an understanding of the state of the world; and no reason why understanding the state of the world should prompt a decision to change it. There is no straightforward road from the fact of looking at a spectacle to the fact of understanding the state of the world; no direct road from intellectual awareness to political action. What occurs instead is a shift. (2009: 75).

8. Bourriaud also follows Mikhail Bakhtin and Marcel Duchamp, highlighting how a 'venturing into the mysteries of creation' allows for the *felt* moment of apprehension/comprehension where Bakhtin's '"matter of expression" becomes "formally creative", a split second in the telltale passage between author and beholder'. Here Duchamp's '"coefficient of art" which is the "difference between what (the artist) had planned to make and what he did"' comes to the forefront, acknowledging and celebrating the receiver's field of interactivity within any experience and appreciation of a work of art (see Bourriaud, 2002: 99).

9. Punchdrunk was initially described as a 'site-specific' company, a term that Barrett resisted, preferring 'site-sympathetic' as more applicable to the nature of Punchdrunk's work, in that the company respond sensually to the tones, textures and narratives of a site. The site defines, influences and shapes the work that is produced. Consequently, where a Punchdrunk production is 'revived', as with *Sleep No More* (2003–4, 2010, 2011–12) or any Punchdrunk Enrichment project, such as *The Uncommerical Traveller* (2011a, 2011b, 2011c, 2011d), the piece is re-designed, re-worked and becomes a wholly new experience related to its translation to an alternative space, place and community. 'Immersive', a term the company now uses to describe its work, allows for a more expansive understanding of the aesthetic form and function of Punchdrunk's theatre events and embraces the wide range of practice, from travel experiences to online interaction that Punchdrunk currently explores.

10. It is certainly the case that some performance events presented under traditional conditions can be open to more sensual and experimental realisation due to the experiential qualities written into the text and/or the production process, such as the work of Samuel Beckett, Churchill, Kane or numerous dance and physical ensemble productions, hence their affinity with immersive practice due to the experiential quality of the work. Morris considers this in relation to Bausch and Lepage in Part Two and I discuss such work at length in *(Syn)aesthetics* (Machon, 2011).

11. Feld foregrounds the reciprocal interchange between the senses and space and highlights how, simply moving through and within a given space, we

become aware of the intertwined nature of these two phenomena, specifically as motion automatically draws upon a kinaesthetic and proprioceptive interplay of the tactile, haptic, sonic and visual senses; 'emplacement always implicate[s] the intertwined nature of sensual bodily presence and perceptual engagement' (Feld, 2006: 181). Feld emphasises the experience of space *as/through* sound, which is a feature exploited within immersive practice.

12. 'Acoustemology means an exploration of sonic sensibilities, specifically of ways in which sound is central to making sense, to knowing, to experiential truth. ... [A]coustic time is always spatialized; sounds are sensed as connecting points up and down, in and out, echo and reverb, point-source and diffuse. And acoustic space is likewise temporalized' (Feld, 2006: 185). It is interesting to note that 'architectural sound design' is often assigned to descriptions of immersive practice; sound becomes tangible, textured and spatial in a (syn)aesthetic manner.

13. This develops from Etienne Balibar's idea of 'transindividuality' which proposes the impossibility of individuals having 'a strong notion of singularity without *at the same time* having a notion of the interaction and interdependence of individuals' (in Massey, 2010: 188; emphasis original). For Gatens and Lloyd 'a basic sociability...is inseparable from the understanding of human individuality' (in Massey, 2010: 188).

14. In addition to the conversations with Barrett, Higgin et al and Sharps in Part Two, see my earlier interviews with Barrett and Doyle, for more detailed illustration of this (Machon, 2011: 89–99; Barrett and Machon, 2007; Doyle and Machon, 2007).

15. With *The Pleasure of Being: Washing, Feeding, Holding*, 'the intimacy of the room becomes our intimacy...intimate space has become so quiet, so simple, that all the quietude of the room is localized and centralized in it. The room is very deeply our room, it is in us.... And all our former rooms come and fit into this one' (Bachelard, 1994: 226).

Part Two   Immersion, Intimacy and Immediacy in Practice

Conversations two

Lundahl & Seitl

1. Hosted by Experience Design Group, Stockholm October, 2011.
2. For Bourriaud the contemporary artist is a 'semionaut', one who 'invents trajectories between signs' (Bourriaud, 2002: 113). DJs, internet surfers and post-production artists, configure knowledge and creative play 'characterized by the invention of paths through culture' to produce 'original pathways through signs...issued from a script that the artist projects onto culture', which in turn 'projects new possible scripts, endlessly' (Bourriaud, 2005: 19).

In occupying spaces of communication and artistic practice, semionauts subvert ideas around artists and artworks offering closed representations of the 'real', whereas the semionaut provides a trajectory of artistic works which is eternally evolving and relational with its audience; the semionaut 'imagines the links, the likely relations between disparate sites' (see Bourriaud, 2005: 19).

3. Plato's allegory for the philosopher's plight describes people who have only ever lived chained to the wall of a cave, facing a blank wall on which they watch flickering shadows projected on the wall, without realising that these are created by objects passing in front of a fire behind them. They attempt to ascribe forms to these shadows, which is as close as they get to viewing reality. The philosopher is like the person who is freed from the shackles of the cave, follows the light to the outside and experiences reality directly. The task lies in returning to the cave and getting the other people to believe this knowledge.

Conversations three

Tassos Stevens of Coney

1. Resilience is the ability of people to respond well to change and setback. It's an ability that can be learnt. Resilience approaches focus on providing support and creating opportunities to promote success, rather than working only to eliminate factors, as they occur, that promote failure.

2. The audience was tricked into believing a youth theatre performance had been sabotaged by 'Ash', an absent fictional performer, which led to them being genuinely caught up in the consequent action.

Conversations four

Bill Mitchell and Sue Hill of WildWorks

1. Latin *munus*, 'the gift', and *cum*, 'together, among each other'. Community, 'to give among each other'.

2. In a personal email following our discussion Bill added a postscript: 're: your question about winged creatures. they are not just about imagination they are messengers of the "gods", bringing us ideas, gifts and wonder' (29 November 2011).

Recommended Reading and Research

Please also refer to the bibliography for wider sources and relevant reading material. The information below has been compiled to assist web-based research as well as directing the reader to accessible texts on certain subjects.

On contributing artists

There are a range of broadsheet profiles and reviews on these artists and/or their work available on the web. Below lists authorised websites, all of which provide details on the history and mission alongside visual documentation of the work and links to reviews. I have also included relevant additional archive material where available.

Artangel: http://www.artangel.org.uk/home

This is an extensive archive that provides detailed information on the mission and history of the organisation and includes a wealth of resources related to all Artangel produced projects since 1992.

- On Wilson and Kuhns's *H.G.* (1995): http://www.artangel.org.uk/projects/1995/h_g/about_the_project/h_g
- On Janet Cardiff's *Missing Voice (case Study B)* (1999): http://www.artangel.org.uk//projects/1999/the_missing_voice_case_study_b/about_the_project/about_the_project

Back To Back Theatre: http://backtobacktheatre.com/

Coney: http://www.youhavefoundconey.net/home/
- Coney principles: http://www.youhavefoundconey.net/2012/01/18/principles/

- *A Small Town Anywhere*, including video footage: http://www.youhave-foundconey.net/2012/01/21/a-small-town-anywhere-2/
- On *The Gold-bug*, the Coney immersion within Punchdrunk's *Masque of the Red Death*, including evocative blogs on the experience and the initial intriguing postcard from Rabbit:

   http://www.youhavefoundconey.net/2011/11/02/the-gold-bug/
   http://inspirationsofpoe.blogspot.co.uk/
   http://goldbug1843.wordpress.com/
   http://goldbug1843.wordpress.com/tales-from-inside-masque-of-the-red-death/inside-morays-chamber/
   Make friends with **Rabbit**: http://www.hellothisisrabbit.org
- See also **Tassos Steven**'s blog: allplayall.blogspot.com.

dreamthinkspeak: http://www.dreamthinkspeak.com/

Howells, Adrian: although Howells does not have an authorised website, the following are archived interviews with him on his practice:

- Part 1: http://www.youtube.com/watch?v=C7btf8Tdg_s
- Part 2: http://www.youtube.com/watch?v=SLwD3APw2F8&feature=relmfu
- On ethics:
   http://www.youtube.com/watch?v=CHhVlTDzE1g&feature=related
- On *Foot Washing for the Sole*:
   http://www.youtube.com/watch?v=y9PPEbAU5z8&feature=related
- On *Salon Adrienne*:
   http://www.youtube.com/watch?v=M7XcWo2GzSo&feature=related

Lundahl & Seitl: http://lundahl-seitl.com/

- *Rotating in a Room of Images*: http://www.youtube.com/watch?v=Dd9w9SB71RU
- *Symphony of a Missing Room*: http://www.youtube.com/watch?v=xuyYhVxnwQg

Mercuriali, Silvia: http://www.silviamercuriali.com
and Autoteatro: http://www.rotozaza.co.uk/autoteatro.html

- *Etiquette*, created by Rotozaza: http://www.rotozaza.co.uk/etiquette.html

- *Wondermart*, created by Mercuriali, Matt Rudkin and Tommaso Perego: http://www.wondermart.co.uk

and **Berlin Nevada**, with Gemma Brockis: http://www.berlinnevada.com

- *Pinocchio*: http://www.berlinnevada.com/PINOCCHIO.html
- http://www.youtube.com/watch?v=_6dW_afiRks

and **Il Pixel Rosso**, with Simon Wilkinson: http://www.ilpixelrosso.org.uk

and **Rotozaza**, with Ant Hampton: http://www.rotozaza.co.uk

(see also **Inconvenient Spoof**, with Matt Rudkin: http://inconvenientspoof.co.uk)

Nimble Fish: http://nimble-fish.co.uk
- *Einstein's Dreams*: http://www.youtube.com/watch?v=k-cAoNhYCoA

Punchdrunk: http://www.punchdrunk.org.uk

See also Machon, 2011, in particular: 89–99; Barrett and Machon, 2007; Doyle and Machon, 2007.

- Archive footage from *Faust* (2006–7): http://vimeo.com/19408848

Punchdrunk Enrichment: http://www.punchdrunk.org.uk and click on the Enrichment and Enrichment Archive section under the navigation icon.

- *Under the Eiderdown* – Video footage of the project: http://www.youtube.com/watch?v=L_BKN6tzrYI
- *The Uncommercial* Traveller – Audio journey: http://soundcloud.com/arcolatheatre/sets/the-uncommercial-traveller
- Arcola 60+ and *The Uncommercial Traveller*: http://www.arcolatheatre.com/creative-learning/the-uncommercial-traveler-arcola-punchdrunk

Wilson, Louise Ann: http://www.louiseannwilson.com
- See also **wilson+wilson**: http://www.wilsonandwilson.org.uk/

WildWorks: http://www.wildworks.biz/
- See also Raynaud (2008)

For wider research on related immersive practice and the immersive inheritance

Artaud, Antonin: Artaud (1993); Barber (2001); Scheer (2000).

Grotowski, Jerzy: see Grotowski (1996); Grimes's overview of the 'Theatre of Sources' (1981) and the Workcenter website dedicated to continuing his practice and analysis: http://www.theworkcenter.org/

Happenings: Kaprow (2006); Sandford (1995). See also the wider history of Fluxus in Friedman (1998) and http://www.fluxus.org/

Installation art: Bishop (2005, 2006, 2010); Bourriaud (2002); Rudolf Frieling et al. (2008); Grau (2003).

Littlewood, Joan: Littlewood (1995). See Matthews (2005, 2007) for a colourful examination of Cedric Price's architecture including his plans to realise Littlewood's ideas.

Site-responsive practice: Kaye (2008); Kloetzel and Pavlik (2009); Kwon (2004); Pearson (2006, 2011); Pearson and Shanks (2001); and Rugg (2010).

One-on-one practice: see Rachel Zerihan's learning resource on the history of one-to-ones, available via the Live Art Agency, London (Zerihan et al., 2009).

Technologies and performance: Berghaus (2005); Broadhurst and Machon (2009, 2011, 2012); Chatzichristodoulou and Zerihan (2011); Dixon (2007); Moser and MacLeod (1996); Peachey and Childs (2011); and Salter (2010).

Pervasive gaming (transmedia and cross platform design): Montola, Stenros and Waern (2009) and the companion website: http://pervasivegames.wordpress.com/

Part One: cited company websites

Badac Theatre: www.badactheatre.com/

Blast Theory: www.blasttheory.co.uk

Brith Gof: http://brithgof.org/

- see also Pearson (2006, 2011) and Pearson and Shanks (2001)

De La Guarda – see also Fuerzabruta below.

- *Maracana*: http://www.youtube.com/watch?v=bbc3de0Zlng
- *Villa! Villa!*: http://www.youtube.com/watch?v=mDgF9ep2Vus

Dogtroep: http://www.dogtroep.nl/eng/index3.html A range of visual material can be found via You Tube, for example:

- http://www.youtube.com/watch?v=LihMJSrImOw
- http://www.youtube.com/watch?v=9nfRWo3rT5c
  http://www.youtube.com/watch?v=_-ukWsEodN8&feature=relmfu

Extant Theatre Company: http://www.extant.org.uk/

Forster & Heighes: http://www.forster-heighes.org.uk/

Fuerzabruta: http://fuerzabruta.net/

- http://www.youtube.com/watch?v=7lB_3wQ88eQ&feature=related

La Fura Dels Baus: www.lafura.com

Lotos Collective: http://www.lotoscollective.org
- *The Trial of the Ancient Mariner* gallery archive: http://www.flickr.com/photos/hoxton-hall/sets/72157626743104354/

Oily Cart: www.oilycart.org.uk/

Ontroerend Goed: www.ontroerendgoed.be

Periplum: www.periplum.co.uk

Pilgrim, Geraldine (Corridor); http://www.geraldinepilgrim.com/

Redmoon Central: http://www.redmoon.org/

Reial Companyia de Teatre de Catalunya: http://www.lareial.net

Royale de Luxe: http://www.royal-de-luxe.com

Shunt: http://www.shunt.co.uk/

Skewed Visions: http://vimeo.com/skewedvisions

Sound & Fury: http://www.soundandfury.org.uk/

- Film version of *Kursk*: http://thespace.org/items/e0000hhn?t=zyc6

Walkabout Theatre: http://www.walkabouttheater.org

Warner, Deborah, *St Pancras Project: A Fantastical Walk*: http://www.bbc.co.uk/radio3/johntusainterview/warner_transcript.shtml

Welfare State: http://www.welfare-state.org/

- See also Craig (1980) and the Welfare State Research Archive at Bristol University: http://www.bris.ac.uk/theatrecollection/welfarestate.html

You Me Bum Bum Train: http://www.bumbumtrain.com/

- http://www.youtube.com/watch?v=f_4A2wTrqgg or http://www.youtube.com/watch?v=uwgYhpsBeFo

Bibliography

Artaud, Antonin. 1971. *Collected Works Volume 2*. Trans. Victor Corti. London: Calder & Boyars.

——. 1993. *The Theatre and Its Double*. Trans. Victor Corti. London: Calder & Boyars.

Auslander, Philip. 1999. *Liveness – Performance in a Mediatized Culture*. London and New York: Routledge.

Bachelard, Gaston. 1994. *The Poetics of Space*. Trans. Maria jolas. Foreword John R. Stilgoe. Boston, MA: Beacon Press.

——. 2011. *Air and Dreams: An Essay on the Imagination of Movement*. Trans. Edith R. Farrell and C. Frederick Farrell. Dallas, TX: Dallas Institute Publications.

Banes, Sally. 2007. 'Olfactory Performances', in Sally Banes and André Lepecki (eds). *The Senses in Performance*. London and New York: Routledge, 29–37.

Banes, Sally and André Lepecki. (Eds). 2007. *The Senses in Performance*. London and New York: Routledge.

Barber, Stephen. 2001. *Artaud – The Screaming Body*. London: Creation Books.

Barrett, Felix and Josephine Machon. 2007. 'Felix Barrett in Conversation with Josephine Machon', *Body, Space & Technology Journal*, 7.1. Brunel University: http://people.brunel.ac.uk/bst/vol0701/home.html (accessed June 2008).

Barthes, Roland. 1987. 'The Death of the Author', *Image – Music – Text*. Selected and trans. Stephen Heath. London: Fontana Press, 142–8.

Bayley, Clare. 2007. *The Container*. London: Nick Hern Books.

Benford, Steve et al. 1999. *Pushing Mixed Reality Boundaries*. Co-authors. Sally Jane Norman, John Bowers, Matt Adams, Ju Row–Farr, Boriana Koleva, Ian Taylor, Marie–Louise Rinman, Katja Martin, Holger Schnädelbach and Chris Greenhalgh. Stockholm, Sweden: CID, Centre for User-Oriented IT Design.

Bennett, Susan. 2003. *Theatre Audiences – A Theory of Production and Reception*, 2nd edn. London and New York, Routledge.

Berghaus, Günter. 2005. *Avant-Garde Performance – Live Events and Electronic Technologies*. Basingstoke and New York: Palgrave Macmillan.

Billington, Michael. 2012. 'E is for experiment', *The Guardian Online*, Tuesday 10 January (accessed January 2012).

Bishop, Claire. 2005. Installation Art: A Critical History. London: Routledge.

——. (Ed.) 2006. *Participation*. London, Whitechapel Gallery and Cambridge, MA: MIT Press.

——. 2010. *Installation Art*. London: Tate Publishing.

Bouchard, Gianna. 2009. 'Haptic Visuality: The Dissective View in Performance', in Alison Oddey and Christine White (eds). *Modes of Spectating*. Bristol and Chicago: Intellect, 161–76.

Bourriaud, Nicolas. 2002. *Relational Aesthetics*. Trans. Simon Pleasance and Fronza Woods with Mathieu Copeland. Dijon: Les Presses du Réel.

——. 2005. *Postproduction Culture as Screenplay: How Art Re-Programs the World*. Trans. Jeanine Herman. New York: Lukas & Sternberg.

——. 2006. 'Relational Aesthetics//1998', in Claire Bishop (ed.). *Participation*. London: Whitechapel Gallery; Cambridge, MA, MIT Press: 160–71.

Broadhurst Susan and Josephine Machon. (Eds). 2009. *Sensualities/Textualities and Technology: Writings of the Body in 21st Century Performance*. Basingstoke and New York: Palgrave Macmillan.

——. 2011. *Performance and Technology: Practices of Virtual Embodiment and Interactivity*. Basingstoke and New York: Palgrave Macmillan.

——. 2012. *Identity, Performance and Technology: Practices of Empowerment, Embodiment and Technicity*. Basingstoke and New York: Palgrave Macmillan.

Calleja, Gordon. 2011. *In-Game – From Immersion to Incorporation*. London and Cambridge, MA: MIT Press.

Chatzichristodoulou, Maria and Rachel Zerihan. (Eds). 2011. *Intimacy Across Visceral and Virtual Performance*. Basingstoke and New York: Palgrave Macmillan.

Chatzichristodoulou, Maria, Janis Jefferies and Rachel Zerihan, 2009. *Interfaces of Performance*. London: Ashgate.

Churchill, Caryl. 1994. *The Skriker*. London: Nick Hern Books.

——. 2000. *Far Away*. London: Nick Hern Books.

——. 2012. *Love and Information*. London: Nick Hern Books.

Coveney, Michael. 2010. 'Stage Directions: Immersive Theatre', *Prospect Magazine Online*, 19 August (accessed January 2012).

Craig, Sandy. 1980. *Dreams and Deconstructions – Alternative Theatre in Britain*. Derbyshire: Amber Lane Press.

Cytowic, Richard E. 2002. *Synesthesia: A Union of the Senses*, 2nd edn. Cambridge, MA: MIT Press.

Damasio, Antonio. 2000. *The Feeling of What Happens – Body, Emotion and the Making of Consciousness*. London: William Heinemann.

Debord, Guy. 2010. *Society of the Spectacle*. Trans. Various. Detroit, MI: Black & Red.

Deleuze, Gilles. 2001. *Pure Immanence – Essays on A Life*. Intro. John Rajchman. Trans. Anne Boyman. New York: Zone Books.

——. 2004. *Francis Bacon – The Logic of Sensation*. Trans. Daniel W. Smith. London and New York: Continuum.

——. 2010. *The Logic of Sense*. Ed. Constantin. V. Boundas. Trans. Mark Lester with Charles Stivale. London: Continuum.

Deleuze, Gilles and Félix Guattari. 1999. *What is Philosophy?* Trans. Graham Burchell and Hugh Tomlinson. London and New York: Verso.

Di Benedetto, Stephen. 2007. 'Guiding Somatic Responses within Performative Structures: Contemporary live art and sensorial perception', in Sally Banes and André Lepecki (eds). *The Senses in Performance*. London and New York: Routledge, 124–34.

Dixon, Steve. 2007. *Digital Performance: A History of New Media in Theater, Dance, Performance Art, and Installation*. London and Cambridge, MA: MIT Press.

Doyle, Maxine and Josephine Machon. 2007. 'Maxine Doyle in Conversation with Josephine Machon', *Body, Space & Technology Journal*, 7.1. Brunel University: http://people.brunel.ac.uk/bst/vol0701/home.html (accessed June 2011).

Driscoll, Rosalyn. 2011. 'Aesthetic Touch', in Francesca Bacci and David Melcher (eds). *Art and the Senses*. Oxford: Oxford University Press, 107–14.

Eco, Umberto. 1989. *The Open Work*. Trans. Anna Cancogni. Cambridge, MA: Harvard University Press.

——. 2006. 'The Poetics of the Open Work // 1962', *Participation*. Ed. Claire Bishop. London, Whitechapel Gallery; Cambridge, MA, MIT Press, 20–40.

Esslin, M. *Antonin Artaud – The Man and His Work*. London: John Calder, 1976.

Etchells, Tim. *Certain Fragments*. London and New York: Routledge, 2004.

Eyre, Richard and Nicholas Wright. 2000. *Changing Stages*. London: Bloomsbury.

Feld, Steven. 2006. 'Places Sensed, Senses Placed: Toward a Sensuous Epistemology of Environments', in David Howes (ed.). *Empire of the Senses – The Sensual Culture Reader*. Oxford and New York: Berg: 179–91.

Fraleigh-Horton, Sandra. 1999. *Dancing into Darkness: Butoh, Zen and Japan*. Pittsburgh, PA: University of Pittsburgh Press.

Friedman, Ken. (Ed.) 1998. *The Fluxus Reader*. Chichester: Academy Editions /John Wiley & Sons.

Frieling, Rudolf, Boris Groys, Robert Atkins and Lev Manovich. 2008. *The Art of Participation 1950 to Now*. New York and London: Thames & Hudson/San Fransico Museum of Modern Art.

Geurts, Kathryn Linn. 2003. *Culture and the Senses: Bodily Ways of Knowing in an African Community*. Berkeley and Los Angeles, CA, and London: University of California Press.

——. 2006. 'Consciousness as "Feeling in the Body" – A West African Theory of Embodiment, Emotion and the Making of Mind', in David Howes (ed.). *Empire of the Senses – The Sensual Culture Reader*. Oxford and New York: Berg: 164–78.

Goldberg, RoseLee. *Performance Art*. London: Thames & Hudson, 1996.

Goulish, Matthew. *39 Microlectures in Proximity of Performance*. London and New York: Routledge, 2001.

Grau, Oliver. 2003. *Virtual Art: From Illusion to Immersion*. Trans. Gloria Custance. Cambridge, MA: MIT Press.

Grimes, Ron. 1981. 'The Theatre of Sources', *The Drama Review: TDR*, 25.3, Actor/Director Issue (Autumn), 67–74.

Grotowski, Jerzy. 1996. *Towards a Poor Theatre*. London: Methuen.

Hannah, Dorita. 2011. 'Event-space: Performance space and spatial performativity', in Jonathan Pitches and Sita Popat (eds). *Performance Perspectives – A Critical Introduction*. Basingstoke and New York: Palgrave Macmillan: 54–62.

Hayman, Ronald. *Artaud and After*. Oxford : Oxford University Press, 1977.

Hill, Leslie. 2006. '(Dis)placing the senses: Introduction', *Performance and Place*. Leslie Hill and Helen Paris (eds). Basingstoke and New York: Palgrave Macmillan, 47–51.

Hill, Leslie and Helen Paris. 2006. *Performance and Place*. Basingstoke and New York: Palgrave Macmillan.

Howes, David. (Ed). 2006. *Empire of the Senses – The Sensual Culture Reader*. Oxford and New York: Berg.

Huxley, Michael and Noel Witts. (Eds). *The Twentieth Century Performance Reader*.

Jubb, David. 2010. Keynote speaker, unpublished paper. *The Epic and the Intimate*. Chair: Lyn Gardner. Other panel members: Adrian Howells, Deborah Warner, Dries Verhoeven, Helen Marriage. London. ICA. 1 July.

Kaprow, Allan, 1995. 'Excerpts from "Assemblages, Environments & Happenings"', in Mariellen R. Sandford (ed.). *Happenings and Other Acts*. London and New York: Routledge, 235–45.

Kaprow, Allan. 2006. 'Notes in the Elimination of the Audience', in Claire Bishop (ed.). *Participation*. London, Whitechapel Gallery; Cambridge, MA: MIT Press: 102–4.

Kaye Nick, (2008). *Site-Specific Art*. London and New York: Routledge.

Kent, Alan M. 2010. *The Theatre of Cornwall – Space, Place, Performance*. Bristol: Westcliffe Books.

Kershaw, Baz. 1999. *The Radical In Performance: Between Brecht And Baudrillard*. London and New York: Routledge.

Kloetzel, Melanie and Caroline Pavlik. (Eds). 2009. *Site Dance: Choreographers and the Lure of Alternative Spaces*. Gainesville, FL: University Press of Florida.

Knapp, Bettina. L. *Antonin Artaud: Man of Vision*. Preface by Anaïs Nin. Athens, OH: Swallow Press, 1980.

Kwon, Miwon. 2004. *One Place After Another – Site-Specific Art and Locational Identity*. Cambridge, MA: MIT Press.

Littlewood, Joan. 1995. *Joan's Book – Joan Littlewood's Peculiar History As She Tells It*. London: Minverva.

Logan, Brian. 2008. 'Edinburgh Festival: The Factory', *The Guardian Online*, 20 August (accessed September 2011).

Lorentz, Diana. 2006. *A Study of the Notions of Immersive Experience in Museum Based Exhibitions*. Unpublished Thesis for Master of Design. University of Technology, Sydney. Faculty of Design, Architecture & Building.

Machon, Josephine. 2011. *(Syn)aesthetics Redefining Visceral Performance*. Basingstoke and New York: Palgrave Macmillan.

Marks, Kathy and Daniel Howden. 2008. 'Environment: The world's rubbish dump: A tip that stretches from Hawaii to Japan', *The Independent*. Online Archives. Tuesday 5 February (accessed June 2011).

Marks, Laura. 2000. *The Skin of the Film: Intercultural Cinema, Embodiment, and the Senses*. Durham, NC, and London: Duke University Press.

——. 2002. *Touch: Sensuous Theory and Multisensory Media*. Minnesota, MN: University of Minnesota Press.

Massey, Doreen.. 2010a. *For Space*. London: SAGE Publications.

——. 2010b. *Landscape/Space/Politics: An Essay*. Unpublished paper. Part of an AHRC-funded research project: 'The future of landscape and the moving image' (AH/E510566/1).

Mathews, Stanley. 2005. 'The Fun Palace: Cedric Price's experiment in architecture and technology', *Technoetic Arts: A Journal of Speculative Research*, 3.2 (September).

——. 2007. *From Agit-Prop to Free Space: The Architecture of Cedric Price*. London: Black Dog Publishing.

Mitchell, Robert. 2010. *Bioart and the Vitality of Media*. Washington: University of Washington Press.

Montola, Markus, Jaako Stenros and Annika Waern. 2009. *Pervasive Games: Theory and Design*. Burlington, MA: Morgan Kaufmann Game Design Books.

Moser, Mary Anne with Douglas MacLeod. (Eds). 1996. *Immersed in Technology: Art and Virtual Environments*. London and Cambridge, MA: MIT Press.

Nanako, Kurihara. 2000. 'Hijikata Tasumi – The Words of Butoh', *The Drama Review*, 44.1 (T165), (Spring), 12–28.

Nield, Sophie. 2006. 'There is another world: Space, theatre and global anti-capitalism', *Contemporary Theatre Review*, 16.1, 51–61.

——. 2008. 'The Rise of the Character Named Spectator', *Contemporary Theatre Review*, 18.4, 531–44.

Oddey, Alison. 2009. 'Tuning-in to Sound and Space: Hearing, Voicing and Walking', in Alison Oddey and Christine White (eds). *Modes of Spectating*. Bristol and Chicago: Intellect, 133–46.

Oddey, Alison and Christine White (eds). 2009. *Modes of Spectating*. Bristol and Chicago, IL: Intellect.

Pallasmaa, Juhani. 2000. 'Hapticity and Time: Notes on a Fragile Architecture', *The Architectural Review*, 207.1239 (May), 78–84.

——. 2005. *The Eyes of the Skin: Architecture and the Senses*. Chichester: John Wiley & Sons.

——. 2009. *The Thinking Hand – Existential and Embodied Wisdom in Architecture*. Chichester: John Wiley & Sons.

——. 2011. *The Embodied Image – Imagination and Imagery in Architecture*. Chichester: John Wiley & Sons.

Palmer, Scott. 2011a. 'Audience space/scenographic space', in Jonathan Pitches and Sita Popat (eds). *Performance Perspectives – A Critical Introduction.* Basingstoke and New York: Palgrave Macmillan, 74–84.

——. 2011b. 'Space – Introduction', in Jonathan Pitches and Sita Popat (eds). *Performance Perspectives – A Critical Introduction.* Basingstoke and New York: Palgrave Macmillan, 52–4.

Peachey, Anna and Mark Childs. (Eds). 2011. *Reinventing Ourselves: Contemporary Concepts of Identity in Virtual Worlds* (Springer Series in Immersive Environments). London, Dordrecht, Heidelberg and New York: Springer.

Pearson, Mike. 2006. *In Comes I: Performance, Memory and Landscape.* Exeter: University of Exeter Press.

——. 2011. *Site-Specific Performance.* Basingstoke and New York: Palgrave Macmillan.

Pearson, Mike and Michael Shanks. 2001. *Theatre/Archaeology.* London and New York: Routledge.

Phelan, Peggy & Jill Lane. Eds. 1998. *The Ends of Performance.* New York & London: New York University Press.

Pitches, Jonathan and Sita Popat. Eds. 2011. *Performance Perspectives – A Critical Introduction.* Basingstoke and New York: Palgrave Macmillan.

Rajchman, John. 2001. 'Introduction', in Gilles Deleuze. *Pure Immanence – Essays on A Life.* Trans. Anne Boyman. New York: Zone Books, 7–23.

Rancière, Jacques. 2006. 'Problems and Transformations in Critical Art//2004', in Claire Bishop (ed.). *Participation.* London, Whitechapel Gallery; Cambridge, MA: MIT Press, 83–93.

——. 2009. *The Emancipated Spectator.* Trans. Gregory Elliott. London and New York: Verso.

Raynaud, Savine. 2008. *Landscape Theatre* (*Théâtre de Paysage*). Montpellier: Édition l'entretemps.

Roose-Evans, James. 1989. *Experimental Theatre from Stanislavsky to Peter Brook.* London: Routledge.

Roth, Maya E. 2007. 'A Doubly "Environmental" Sensorium – Omaha Magic Theatre's *Sea of Forms*', in Sally Banes and André Lepecki (eds). *The Senses in Performance.* London and New York: Routledge, 156–65.

Rugg, Judith. 2010. *Exploring Site-Specific Art – Issues of Space and Internationalism.* London and New York: I. B. Tauris/Palgrave Macmillan.

Salter, Chris. 2010. *Entangled: Technology and the Transformation of Performance.* Foreword by Peter Sellars. Cambridge, MA, and London: MIT Press.

Sandford, Mariellen. R. (Ed.) 1995. *Happenings and Other Acts.* London and New York: Routledge.

Scarry, Elaine. 1985. *The Body In Pain – The Making and Unmaking of the World.* New York and Oxford: Oxford University Press.

Schechner, Richard. 1994. *Environmental Theatre.* New York and London: Applause Theatre Book Publishers.

——. 1995. *The Future of Ritual – Writings on Culture and Performance.* London and New York: Routledge.

——. 2007. 'Rasaesthetics', in Sally Banes and André Lepecki (eds). *The Senses in Performance*. London and New York: Routledge, 10–28.

Scheer, Edward. (Ed.) 2000. *100 Years of Cruelty: Essays on Artaud*. Sydney: Power Publications.

Schneider, Rebecca. 1997. *The Explicit Body In Performance*. London and New York: Routledge.

Schumacher, Claude. (Ed.) *Artaud on Theatre*. London : Methuen, 1989.

Sklar, Deidre. 2007. 'Unearthing kinesthesia: Groping among cross-cultural models of the senses in performance', in Sally Banes and André Lepecki (eds). *The Senses in Performance*. London and New York: Routledge, 38–46.

Steinman, Louise. 1995. *The Knowing Body*. Berkeley, CA: North Atlantic Books.

Svich, Caridad. 2003. *Trans-Global Readings – Crossing Theatrical Boundaries*. Manchester and New York: Manchester University Press.

Welton, Martin. 2011. *Feeling Theatre*. Basingstoke and New York: Palgrave Macmillan.

White, Gareth. 2009. 'Odd Anonymized Needs: Punchdrunk's Masked Spectator', in Alison Oddey and Christine White (eds). *Modes of Spectating*. Bristol and Chicago, IL: Intellect, 219–29.

Wilson, Louise Ann. 2011. 'Scenographic space and place – in conversation with Scott Palmer', in Jonathan Pitches and Sita Popat (eds). *Performance Perspectives – A Critical Introduction*. Basingstoke and New York: Palgrave Macmillan, 63–74.

Zarilli, Phillip B. 2007. 'Senses and Silence in actor training and performance', in Sally Banes and André Lepecki (eds). *The Senses in Performance*. London and New York: Routledge: 47–70.

Zarilli, Phillip B.. 2009. *Psychophysical Acting*. London and New York: Routledge.

Zerihan, Rachel. 2006. 'Intimate Inter-Actions: Returning to the Body in One to One Performance', *Body, Space, Technology Journal*, 6.1. Brunel University. http://people.brunel.ac.uk/bst/vol0601/home.html (accessed June 2008).

——. 2009. 'Introduction', in Rachel Zerihan et al. *Live Art Development Agency Study Room Guide on One to One Performance*. Unpublished document. London: Live Art Development Agency, 3–7.

Zerihan, Rachel et al. 2009. *Live Art Development Agency Study Room Guide on One to One Performance*. Including interviews with Oreet Ashery, Franko B, Ang Bartram, Jess Dobkin, Davis Freeman/Random Scream, Adrian Howells, Dominic Johnson, Eirini Kartsaki, Leena Kela, Berni Louise, Susana Mendes-Silva, Kira O'Reilly, Jiva Parthipan, Michael Pinchbeck, Sam Rose, Samantha Sweeting and Martina Von Holn. Unpublished document. London: Live Art Development Agency. Available to download via: www.thisisliveart. co.uk/resources/Study_Room/guides/Rachel_Zerihan.html.

Unpublished interviews

Gardner, Lyn and Josephine Machon. 2011. Young Vic Theatre, London, 13 September.

Higgin, Pete and Josephine Machon. 2011. Elfrida Primary School, Lewisham, London, 10 March.

Jubb, David and Josephine Machon. 2012. BAC, London, 17 April.

Morris, Michael and Josephine Machon. 2012. Notes on a conversation. Artangel Offices, London, 27 April.

Oshodi, Maria and Josephine Machon. 2011. 24 October.

Sanchez-Camus, Roberto and Josephine Machon. 2011. In discussion. Other contributors, Ffion Aynsley and Saul Eisenberg. London, 21 June.

Blogs

Trueman, Matt. 2011. 'Fading Smiles – A Response to the One on One Festival at BAC', *Carousel of Fantasies*, 3 April (first accessed 4 April 2011): http://carouselof-fantasies.blogspot.com/2011/04/fading-smiles-response-to-one-on-one.html.

——. 2010. 'Immersive theatre: Take us to the edge, but don't throw us in', *Guardian Theatre Blog*. Wednesday 7 April (first accessed May 2010): http://www.guardian.co.uk/stage/theatreblog/2010/apr/07/immersive-theatre-terrifying-experience

Online and broadcast archives, films referenced

Edwards, Rupert. 2011a. *Passion in Port Talbot: The Town Tells Its Story*. Director, Rupert Edwards. Artistic directors, Bill Mitchell, Michael Sheen. Executive producer, Fiona Morris. BBC One Wales. Aired on Sunday 5 June, 22:25.

——. 2011b. *Passion in Port Talbot: It Has Begun*. Director, Rupert Edwards. Artistic directors, Bill Mitchell, Michael Sheen. Executive producer. Fiona Morris. BBC One Wales. Aired on Sunday 12 June, 22:25. (Repeated BBC Four, 22:30, Sunday 8 April 2012).

Hemming, Sarah. 2012. Presenter. *It's Fun, but Is It Theatre?* Producer. Sara Jane Hall. BBC Radio 4. Broadcast at 16:00 on Monday 28 May.

McKean, Dave. 2012. *The Gospel of Us*. Director, Dave McKean. Producer, Eryl Huw Phillips. Screenplay, Owen Sheers. Lead performer/producer/co-artistic director, Michael Sheen. Co-artistic director, Bill Mitchell. Distributed by Soda Pictures. General release, April.

Wenders, Wim. 2011. *Pina*. Writer, director, producer, Wim Wenders. In association with Tanztheater Wuppertal, Pina Bausch and The Pina Bausch Foundation. 3-D producer. Erwin M. Schmidt.

Performances

Artangel. 1995. *H.G.* Concept, design, collaboration, Robert Wilson and Hans Peter Kuhn. With Michael Howells. Commissioned and produced by Artangel. Clink Street Vaults, London, UK. 12 September – 15 October.

——. 1999. *The Missing Voice (Case Study B)*. Cocept, text and direction, Janet Cardiff. Commissioned and produced by Artangel. Supported by *Arts Council England, Special Angels and The Company of Angels*. Funders and Collaborators, Bloomberg and Whitechapel Gallery. Whitechapel Library to Liverpool Street Station, London, UK. June onwards.

——. (2011). *Audio Obscura*. Concept, text and direction, Lavinia Greenlaw. Sound design, Tim Barker. Underscore, Harry Escott. Kiosk design, Ingrid Hu. Sound production, Somethin' Else. Commissioned and produced by Artangel and Manchester International Festival. Manchester Piccadilly Station, Saturday 2–Sunday 17 July; Lower concourse, St Pancras International Station, 13 September–23 October.

Back To Back Theatre. 2002. *Soft*. Director/devisor, Bruce Gladwin. Devisors/ performers, Marcia Ferguson, Rita Halabarec, Nicki Holland, Darren Riches, Jim Russell, Sonia Teuben. Dramaturg, Melissa Reeves. Sound design and composition, Hugh Covill. Set design, Dave Morison, Chris Price. Lighting design, Efterpos Soropos. Animation, Rhian Hinkley. Inflatable construction'puppeteer, Mark Cuthbertson. Costume design, Shio Otani. Produced in asociation with Melbourne International Arts Festival. Shed 4, Melbourne Docklands, 19–26 October.

——. 2007. *Small Metal Objects*. Director/devisor, Bruce Gladwin. Devisors/ performers, Simon Laherty, Genevieve Morris, Jim Russell, Sonia Teuben. Sound composer and designer, Hugh Covill. Produced in collaboration with The Barbican, London. Stratford East Station, East London, UK, 31 October – 10 November.

——. 2009. *Tour Guide*. Director/devisor, Bruce Gladwin (project in development, 2011). Produced in association with Linz 09 – European Cultural Capital 09. Volksgarten, Linz, Austria, 10–11 August.

——. 2010. *Food Court*. Director/set design/devisor, Bruce Gladwin. Performers/ devisors, Mark Deans, Rita Halabarc, Nicki Holland, Sarah Mainwaring Scott Price. Music, The Necks; Chris Abrahams Piano, Lloyd Swanton Bass and Tony Buck Drums. Set design/construction, Mark Cuthbertson. Lighting design/ technical direction, Andrew Livingston, bluebottle. Animated design, Rhian Hinkley. Sound design, Hugh Covill. Costume design, Shio Otani. London, Barbican Theatre, 23–25 June.

Coney. 2007–8. *The Gold-bug*. Coney representatives/Tom Bowtell, Gary Campbell, George Collie, Mr Rupert Grandison, Phil McDonnell, Sonia Moray, Tassos Stevens, Megan Walsh, and others. Commissioned by BAC. Hosted by Punchdrunk. Within Punchdrunk's *Masque of the Red Death* (2007–8). London, BAC, October–March.

——. 2009. (ongoing). *A Small Town Anywhere*. Coney representatives/co-authors, Tom Bowtell, Gary Campbell, Tracky Crombie, Annette Mees, Ben Pacey, Tassos Stevens and Melanie Wilson. Co-producers, Coney and BAC. London, BAC, October–November.

——. *The Loveliness Principle*. 2010 (ongoing). Coney representatives, Rhiannon Armstrong, Rachael A Smith and Tassos Stevens. Co-producers, Coney and BAC. BAC's One-on-One Festival. London, BAC, 6–18 July.

dreamthinkspeak. 2004. *Don't Look Back*. Director/film and design conception, Tristan Sharps. Co-designer, Naomi Wilkinson. Composer, Max Richter. Commissioned by Brighton Festival 2003, South Hill Park Arts Centre, The Hazlitt Theatre and Corn Exchange Maidstone. London, Somerset House. 28 May–14 June.

——. 2009. *Absent*. Director/designer, Tristan Sharps. Composer, Max Richter. Commissioned by Ignite 09. London, Royal Opera House, Covent Garden, September.

——. 2010. *Before I Sleep*. Director/designer, Tristan Sharps. Composer, Max Richter. Sound designer, Pendle Poucher. Commissioned by The Brighton Festival 2010. London Road, Brighton. The Co-operative Building. May–July.

——. 2012. *The Rest Is Silence*. Director, Tristan Sharps. Designers, Robin Don, Tristan Sharps. Sound design, Pendle Poucher. Co-commissioned by Brighton Festival 2012, London International Festival Of Theatre Lift 2012 and The Royal Shakespeare Company (RSC for the World Shakespeare Festival as part of the London 2012 festival). (Brighton Festival, May – June; Newcastle Playhouse, RSC Season, June). London, Riverside Studios, 12–23 June.

Extant Theatre Company. 2010a. *The Question*. Research and Development Project. In collaboration with BAC and the Open University. Director/writer, Maria Oshodi. Haptic technology device designer/engineer, Adam Spiers. Haptic device design assistant, David McGoran. Haptic device technical assistant, Paul O'Dowd. Sound design/engineer, Peter Bosher. Set design, Lynn Cox. BAC, London, June.

——. 2010b. 'The Question', *Digital Resources in the Humanities & Arts 2010: Sensual Technologies*. Research and Development Project. In collaboration with BAC and the Open University. Director/writer, Maria Oshodi. Haptic technology device designer/engineer, Adam Spiers. Haptic device design assistant, David McGoran. Haptic device technical assistant, Paul O'Dowd. Sound design/ engineer, Peter Bosher. Set design, Lynn Cox. Brunel University, Uxbridge, UK, 8–9 September.

——. 2012. *Sheer*. Director/writer, Maria Oshodi. Dramaturg advisor, Alex Bulmer. Burlesque consultant, Jo King. Comedy consultant, Spymonkey's Petra Massey. Costume design, Andrea Carr. Sound design, Peter Bosher. Lighting design, Lawrence Stromski. Set design, Stephanie Johns. Cast, Sarah Caltieri, Amelia Cavallo, Tim Gebbels, Heather Gilmore. ArtsDepot, North Finchley, London, 3–4 April.

Headlong Theatre. 2011. *Decade*. Director, Rupert Goold. Produced in association with the National Theatre and Chichester Festival Theatre. St Katharine Docks, London, September–October.

Howells, Adrian. 2008 (ongoing). *Foot Washing for the Sole*. Creator/performer, Adrian Howells. Attic room, Arab guest house. Nazareth, Israel, October.

———. 2009. *The Garden of Adrian*. Creator/performer, Adrian Howells. Installation by Mike Brookes, Minty Donald, Nick Millar, Nicola Scrutton. Presented in association with G12/University of Glasgow. Gilmorehill G12, Glasgow, 15–20 June.

———. 2011a. *May I have the Pleasure...?* Creator/performer, Adrian Howells. The Point Hotel Conference Centre. Edinburgh Festival, August.

———. 2011b (ongoing). *The Pleasure of Being: Washing, Feeding, Holding*. Creator /performer, Adrian Howells. BAC One-on-One Festival, London, 29 March – 9 April.

———. 2012 (ongoing). *Lifeguard*. Creator/performer, Adrian Howells. Co-performer, Ira Mandela Siobhan. Collaborators, Mike Brookes, Minty Donald, Rob Drummond, Nick Millar and Nichola Scrutton. Presented by the National Theatre of Scotland and The Arches, Glasgow. In association with Govanhill Baths Community Trust and the Centre for Community Practice. Govanhill Baths, Glasgow 5–27 October.

Lotos Collective. 2011. *Trial of The Mariner*. Artistic director, Roberto-Sanchez-Camus. Produciton design/animation, Sarah-Jane Blake. Wordsmith, John Michael Rossi. Project manager, Ffion Aynsley. Graphic design/research, Jenna Rossi-Camus. Music director/original music /performer/collaborator, Saul Eisenberg as The Junk Orchestra. Presented by Lotos Collective and Hoxton Hall. London, Hoxton Hall, 21 May.

Lundahl & Sietl. 2011a (ongoing). *Rotating in a Room of Images*. Artistic directors, Christer Lundahl, Marina Seitl. Choreographer, Martina Seitl. BAC One-on-One Festival, London, 29 March – 9 April.

———. 2011b (ongoing). *Symphony of a Missing Room*. Artistic directors, Christer Lundahl, Marina Seitl. Choreographer, Martina Seitl. Collaborators, Julie Bower, Lisette Drangert, Laura Hemming-Lowe, Catherine Hoffmann, Colin Mclean, Marie-Gabrielle Rotie. Assistant artist, Genevieve Maxwell. Birmingham Museum and Art Gallery, 22–27 March.

———. 2011c (ongoing). *The Infinite Conversation*. Artistic directors, Christer Lundahl, Marina Seitl. Stockholm, Magasin 3, May.

Mercuriali, Silvia. *Pinocchio*. 2007. Co-artistic directors/performers, Gemma Brockis, Silvia Mercuriali. Produced by Berlin Nevada. London, BAC, 20–21 September.

———. 2009 (ongoing). *Wondermart*. Concept/director/writer, Silvia Mercuriali. In collaboration with Matt Rudkin Original music, Tommaso Perego. Various supermarket locations.

———. 2010. *Etiquette*. Co-artistic directors/writers, Ant Hampton, Sylvia Mercuriali. Produced by Rotozaza. BAC One-On-One Festival, London, 6–18 July.

———. 2011a. *And the Birds Fell from the Sky...* Co-artistic directors, Silvia Mercuriali, Simon Wilkinson. Produced by Il Pixel Rosso. BAC One-on-One Festival, London, 29 March – 9 April.

——. 2012a. *Still Night*. Co-artistic directors/performers, Gemma Brockis, Sylvia Mercuriali. Produced by Berlin Nevada. London, BAC, 20–21 September.

——. 2012b. *The Great Spavaldos*. Co-artistic directors/performers, Sylvia Mercuriali, Simon Wilkinson. Produced by Il Pixel Rosso. The Roundhouse, London, 28 March – 28 April.

Nimble Fish. 2007a. *Einstein's Dreams*. Co-producers/designers/collaborators, Nimble Fish. Co-producers, Creative Partnerships Thames Gateway (Basildon and Thurrock). Creative director, Sue Lawther. Performers/collaborators, pupils and staff at Woodlands School in Basildon.

——. 2007b. *The Container*. Designers/producers, Nimble Fish. Writer, Clare Bayley. Performers, Doreen Blackstock, William El-Gardi, Deborah Leveroy, Omar Mostafa, Mercy Ojelade, Chris Spyrides. London, April. (Edinburgh Festival, Edinburgh, August.)

——. 2010. *re:bourne*. Commissioning producers, co-producers, collaborators, designers. Co-producers, Workers of Art. re:bourne Festival Sittingbourne. August.

Periplum. 2011. *Journey Through the Afterlife: Ancient Egyptian Book of the Dead*. Curators/contributors, Periplum. Other contributors, 815 agency, Katherine Hoare, Daemon Or Doppelganger?, Delia Pemberton, Janet Johnstone, Juliana Brustik and Al Malikat dance troupe, Juliet Russell (Vocal Explosion) Irving Finkel, Phil Minton with the Feral Choir, Samira Kirollos, Substantial Film. London, British Museum, 17 February.

Punchdrunk. 2003–4. *Sleep No More*. Co-director, Felix Barrett. Co-director/choreographer, Maxine Doyle. The Beaufoy Building, Kennington, London, November 2003 – January 2004.

——. 2005. *The Firebird Ball*. Co-artistic director/designer, Felix Barrett. Co-artistic director/choreographer. Maxine Doyle. Producer, Colin Marsh. Designers, Beatrice Minns, Livi Vaughan. Lighting designer, Paul Normandale. Sound designer, Stephen Dobbie. Costume designer, Tina Bicât. Offley Works. London, January–March.

——. 2006–7. *Faust*. Co-director/designer, Felix Barrett. Co-director/choreographer, Maxine Doyle. Producer, Colin Marsh. In association with the National Theatre. 21 Wapping Lane, London, October 2006 – March 2007.

——. 2007–8. *The Masque of the Red Death*. Co-artistic director/designer, Felix Barrett. Co-artistic director/choreographer, Maxine Doyle. Producer, Colin Marsh. Designers, Beatrice Minns, Livi Vaughan. Lighting designer, Paul Normandale. Sound designer, Stephen Dobbie. Costume designer, Tina Bicât. In association with the National Theatre. BAC, September 2007 – April 2008.

——. 2009. *Tunnel 228*. In collaboration with The Old Vic.

——. 2010 *Sleep No More*. Co-director/designer, Felix Barrett. Co-director/choreographer, Maxine Doyle. Produced by Punchdrunk and American Repertory Theatre (ART), Old Lincoln School, Brookline, Massachusetts.

———. 2011–12 *Sleep No More*. Co-director/designer, Felix Barrett. Co-director/ choreographer, Maxine Doyle. Associate designers, Beatrice Minns, Livi Vaughan. Lighting designer, Paul Normandale. Sound designer, Stephen Dobbie. Produced by Punchdrunk and Emursive. New York City, New York, The McKittrick Hotel.

———. 2011a. *....And Darkness Descended*. Director, Felix Barrett. Produced by Punchdrunk and Sony PlayStation. Waterloo Station Arches, London, 1–4 September.

———. 2011b. *The Crash of the Elysium*. Created by Felix Barrett and Tom MacRae. Written by Tom MacRae. Based on an original idea by Steven Moffat. Director, Felix Barrett. Enrichment director, Pete Higgin. Designer, Livi Vaughan. Lighting designer, Paul Normandale. Sound designer, Stephen Dobbie. Commissioned by Manchester International Festival, BBC, London 2012 Festival and Salford City Council. Produced by Manchester International Festival, Punchdrunk and BBC Wales. MediaCityUK, Manchester, 1–17 July.

———. 2011c. *The Uncommercial Traveller*. Performed by actors from Arcola Theatre's 60+ Community Company. Directors, Owen Calvert-Lyons, Peter Higgin, Jen Thomas. Designers, Olivia Altaras, Sean Turner. Sound designer, Stephen Dobbie. Produced by Arcola Theatre and Punchdrunk Enrichment. Hackney, London, 25 June – 17 July.

———. 2011d. *Under the Eiderdown*. Enrichment Projects. (London schools, various, 2009–2011). Elfrida Primary School, Lewisham. Thursday 10 March.

———. 2012a. *The Uncommercial Traveller*. Performed by past and present students of Karachi's National Academy of Performing Arts (NAPA). Directors, Owen Calvert-Lyons, Peter Higgin. Produced by The British Council as part of the Dickens 2012 Programme. Karachi, Pakistan, 10–12 February: http://literature.britishcouncil.org/projects/2011/dickens-2012/punchdrunk-the-uncommercial-traveller.

———. 2012b. *The Uncommercial Traveller*. Performed by local community non-professional actors. Directors, Owen Calvert-Lyons, Peter Higgin. Original text by playwrights from St Martin's and Courthouse Arts. Produced by The British Council as part of the Dickens 2012 Programme/ Karachi National Play Festival. Melbourne, Australia, 21 February: http://literature.britishcouncil.org/projects/2011/dickens-2012/punchdrunk-the-uncommercial-traveller.

———. 2012c. *The Uncommercial Traveller*. Performed by local community non-professional actors. Directors, Owen Calvert-Lyons, Peter Higgin. Produced by The British Council as part of the Dickens 2012 Programme, George Town, Penang, Malaysia, 10–15 April: http://literature.britishcouncil.org/projects/2011/dickens-2012/punchdrunk-the-uncommercial-traveller.

———. 2012d. *The Uncommercial Traveller: Singapore*. Performed by local community non-professional actors. Directors, Owen Calvert-Lyons and Peter Higgin. Produced by The British Council as part of the Dickens 2012 Programme,

Singapore, 2–9 April: http://literature.britishcouncil.org/projects/2011/dickens-2012/punchdrunk-the-uncommercial-traveller.

——. 2012e. *The Game*. Research & Development Project in collaboration with Rose Bruford College. Supported by Digital Research & Development Fund for Arts and Culture (a partnership between the Arts Council England, Arts & Humanities Research Council (AHRC) and NESTA). Rose Bruford College buildings and grounds, Sidcup, England, 17 March.

——. 2012f. *Sleep No More*. Real World Online Connection, Research & Development Project. Produced by Punchdrunk and MIT Lab. Supported by MIT, Digital Research & Development Fund for Arts and Culture (a partnership between the Arts Council England, Arts & Humanities Research Council (AHRC) and NESTA). 18 May.

Sound & Fury. 2009. *Kursk*. Created by Mark Espiner and Dan Jones. Collaboration with Bryony Lavery. Performers, Ian Ashpitel, Bryan Dick, Tom Espiner, Dan Jones, Laurence Mitchell. Soundscore, Dan Jones. A Young Vic and Fuel Production. Commissioned by The Junction, Cambridge. Young Vic Theatre, London, June.

——. 2012. *Going Dark*. Written by Hattie Naylor in collaboration with Sound&Fury. Performer, John Mackay. Directors, Mark Espiner, Dan Jones. Designer, Ales Valasek. Lighting, Guy Hoare. Produced by Fuel. Young Vic Theatre, London, March.

Warner, Deborah. 1995. *The St Pancras Project: A Fantastical Walk*. Concept/director, Deborah Warner. Designer, Hildegard Bechtler. Produced by LIFT 95. London, The Midland Grand Hotel, St. Pancras, August.

WildWorks. 2003. *A Very Old Man With Enormous Wings: 3 Island Project*. Artistic director, Bill Mitchell. Associate director, Sue Hill. Associate director/Community and research, Mercedes Kemp. Associate designer, Myriddin Wannell. Performers/WildWorks' artists, Lucy Fontaine, Anna Lindgren. WildWorks' designer/ artist, Pete Hill. Executive director, Sunita Pandya. In collaboration with Kneehigh Theatre Company, Cornwall, UK, and St James Centre for Creativity, Malta.

——. 2004. *A Very Old Man With Enormous Wings: 3 Island Project*. Artistic director, Bill Mitchell. Associate director, Sue Hill. Associate director/Community and research, Mercedes Kemp. Associate designer, Myriddin Wannell. Performer/WildWorks' artists, Lucy Fontaine, Anna Lindgren. WildWorks' designer/ artist, Pete Hill. Executive director, Sunita Pandya. In collaboration with Kneehigh Theatre Company, Cornwall, UK and The Cyprus Theatre Organisation, Cyprus.

——. 2005. *A Very Old Man With Enormous Wings: 3 Island Project*. Artistic director,. Bill Mitchell. Associate director, Sue Hill. Associate director/ Community and research, Mercedes Kemp. Associate designer, Myriddin Wannell. WildWorks' designer/artist, Tom Barnecut. Performers/WildWorks' artists, Lucy Fontaine, Anna Lindgren, Steve Jacobs. WildWorks' designer/artist, Pete Hill. Executive director, Sunita Pandya. In collaboration with Kneehigh Theatre Company, Cornwall, UK. Hayle, and Cornwall, UK.

——. 2006–7. *Souterrain*. Artistic director, Bill Mitchell. Associate director, Sue Hill. Associate director/Community and research, Mercedes Kemp. Associate designer, Myriddin Wannell. WildWorks' designer/artist, Tom Barnecut. Performers/WildWorks' Artists, Agnieszka Blonska, Lucy Fontaine, Anna Lindgren, Steve Jacobs. WildWorks' designer/artist, Pete Hill. Musical director/WildWorks' artist, Claire Ingleheart. Visual artist/ designer, Ellie Williams. Executive director, Sunita Pandya. Gosnay, France; Hastings, UK; Colchester, UK; Amiens, France; Brighton, UK; Dolcoath, Cornwall, UK.

——. 2008. *Woman in the Room*. Artistic director, Bill Mitchell. Associate director, Sue Hill. Associate designer, Myriddin Wannell. Executive director, Sunita Pandya. Commissioned by BAC. Hosted by Punchdrunk. Within Punchdrunk's *Masque of the Red Death* (2007–8), London, BAC.

——. 2009. *The Beautiful Journey*. Artistic director, Bill Mitchell. Associate director, Sue Hill. Associate director/Community and research, Mercedes Kemp. Associate designer, Myriddin Wannell. WildWorks' designer/artist, Tom Barnecut. Performers/WildWorks' artists, Agnieszka Blonska, Lucy Fontaine. WildWorks' designer/artist, Pete Hill. Musical director/WildWorks' artist, Claire Ingleheart. WildWorks' visual artist/designer, Ellie Williams. North East, The River Tyne, Wallsend; South West, Devonport Royal Navy Dockyard.

——. 2010–12. *The Enchanted Palace*. Artistic director, Bill Mitchell. Associate director, Sue Hill. Associate director/Community and research, Mercedes Kemp. Associate designer, Myriddin Wannell. WildWorks' designers/artists, Tom Barnecut, Pete Hill. Performers/WildWorks' artists, Agnieszka Blonska, Lucy Fontaine, Steve Jacobs, Anna Lindgren. Visual artist/designer, Ellie Williams. Executive director, Sunita Pandya. In collaboration with Historic Royal Palaces. London, Kensington Palace.

——. 2011. *The Passion*. Artistic director, Bill Mitchell. Associate director, Sue Hill. Associate director/Community and research, Mercedes Kemp. Associate designer, Myriddin Wannell. WildWorks' designer/artist, Pete Hill. Musical director/WildWorks' artist, Claire Ingleheart. Visual artist/designer, Ellie Williams. Executive director, Sunita Pandya.

——. 2012. *BABEL* Artistic director, Bill Mitchell. Associate director, Sue Hill. Associate director/Community and research, Mercedes Kemp. Associate designer, Myriddin Wannell. Performers/WildWorks' artists, Agnieszka Blonska, Anna Lindgren. WildWorks' designer/artist, Pete Hill. WildWorks' visual artist/designer, Ellie Williams. Executive director, Sunita Pandya. Produced by WildWorks and Battersea Arts Centre. In collaboration with Lyric Hammersmith, Theatre Royal Stratford East and Young Vic Theatre. Caledonian Park, London, 8–20 May.

Wilson, Louise Ann. 2008. *Still Life.* Co-production with Sap Dance. Co-director/ scenographer/performer, Louise Ann Wilson. Co-director/choreographer/ dancer, Nigel Stewart. Far Arnside, Morecambe Bay, England, September.

——. 2010. *Jack Scout.* Co-director/scenographer/performer, Louise Ann Wilson. Co-director/choreographer/dancer, Nigel Stewart. Vocalist, Steve Lewis. Musician, Matt Robinson. Dancer, Natasha Fewings. Music advisor, Peter Moser. Artistic advisor, Mark Whitelaw. Co-production with Sap Dance. Jack Scout, Silverdale, Morecambe Bay, England, September.

——. 2011. *Fissure.* Creator/director, Louise Ann Wilson. Writer, Elizabeth Burns. Composer, Jocelyn Pook. Choreographer, Nigel Stewart. Expert advisors/voices, Professor Michael Brada (neuro-oncologist), Andrew McEvoy (neuro-surgeon), Dr Chris Clark (neuro-imager), Dr Mike Kelly (geologist), Colin Newlands (conservationtionist), Duncan Morrison (caver), and mountain leaders. Dancers, Jennifer Essex, Julia Griffin, Fania Grigoriou, Noora Kela, Luisa Lazzaro, Sonja Perreten. Singers/musicians: Alice Grant, Martina Schwarz, Mikhail Karikis, Olivia Chaney, Sally Davies, Vivien Ellis. Choir: Alisun Pawley, Jeff Wallcook, Cara Curran, Sarah Wallcock. Bellringers: The Kirby Lonsdale Handbell Ringers; St James Church, Clapham Bell Ringers. Co-production with Artevents. Commissioned by Artevents for national *Re-enchantment.* Supported by Yorkshire Dales National Park, Ingleborough Nature Reserve, Natural England, Ingleborough Estates, Ingleborough Cave, Above and Below, Settle to Carlisle Railway, 21–23 May.

——. 2012. *Ghost Bird.* Creator/designer/producer, Louise Ann Wilson. Choreographer, Nigel Stewart of Sap Dance. Performer/dance artist, Julia Griffin. Commissioned by Green Close. Co-commissioned by Live at LICA. Produced by the Louise Ann Wilson Company Ltd. Made with the support of land-owners United Utilities Estates and tenants, the Forest of Bowland Area of Outstanding Natural Beauty and the RSPB. Trough of Bowland, Lancashire, England, 11am–3pm, 15 and 16 September.

wilson+wilson. 1998. *House.* Co-creator/co-director/designer, Louise Ann Wilson. Co-creator/co-director, Wils Wilson. Writer, Simon Armitage. Composer, Robin Rimbaud aka Scanner. Co-producers: wilson+wilson, Huddersfield Contemporary Music Festival and The Lawrence Batley Theatre, Huddersfield. Eighteenth-century workers' cottages, Goldthorp's Yard, Huddersfield, England.

——. 2001. *Mapping the Edge.* Co-creator/co-director/designer, Louise Ann Wilson. Co-creator/co-director, Wils Wilson. Writers, Amanda Dalton, Bernardine Evaristo, Alison Fell. Composer, Kuljit Bhamra. Co-producers, wilson+wilson and Sheffield Crucible Theatre. Sheffield, various locations, England.

——. 2003. *News from the Seventh Floor,* Clements Dept Store, Watford. Co-creator /co-director/designer, Louise Ann Wilson. Co-creator/co-director, Wils Wilson. Writers, Peter Straughan, Bridgette O'Conner. Composer, Olly Fox. Co-producers, wilson+wilson, Watford Palace Theatre, Watford, England.

——. 2005. *Mulgrave*, Co-creator/co-director/designer, Louise Ann Wilson. Co-creator/co-director, Wils Wilson. Writer, Amanda Dalton. Composer, Hugh Nankivel. Producers, wilson+Wilson. Mulgrave Woods, Lythe, North Yorkshire.

——. 2010 (ongoing). *You Me Bum Bum Train*. Concept/design/directors, Kate Bond, Morgan Lloyd. Produced by Barbican Bite 2010 and Create 2010. London, LEB Building, Bethnal Green, July.

Index